NEW CANADIAN VOICES

Jessie Porter
Editor

Jarvis Collegiate Institute

Toronto

WALL & EMERSON, INC.

Toronto, Ontario • Middletown, Ohio

Photographs: Henry Butt and Doug Derma, Technical Aids, Toronto Board of Education, Jessie Porter, and Nancy Yam.

Portions of this book were previously published as *The Search for Self: Thoughts and Feelings of New Canadian Teenagers,* Toronto Board of Education, 1983. Reprinted with the permission of the Toronto Board of Education.

Requests for permission to make copies of any part of this work should be sent to: Wall & Emerson, Inc., Six O'Connor Drive, Toronto, Ontario, Canada M4K 2K1

Orders for this book may be directed to either of the following addresses:

For Canada and the rest of the world:	*For the United States:*
Wall & Emerson, Inc.	Wall & Emerson, Inc.
Six O'Connor Drive	806 Central Ave.
Toronto, Ontario, Canada	P. O. Box 448686
M4K 2K1	Middletown, Ohio 45044-8686

By telephone or facsimile (for both addresses):

Telephone: (416) 467-8685
Fax: (416) 696-2460

Canadian Cataloguing in Publication Data

Main entry under title:

New Canadian voices

ISBN 1-895131-05-7

1. Canadian essays (English) - Minority authors.*
2. School prose, Canadian (English) - Ontario - Toronto.*
3. Minorities - Canada - Literary collections.
4. English language - Textbooks for second language learners.*
5. Jarvis Collegiate Institute (Toronto, Ont.).
I. Porter, Jessie, 1938-

PS8235.M56N4 1991   C810'.8'092375   C91-093269-7
PR9194.5.M56N4 1991

ISBN 1-895131-05-7
Printed in Canada by Hignell Printing Limited, Winnipeg.

1 2 3 4 5   94 93 92 91

Dedication

To the New Canadian students from
Jarvis Collegiate Institute, Toronto

Acknowledgements

Students of English as a Second Language at Jarvis Collegiate Institute: those who contributed their stories to this book and those who inspired them.

Winston and Alexander Loui, who created the Multicultural Society, a group of graduates who support financially and emotionally ESL students at Jarvis Collegiate. Francis Poon, whose computer expertise was invaluable to me.

My colleagues at Jarvis Collegiate and in the Toronto Board of Education who have encouraged New Canadian students to develop their "voices." And special thanks to the teachers in the Department of English as a Second Language at Jarvis Collegiate, who have taught many of these students and offered useful ideas for this book.

Bruce Porter, my husband, and Julie Gibson, my friend, both of whom helped me.

Martha and Byron Wall of Wall & Emerson, Inc. who enjoyed these stories, believed they should be preserved, edited and produced this book.

Contributors

Abou Dan, Hussam, *Egypt*
Ang, Edwin, *Cambodia*
Ang, Tong, *Cambodia*
Blentich, Haris, *Yugoslavia*
Bui, Long, *Vietnam*
Bui, Van Tung, *Vietnam*
Cawagas, Clara, *The Philippines*
Cen, Xuan, *China*
Chan, Lois, *Hong Kong*
Chan, Margaret, *Hong Kong*
Chan, Victor, *Hong Kong*
Chao, Nora, *China*
Chen, Jodie, *Burma*
Cheng, Wayne, *Taiwan*
Cho, Armando, *Brazil*
Chou, Kenny, *China*
Chung, Monica, *Korea*
Chung, So Yi, *Korea*
Csermak, Joseph, *Hungary*
Doan, Khuong An, *Vietnam*
Dombi, Agnes, *Romania*
Ebenezer, Ranjit, *India*
Fang, Hsia Ying, *China*
Fong, Yuan, *China*
Fu, William, *Hong Kong*
Giang, Dan So, *Vietnam*
Golshani, Keshavarez, *Iran*
Hoang, Tim, *Vietnam*
Hong, Sung Ja, *Korea*
Hsiung, Snow, *China*
Hsiung, Tung Shiang, *China*
Kawamoto, Reiko, *Japan*
Kawamoto, Yuichi, *Japan*
Khan, Asif, *Pakistan*
Khan, Mohammed, *Pakistan*
Kharabian, Nadine, *Lebanon*

Khosrovaneh, Amir, *Iran*
Kim, Chong Yool, *Korea*
Kim, Monica, *Korea*
Kim, Sung Hoon, *Korea*
Ko, Yu Chung, *Hong Kong*
Krisztics, Krisztina, *Hungary*
Kwong, Shirley, *Hong Kong*
La, Kyung Ju, *Korea*
Lam, Ba Hong, *Vietnam*
Lee, Hwan, *Korea*
Lee, Steve, *Korea*
Li, Fa Jung, *India*
Li, Hai Bo, *China*
Lien, Chau, *Vietnam*
Lien, Jason, *Vietnam*
Lien, Thuan, *Vietnam*
Lim, Johnny, *The Philippines*
Liu, Ted, *China*
Lok, Peggy, *Hong Kong*
Loui, Winston, *Trinidad*
Luc, To Phan, *Vietnam*
Luong, Thuy Van, *Vietnam*
Ly, Juliana, *Vietnam*
Ly, Mit, *Vietnam*
Ly, Quang, *Vietnam*
Ma, Henry, *Hong Kong*
Ma, James, *Hong Kong*
Ma, Kirby, *Hong Kong*
Madarang, John, *The Philippines*
Manickam, Nimalan, *Sri Lanka*
Meng, Ang *Laos*
Miao, Xiao, *China*
Mikas, Joy, *Greece*
Missaghi, Farshid, *Iran*
Mok, Maria, *Hong Kong*
Monroy, Annelise, *Columbia*

Morad, Michael, *Lebanon*
Moraes, Caroline, *Brazil*
Morales, Alma, *The Philippines*
Nagaranthy, Matheyalagan,
            Sri Lanka
Nazarian, Janet, *Iran*
Ngo, Viet Kiem, *Vietnam*
Ngo, Michael, *Burma*
Nguyen, Dao, *Vietnam*
Nguyen, Hung, *Vietnam*
Nguyen, Tuan, *Vietnam*
Oue, Gary, *China*
Park, Joseph, *Korea*
Park, Laura, *Korea*
Phan, Phu Ha, *Vietnam*
Phung, Donna, *Vietnam*
Pong, Mi Suk, *Korea*
Pui, Shirley, *China*
Queh, Robert, *Burma*
Ramirez, Karla, *Costa Rica*
Rivera, Loida, *The Philippines*
Saupan, Analyn, *The Philippines*
Shabani, Esmaeil, *Iran*
Shiu, Ephrem, *Hong Kong*
Skalamara, Marta, *Yugoslavia*
So, Cecelia, *Hong Kong*
So, Joey, *Hong Kong*
Sok, Sangva, *Cambodia*
Song, Jonathon *China*
Szeto, Esmond, *Hong Kong*
Szeto, Ming, *Hong Kong*
Tai, Chris, *China*
Tam, Amy, *Hong Kong*
Tam, Kit Yin, *Hong Kong*
Tam, Li Yuin, *China*

Tam, Maggie, *Hong Kong*
Tam, Pui Yu, *Hong Kong*
Tang, Chauncee, *Cambodia*
Tang, Diana, *Vietnam*
Teymouri, Peyman, *Iran*
Thangarajah, Rajakumar, *Sri Lanka*
Thurairajah, Jeyanthy, *Sri Lanka*
Tran, Cam Thanh, *Vietnam*
Tran, Le Trang, *Vietnam*
Truong, Cach, *Cambodia*
Truong, Chris, *Vietnam*
Tseng, Li Minh, *China*
Van, Sam, *Vietnam*
Vu, Cuong, *Vietnam*
Vuong, Cam Hung, *Vietnam*
Wang, Binhua, *China*
Wang, Bobby, *China*
Wang, Lin, *China*
Wang, Su, *China*
Wat, Iva, *Hong Kong*
Wong, Fung Yue, *Hong Kong*
Wong, Hau Yu, *Hong Kong*
Wong, John, *Hong Kong*
Wong, Kit, *Hong Kong*
Wu, Rei Zhong, *China*
Yeh, Fee Mei, *India*
Yeo, Tze Kan, *Burma*
Yeoh, Huey Seen, *Malaysia*
Yu, Emma, *China*
Yu, Jennifer, *China*
Yu, Richard, *Hong Kong*
Yuan, Fong, *China*
Zarankin, Julia, *Russia*
Zhang, Qi, *China*
Zheng, Shuang, *China*

Contents

BECOMING CANADIAN 269

INTRODUCTION

To the Student

The stories in *New Canadian Voices* were written by adolescents and young adults. All speak English as a second language and most had been in Canada less than five years when they wrote these stories. Many were refugees from Vietnam, Cambodia, China, Iran, Sri Lanka, Latin America, and South America. They left their families behind in war-torn countries, and after many escape attempts and long months in refugee camps, came to Canada alone. Others came from Eastern Europe, Korea, Hong Kong, the Philippines, and India with their families. The excitement of the first months, the frustration of learning a new language and understanding a new country, the tensions at school, at home, and on the job, the on-going struggle to live between cultures, the growing appreciation of the cultural heritage—all these experiences are shared through the stories in this book.

This collection also includes some writing by high school graduates in their twenties and early thirties who are now working, continuing their studies, or raising families. Their stories offer a different perspective and tell of life beyond the early struggles.

At the end of each section are talking and writing activities which will help you better understand the stories, explore your own feelings and ideas, and develop your communication skills.

If you are a recent immigrant, perhaps after reading about the lives of these young people, you will feel less lonely and isolated and more hopeful about your future in Canada. The students who express their thoughts and feelings here felt just as self-conscious and tongue-tied as you may feel now, but they have succeeded in learning English, making friends, finishing school, getting jobs, entering college or university, and feeling more and more at home in Canada.

You will also enjoy reading these accounts even if you are not a recent immigrant but wish to understand the problems faced by young immigrants and refugees, the reasons why they came to Canada, their cultural backgrounds and values, their hopes and dreams. The material in this book provides valuable information on various topics related to Canadian immigration. Some of the themes explored in the writings include: the effect of war on families, the effect of immigration on family relationships, problems of adjustment to Canada, the need to integrate two cultures, multiculturalism, discrimination in Canada, the help society should give immigrants, and the importance of family roots and cultural heritage.

Whether you are a newcomer to Canada or not, as you read about the experiences of these young people, you will be struck by their honesty and inspired by their determination and courage.

To the Teacher

New Canadian Voices is a collection of writings drawn from the journals, biographies, autobiographies, personal narratives, and essays of students from Jarvis Collegiate Institute in Toronto. The student writers speak English as a second language and most of the writing was done in English as a Second Language classes. The book also contains a small section of letters from graduates of Jarvis Collegiate's English as a Second Language program. Accompanying the student writings are activities intended to encourage interaction with the text and develop oral and written language skills.

This collection of personal accounts is intended primarily for use with ESL students from Grades 9 to 12, but can also be used with adult learners whose first language is not English. In addition, it is of interest to anyone who wishes to explore issues related to immigration and multiculturalism.

I have collected these writings, mainly from my own students, over a period of twelve years, while teaching English as a Second Language in a large urban high school which attracts many immigrants and refugees. The writings include the students' memories of life in their native countries, their thoughts and feelings about immigrating to Canada, and their reactions to living between two different cultures.

Some of the material in this collection was developed by students from incidents first recorded in their journals in response to class discussion about day-to-day survival in a new culture. The stories in "Adjusting to Canada" are examples of writing that originated in this way. In the advanced ESL classes, the motivation for the narratives and the autobiographical writing in "Memories" came from the literature read in class. Excerpts from biographies or newspaper articles that focused on New Canadians, *The Diary of Anne Frank, The Joy Luck Club,* and *Fifth Chinese Daughter* are some of the materials that were used to motivate personal responses.

Literature studied in class provided a model for improving style of first drafts. For example, after reading dramatically the dialogue in novels or stories, or role-playing situations in these stories, students were able to include realistic dialogue in their personal narratives. After reading essays or editorials, discussing the ideas in groups, and analyzing essay form, students were able to write a more persuasive essay supporting their opinion with vivid illustrations. Students reworked and rewrote first drafts after student and teacher reaction and feedback to the ideas and the style.

I have used these stories and the activities in my classes to promote student interaction and to encourage ESL students to explore their feelings, analyze their beliefs, and develop their language skills. Consequently, the original stories have, in turn, inspired more writing from each new group of students.

Through the honesty and power of their writing students have taught me much about their cultures, their family values, their determination to adapt to a new society, and have strengthened my belief in the resilience and insight of young people.

Why Use *New Canadian Voices* in the ESL Classroom

The impact of these stories on ESL students is strong and immediate because they describe experiences that their readers share. Thus the stories motivate ESL students to talk and write about their lives. When students see language which expresses their thoughts and feelings, they have a powerful incentive to master this language so that they can speak with their own voices. The style of the writing is simple and direct and provides students with the language models they need to tell and record their experiences.

As students respond to these stories, they begin to analyze their own attitudes and values as they try to relate to and understand a new culture. The recognition that their feelings are shared by others may help students work through their anxiety and culture shock. They talk about their painful, amusing, or embarrassing experiences as they focus on the profound changes they are undergoing in their adjustment to life in Canada. In the process they form new friendships and begin to feel less unhappy and less alienated.

As students listen to each other, share personal responses, and help each other struggle to express ideas, they begin to build the confidence and skills necessary to learn a new language. As students continue to discuss and write about topics important to them, they begin to trust each other and risk more—an essential prerequisite for language learning. Communication becomes important, and language becomes a necessary tool for communication.

How to Use *New Canadian Voices* in the ESL Classroom

This anthology may be used with students at the beginning, intermediate, and advanced levels of English proficiency, and is intended to supplement literature and other classroom reading materials in order to develop communication skills. I also use the stories as resource material to support the themes of "Personal Identity" and "Multiculturalism" in a history course for ESL students in their first year in school in Canada.

At the end of each section are specific ideas on how to use this book in the classroom. The questions and activities have been designed for young people who speak English as a second language and who have been in Canada five years or less. The teacher will not have the time to do all the activities. It is expected that she or he will select from among the activities those which are most appropriate to the abilities and interests of the class. Teachers can introduce the sections in any order.

Adjusting Activities to the Language Level of the Student

The stories in each section progress gradually from shorter to longer and from easier to more difficult. At the beginners' level, these stories can be used as a springboard both for journal writing and for discussion about problems of adjustment. In addition, the simpler stories can be used profitably by students with more English proficiency who may wish to read and discuss them independently or in small groups.

Beginners need much help with vocabulary and grammatical structures before and during the initial reading of each story. They also need considerable teacher-directed practice with the vocabulary and structures, with the text in front of them, before they are familiar enough with both to discuss and to write freely.

At the end of each section, questions and activities for beginning students are identified by a single asterisk [*].

At the intermediate and advanced levels, particularly in the first month of school, the stories enable the teacher to draw out students and get them talking about themselves. As a result, students come to know each other more intimately, as do the teacher and the students, and a class cohesiveness develops. The talking and writing responses allow the teacher an opportunity to diagnose areas of strength and weakness and to develop a writing program to fit class and individual needs.

At the intermediate and advanced levels, the questions and activities are marked by two asterisks [**].

When working with the longer, more complex stories, students need extra assistance from the teacher and more reinforcement of language structures. At the intermediate level, class discussion of new structures and vocabulary or independent reading for homework is usually necessary before students are able to talk or write in response to the ideas in the stories and before they can use new vocabulary and structures freely, spontaneously, and creatively. Advanced students may be able to react to the ideas contained in essays or heard during class discussion without these preliminary language and comprehension exercises.

What works best in class is a varied approach with intensive and extensive reading, partner, group, and class discussion, and independent and teacher-directed analysis. Many students need to write new words and structures before they are confident enough to use them orally. Thus, a typical sequence of instruction could include reading a few new selections to the students, working on new vocabulary in class, and assigning for homework the rereading of the stories with written answers to accompanying questions. On the following day, the students would be expected to discuss the stories without looking at the text for help, and to become more involved in freely expressing feelings and presenting arguments to support opinions.

Introducing the Text

The following methods may be used to introduce students to each new section of the text or to the individual stories.

- *Teacher Reading.* The teacher's enthusiasm and dramatic presentation can serve to spark interest in the stories. At the same time, the teacher's pronunciation, enunciation, and rhythm provide correct models for students. At the beginning and intermediate levels, prior to reading, the teacher may need to present and explain words and structures that may be difficult and cause confusion. However, the advantage of these stories is that they speak directly to the reader, and explanation can be kept to a minimum. Also before reading, the teacher may ask the students to predict what the story will be about from the title. Another way to involve students is to stop during the reading and ask the class to predict what may happen next.

- *Student Reading.* Students at the advanced level who enjoy oral reading can read stories aloud to the class or to a small group. However, first readings should only be done by the confident, fluent reader.

- *Independent, Extensive Reading.* Students read passages for homework in preparation for class discussion. The teacher may suggest that, in addition to a first silent reading, students reread passages with a dictionary and make a vocabulary list. Then students might answer comprehension questions to prepare for class discussion.

- *Silent Reading in Class.* Students read silently in response to leading questions set by the teacher. During this reading they attempt to locate the information required to answer the questions. These questions may vary from simple, factual inquiries to those that demand more complex, higher level inference and analysis skills.

- *Talking with Partners or in Groups.* Students first discuss their own experiences before reading about those of others and responding to them. If students have trouble beginning, a few teacher-prepared questions may be
  helpful.

Talking and Writing

The talking and writing activities at the end of each section include a series of
questions designed to increase comprehension and elicit personal response. Questions for beginning students are marked [*]. Questions for intermediate and advanced students are marked [**]. Although these questions are divided into two
levels of difficulty, the division should be disregarded at times. For example, beginners may enjoy working at longer, more difficult passages. When they are interested
in the ideas of the stories, they are highly motivated to attempt and persist with
more complex reading material and related follow-up assignments. With the assistance of the teacher, they can benefit from reading and discussing the more chal-
lenging material. Intermediate and advanced students also benefit from reading,
discussing, and writing about the earlier stories. By reading at easier levels they are
able to read quickly and independently, or work in small groups with very little
teacher assistance.

The comprehension questions begin by asking the students to focus on the ideas in
the story and then invite them to respond personally to these ideas by comparing
them with their own experiences. Sometimes students answer these questions by
talking, and sometimes by writing. Usually both oral and written language responses are necessary to effectively reinforce the learning of new vocabulary and
structures. Comprehension questions do not follow every reading selection; at times
students are encouraged to read independently and extensively.

To follow any one pattern of instruction quickly becomes boring. A variety or
combination of methods geared to the interests, needs, and rhythm of the class
ensures maximum student involvement.

The following approaches might be used. The teacher

- directs discussion of the questions with the whole class and assigns
  written answers for homework. The primary focus is always on the
  ideas; grammatical structures and vocabulary are examined when they
  are necessary to understand the meaning.

- assigns written answers for homework after stories have been introduced and read in class. The next day, the teacher leads discussion of
  answers with the whole class or assigns questions to small groups for
  discussion. Students are more able to talk freely without the text in
  front of them if they have been given the chance to think about the ma-

terial as directed by comprehension questions.

- groups students who are at a more advanced language level and asks them to discuss questions. Then the teacher assigns written answers for homework.

- asks students to read stories at home, then involves students in group or class discussion, and assigns written answers for homework.

Group Discussion

After each section there are questions which encourage group discussion. The activities have been designed for the intermediate and advanced students, but after six months of English instruction, some students are also able to participate in group discussion of these ideas.

The comprehension questions under *Talking and Writing* allow the students to discuss non-threatening topics until they feel comfortable. Once they know one another better, and have mastered the language they need to express their ideas, they will feel relaxed enough to express their feelings and share and evaluate opinions. At this point the questions from the *Group Discussion* section are appropriate.

Informal conversation groups allow students to express their feelings more freely without the inhibiting and controlling presence of the teacher. Consequently, they tend to talk more. Students are grouped so that different cultures are represented in each gathering in order to spark more interesting exchanges. To encourage the shyer students to express themselves, occasionally try placing them all together in one group where they may feel more comfortable and cannot hide so readily behind the more talkative students.

Writing Folder

For each unit of this book the writing activities have been primarily designed for the intermediate and advanced student. The teacher may, however, simplify some of these activities for students in their first year of learning English.

Each student has a personal writing folder in which responses, plans, and ideas, first and other drafts, and final editions are kept. By comparing later with earlier work, students are able to see recurring problems in their writing, decide which work is worth developing further, and appreciate their steady progress in expressing ideas. In addition, the teacher has concrete evidence at hand on which to base evaluation and further program design.

The suggestions for writing are intended to challenge students to explore their feelings, describe and analyze their reactions, develop their ideas logically, and marshall evidence in support of their opinions. Student writing is done in a wide variety of forms, including journal, letter, narrative, report, persuasive paragraph, personal essay, formal expository essay, script, writing in role, and poetry.

Autobiography

The stories in the unit "Memories" and in the section "Future Goals" in the unit "Becoming Canadian" are used primarily to motivate the writing of an autobiography. In the past I have found much of the most vivid and powerful writing of students in their autobiographies. This assignment is a long-term project in which students write approximately eight chapters over a period of two months. After reading the stories in the last two units and writing responses in their journals to the questions at the end of each section, students have the confidence and skill to begin writing about their own lives. First drafts are often written in class and revised after teacher and partner feedback. The autobiography is then published in a booklet with accompanying illustrations or photographs.

The writing process involves the following stages.

Pre-writing

In the *Talking and Writing* section, students have been invited to interact with the stories by questions which lead to understanding the ideas and responding to the feelings in the story. They have talked to their partners and written in their journals. In group discussion they have shared their personal experiences with one another and compared them to the conflicts and themes expressed in the stories. Now they have the vocabulary and structures they need to talk about what is important to them. Now they are ready to develop and organize their initial unstructured responses.

Often the teacher can ask students to observe how ideas have been connected in complex sentences. When this informal examination of sentence structure is accompanied by more formal teaching of subordination, students become skillful in linking ideas.

The teacher might direct the students to models in this text or to literature before they write so that they can observe structure, tone, and style. For example, students might examine how

- specific examples and personal anecdotes make writing interesting and persuasive;
- dialogue adds drama and immediacy;
- images spark the imagination;
- rhythmic sentence structure adds persuasiveness;
- transitional words give coherence;
- topic sentences, a strong theme paragraph, and forceful conclusion provide focus and emphasis.

First Drafts

The first draft is written quickly without a dictionary and without concern for mechanics. Some students find it helpful to write the first draft from a plan, but others find it inhibiting. Both methods can be tried. At this stage, the emphasis is on taking risks with language and on developing ideas with many examples. Grammar and spelling are secondary to the clear expression of thought.

Partner Response

Everyone writes better when writing for a specific audience. When their writing is read by their classmates, as well as their teachers, students write more easily. The partner may respond, "I really liked your description of X" or "I don't understand this" or "I had a similar experience when..." or "Can you explain in a little more detail?" Now the writer understands how to edit. Most importantly, in reading what a partner has written, the writer becomes more aware of what works and what does not work in the communication process.

Teacher Response

At this stage most ESL students look forward to reaction from the teacher. The teacher comments on the focus, organization, and development of ideas, and suggests how these might be improved. Recurring errors in grammar and sentence structure are pointed out. No mark is given at this point.

Revision

Students rewrite the first draft, trying to take into account the teacher's and partner's comments. The final draft is then evaluated by the teacher with a mark which takes into account content, style, effort, and progress during the writing process.

Publication

Honest, powerful student writing inspires other students to tell about their experiences. Most of all, publication of student writing through the school newspaper, a class newspaper, the bulletin board, a Remembrance Day service, or a dramatic presentation is a celebration of the importance of the experiences of these students.

ADJUSTING TO CANADA

First Experiences

The young people in the stories that follow describe the excitement they felt when they arrived in Canada. They enjoy the adventure of coming to a new country and delight in the freedom and the choices that exist here. In their first year the students are particularly interested in the many cultural differences; some of these please and excite them, while others disappoint and depress them. They are most struck by the more obvious or dramatic differences in life-style—in food, clothing, housing, transportation, and entertainment.

However, the students gradually become aware of more profound differences in their adopted county. Despite their surface politeness and apparent friendliness, Canadians appear to them to be disinterested in others. Family relationships are less stable and close-knit, and there is little respect for age.

After the first excitement fades, some students feel lost and confused as they try to understand who they are and how they fit into Canada. They wish to become full participating members of their new society, but this appears to be impossible, partly because of the indifference of many Canadians and partly because of the demands of their new lives. They must make difficult decisions. Will they keep names which Canadians find difficult to pronounce or adopt new English-sounding names? Should they take jobs to help their families struggling to survive or concentrate on school studies?

Above all, these young people recognize that, in the process of trying to make sense of a new culture, they have changed significantly. Finding one's own identity is always difficult, but it is even more difficult in the context of trying to fit in to a new country and understand a new people. These students have become more independent and more serious as they try to find a balance in their lives between the old and the new.

As you read the stories in this section, if you are a New Canadian, you might compare your first experiences to those described here. If you were born in Canada, reading these accounts will help you understand the challenges faced by the young people around you who are trying to adjust to Canadian society.

Changes

It seems to me that my immigration to Canada has changed me a great deal. It makes me feel independent when I compare myself to other Canadian teenagers. Because it is a struggle for me to become fluent in English, I am more quiet than I used to be or would like to be. Coming to Canada has also made me more mature than I used to be because I have to worry about many things which I never had to worry about in my native country. For example, I have to worry about my mother. Will she be able to keep her job? I worry about my father. Will he be able to leave Vietnam and join us soon? I worry about our finances. How can we save more money? These questions have gradually made me into a more serious person.

Donna Phung
Vietnam

Too Old?

My immigration to Canada strengthened my determination to get an education. Because the Cultural Revolution in China had interrupted my education in Grade 9, I had been out of school for several years.

My mother felt I was too old to go to school, and she tried to persuade me to work, make some money, and eventually get married. We had many arguments. Eventually I had to move away from home because we could not agree.

The first year in Canada I worked in a factory to earn money for living expenses and saved the money for my first year of school.

In a Canadian high school everything is different from a school in China. I was in a Grade 9 class with students much younger than myself. Sometimes my classmates did much better work in class. This made me feel ashamed, but I continued to study as hard as I could. Always I sat silently in the classes, never answering any questions. In the mathematics class, I did not even know how to say the symbols $+, -, \times, \div,$ but the teacher was extremely patient and helped me.

When I studied at night, often I could not understand a single word from my notebook and textbook. Sometimes I had copied the words incorrectly from the blackboard so that I could not find them in the dictionary. When my mother said that I was just playing around at school, and that I would never finish my education, I became more stubborn, and decided to keep trying.

Shirley Pui
China

Hamburgers and French Fries

Gradually, I adjusted to the Canadian life-style. As time passed, my life became easier and easier every day. For instance, I found out that Canadian food was really very good. I kept telling my mother that I wanted her to cook Canadian food for dinner instead of Chinese food because it took hours to prepare a Chinese dinner and only ten minutes for me to finish it. Now, I would rather eat hamburgers and french fries instead of chow mein and rice.

I would rather wear running shoes than leather shoes. I would rather play hockey, baseball, and football instead of table tennis and basketball. I stay up late at night and get up late in the morning. In winter, I only wear jeans and a coat and I do not feel cold at all.

Although I am used to the Canadian life-style and like it, I must keep my own Chinese tradition. I go to a Chinese school every Saturday morning to study Chinese because my parents do not want me to forget Chinese. I dislike going there, but I believe Chinese is going to help me find a job in the future because it always helps if a person knows more than one language.

Ted Liu
China

Should I Change My Name?

My parents tell me that when I was born, my father looked at me for about half an hour. My mother asked my father, "What's the matter with you? Why are you looking so puzzled?"

My father did not hear what she was saying because he was thinking about what to call me. My father said, "My son...No, no, our son! He is very beautiful—like a moon! And very bright—like a sun!" So my parents decided to give me the name Matheyalagan—Mathey means "moon," "beauty," "sun," and "Stars." Another meaning is "good," "intelligent," and "brave." Alagan means "beauty."

When I was old enough to learn the meaning of my name, I asked my parents, "Why did you choose this name? It embarrasses me. Could you please change it?"

My mom was angry with me. She said, "Don't ever be ashamed of your name. It will bring you good luck in your life." I remember my mother's advice now. When Canadians get impatient with my name because it is hard to say and it is too long, I remember what my name means, and I never consider changing it.

Matheyalagan Nagaranthy
Sri Lanka

Names

Thanks to my father, I received a meaningful name—Ma Chung Yau. My family name is Ma, which means "horse." A horse is known as an intelligent, graceful, powerful animal. Chung means "pine tree." This particular kind of tree is very strong and can resist high winds vigorously. Yau means "rich." The overall meaning is that I have all the characteristics of a horse and a pine tree or that because of my tremendous strength and resistance, finally I will be rich. When I came to Canada, I took the name Kirby. I wonder if I will still have these characteristics!

Kirby Ma
Hong Kong

Sixteen years ago when I was born in Hong Kong, my father gave me the name Cheung Tai. Why did he choose this name? It was because my father had some business in Thailand, Bangkok, and just when I was born he came back from Thailand. So they gave me my name—Tai. The other meaning of Tai in Chinese is "peace." The word Cheung means "fortunate" in Chinese. I love my Chinese name very much. When I entered an English school, the school required me to have an English name. From then on, I was known as William at school.

William Fu
Hong Kong

Don't Forget to Tip

One day my family went to a restaurant downtown. We ordered some food from the waiter. After a moment, the waiter brought our food, and we ate our food. My father paid for the food and we went out of the restaurant. Then the waiter looked strangely at my family. Some time later we knew that it was because we didn't give him a tip. In Korea we don't give tips to waiters.

Chong Yool Kim
Korea

My Father Looked Older

We arrived at the airport where my father, who had come to Canada three years previously, greeted us. Unfortunately, my first impression of Canada was not a pleasing one because of my father, who looked weak and older than he should have. It seemed to me that hard labouring work had taken away the strength, confidence, and dignity which he used to have when he was a colonel in Korea. Well, it might have been our fault because he had been working so hard to bring us to Canada, but that was the way I felt then.

Steve Lee
Korea

Fat or Thin?

When I went to the gym today, I noticed as I have been noticing for some time, that a lot of people in Canada take fitness seriously nowadays. Even older people cycle and swim a lot. In my country, India, and in the Middle East, being fat is a sign of prosperity because only rich people can afford to eat three meals a day. In India, being thin is not considered good although it is scientifically healthy. In Canada, physically fit people are usually well off as only they can afford health club memberships. What a difference there is between two cultures even in the idea of physical beauty!

Ranjit Ebenezer
India

Watching Television and Waiting for a Letter

Everything was new. Everything was strange. These were the feelings in my heart the first few weeks in Canada.

I felt it was hard for me to speak English all the time. I was just like a five-year-old boy learning how to speak. Although I had studied English for ten years, I still could not speak as well as other people. I knew that the main reason for this was that I did not talk English in my daily life in Hong Kong.

I did not have any friends the first two months. I was so bored. Every day the only people I met were my brothers and mother. I always stayed at home and watched television. I longed to talk on the phone for one hour. It was what I always had done in Hong Kong. I did not have a friend to talk with. Every feeling was just kept in my heart. I could not laugh and play with friends.

Every day I waited for the letter carrier. "Is there any letter for me?" I asked this question almost every day. When I received a letter from Hong Kong, I would feel happy to look it through. It brought me the only happiness in the first few months.

September was coming. School was opening. I grew happier. I could talk with friends I knew in class. I would put all my energy to doing well in my school work. I would not feel bored anymore.

William Fu
Hong Kong

Challenges

If people are unable to adapt to the changing environment, they will not survive. I have been struggling to adapt to Canada for ten months with the result that I have lost seven pounds.

Changing from the Orient to the Occident was not as easy as I thought. The earth goes around the sun so that when the east is in the daytime, the west is in the night. In my very first month in Canada I watched TV, or sat up in bed crying when other people slept, and sleeping when others worked. Those were the desperate days I have conquered. There was no friend, nobody to chat with. This cold new world looked hostile to me. I didn't even know who my neighbours were. If there had been no TV, I would have died of loneliness. I remembered what my fourth elder brother had said: "You'll know much more about life when you get to Canada. You don't really know what life is yet. Here, everybody is with you and everything is done for you."

He was absolutely right. My life had started in Canada. For the first two months, I considered life miserable. I desperately needed my mother's company when it was impossible to get it. I missed my nieces and nephews, my brothers, sisters, and my friends. Only then did I realize how important my friends were. In Burma, I had slept between my mother and my sister. When I got here, my sister-in-law told me that all Canadians sleep alone from childhood; therefore, to Canadianize, I had to learn to sleep bravely in my own room, but I prayed a lot before I slept and never watched ghost stories.

My next barrier to overcome is to assimilate into Canadian culture. I disagree with Canadian girls having dates with their boyfriends frequently. It is so easy for them to accept a date, whereas in Burma, girls have to think it over very carefully, as if risking their lives. Especially in the Chinese culture, a person is supposed to have only one man or woman in one's life; therefore, for a girl, caution is essential in choosing a boyfriend. If she dates him, she is engaged to him. Last summer when I was riding on a roller coaster, I saw a young couple kissing right in front of me. I blushed and couldn't find a place to hide my face.

When I attended school, I experienced a new system of teaching and a different relationship between teachers and students. In Burma, when the teacher asks a question, a student must get up and fold hands before answering. Teachers give notes and the students must memorize the notes. Term marks are not counted; the final examination is everything. The exams are quite easy if one memorizes the notes. In Canada, however, the education is a "sticky and tricky" business. I have many sleepless nights because of unfinished homework. I feel frustrated because of poor, poor term marks. I'm in despair to do the play presentation in English since I loathe speaking in public. Now, I know life is a challenge.

Anyway, I have accepted these challenges for my future. I must struggle as best I can.

Jodie Chen
Burma

Please Take Me Home

My parents were born in India. After their marriage they left India for China. I didn't know why. Ten years later, my family moved to Hong Kong. I didn't know why. Three years ago, my family left Hong Kong for another completely different country—Canada. Reasons? Again, I didn't know why. Maybe my parents like to travel from place to place.

When I first heard of our emigration to Canada, I felt as if I were flying to the sky. "Oh! Canada! How lucky you are, Snow. You can go to the famous University of Toronto. You can live with all these blue-eyed, yellow-haired foreigners. You can learn to speak good English. You can live in a white world in winter. Oh, Snow, think of it! Canada! What a wonderful place to go to!" This is what my friends told me. The way they talked made me feel as if I were going to heaven.

When we finally arrived at the airport, I saw there were only two men waiting for us. I was extremely disappointed because in my dream there were always dozens of relatives who waited and welcomed our arrival. The first dream was broken. It made me think that maybe all of my beautiful dreams about Canada would not come true. After all, dreams are dreams! They are not real.

Later, after all the tiresome customs and immigration checks, we got into my uncle's car. The car moved at tremendous speed, passing one green field after another, one magnificent tree after another, one elegant house after another, one blond creature after another. All these things seemed to be having a race with us. I was amused because in Hong Kong you can never drive over 30 miles per hour.

"Oh, run, run, run, our lovely little car. Run faster! Pass them all. Run 500 miles per hour, and take me home, and take me home, and take me home, and take me…" My voice was stuck in my throat. I stopped singing. Fiercely, I repeated the words again and again. Then all of a sudden, a deep bitterness swept over me. The house we used to live in, the school I used to go to, the friends with whom I used to play and talk and laugh came to me vividly. They surrounded me and danced around me. Present images were like a howling sea which wanted to devour me.

Why did I have to leave my house, my friends, and my country to come to this foreign country where I have no home, no friends? Why did I have to come to live with these funny blond strangers and speak the language in which you have to curl your tongue right up to the upper teeth? Oh, no, I don't want to come here. Please take me back.

"Oh, run, run, run, our lovely little car. Run faster! Pass them all. Run 500 miles per hour, and take me home, take me home," I heard myself pleading again.

Snow Hsiung
China

Seeing People's Real Minds

I still remember the day I first arrived in Toronto from my country, Korea. I said to myself with my swollen heart that it was the place where my new life would begin and imagined my bright future.

Everything was surprising and exciting to me from the first day. Everybody was friendly and kind, as I had heard they would be. Especially in my uncle's store, customers always said, "Thank you," to me every time I finished serving them. I was very happy.

However, a few months later, I was depressed, realizing the fact that most people said "Hi," "Thank you," or "I'm sorry," without really meaning it. It was almost a habit. Also I found out that Canadians are somewhat unpredictable. People smiled once and immediately got angry, or liked something very much and then hated it soon after. I found it hard to see people's real minds. It seemed to me that people smiled, greeted, or talked without any "real mind."

When summer came, it was more surprising. Most people walked almost naked, and I found it fascinating that young couples kissed on the street, or even in school, and nobody seemed to be aware or care. However, it became usual and casual to me as I got used to seeing it.

I find that there is little respect for age in Canada. The way of talking to adults is too casual and somewhat rude. When I see how my small nephews and nieces talk to their father or mother, I think it is very rude and too individualistic. Sometimes they ignore their parents. They do not regard me as their uncle; they regard me as their prey. It is really sad to see this rapid change in my family, especially when I think of the next generation.

Joseph Park
Korea

Who Am I?

When I was in China, my mother told me that Canada was so far away it would take us more than 14 hours to get there. Now I am living in Canada, but sometimes I still feel that Canada is so far from me.

Language is my major problem. Although I am able to deal with the assignments and the tests, I feel that I simply can't communicate with other students. Actually, I should say that I am really nervous about misunderstanding others so that I become more and more reticent.

Also, it seems that there is a demarcation line between students who speak English as a first language and students who speak English as a second language. There is even a barrier between the students who speak Mandarin and the students who speak Cantonese. Those Cantonese students stick together and always appear to have a little prejudice against the students who speak Mandarin. You can see many Chinese at school, but most of them go past you like strangers. You wouldn't believe it! Sometimes I feel so depressed and lonely. I don't blame anybody. I just feel it is so hard to really be a member of Canadian society.

Anyway, I don't regret coming to Canada. I should not always think about the negative side. Actually I have learned much during the eight months. For instance, I feel that my English is much better than those days when I was first here.

Also, I have changed a lot during the eight months. I have begun to accept many Canadian values and beliefs that my parents don't understand. For example, I think that it is very important for teenagers to be independent. But my parents say, "What's wrong with you! Remember we are Chinese. We have our own traditions.

It is not necessary to learn those ideas from Canadians. We are going to look after you and fix up everything for you until you get married!"

Yesterday, I received a letter from my Chinese friend. After I finished reading it, I had a strange feeling that my friends were so unfamiliar. No, they hadn't changed. They were still the people I used to know. It is I who have changed so much that I am not the person they used to know. All of a sudden, I just felt that my friends were so far from me and China was so far from me.

I repeated, "Who am I?" Of course, I am not Canadian. But it seems I am no longer Chinese either. Then, who am I? Who will I be? I feel so confused.

Xuan Cen
China

I Lost Myself

Dear Xin:

In Canada everything seems all right, but I still miss you and my other class-mates. Do you remember that night when we finished the last math test and we played cards in my home through the whole night? When we were tired playing, we even went out to play soccer in the street. What a happy night we spent! I'll never forget that.

Don't think I am enjoying a rich life. In your mind, Canada must have lots of gold in the streets. So when I reached Canada, I would not need to work and study at all. Even I indulged in that fantasy before I arrived here. I imagined that my parents would have a furnished room for me. In my own room, I used to fantasize a few times, there would be a TV and a video machine. I had seen how developed the western countries are and how rich these foreigners are on TV in China. Since my parents wanted to stay in Canada, and even take me there, I thought life would be much better than in China.

When I got to Canada and saw my home, I was very disappointed. I could not find my own TV or video machine or record player. I did not even have my own room. I began to wonder why I had come here, why I had left my classmates, my teachers, my friends. I felt I had lost myself.

However, as soon as I knew some special Chinese friends, I changed. They are the same age as I. They have come to Canada by themselves. Some of them didn't even know where they would live when they got off the airplane with only $400 to $500 in their pockets. In Canada, they have to work long hours each day to support themselves while they are in school. They only can sleep four to five hours and cannot find a good job. They, in fact, could live well in China; however, they have saved up everything in China and come here because they want experience and knowledge.

Then I look back at myself. I used to be proud of reaching Canada by myself. Since I am luckier than they, I think I must study harder. I'll never complain about what kind of living condition I am in. After all, my situation is much better than that of lots of others.

In some ways in Canada there is more chance for people to have a good future. There is more freedom of choice, but for me, there is only one choice—science. In China we are forced to study science because in the eyes of our parents, only people who specialize in science or math are considered clever. Since I did not want to be thought of as stupid, and since I was good at math and science, I studied science. But my greatest interest was history. In Canada I must study science because it is impossible to learn English as well as Canadians in a short time; therefore, even here I cannot study history, the subject I love best.

When I first arrived, some Canadians said sympathetically, "Oh, you come from China. How lucky you are. There must be lots of teenagers the same age as you who are suffering."

I could not say anything. People believe that China is a hell, and I had just escaped from hell. How could I explain to them? China is a poor country, and it is not a democratic country, but they are not cruel people. Although there is great suffering in this country, the Chinese also know how to laugh and joke. The Chinese are poor. That does not mean we are homeless and always hungry. China is not democratic. That does not mean the Chinese are in prison.

At present I have no time to experience society. What I am supposed to do and must do is study, study, study in order that I can go to university. It's supposed to be the most important goal for me. What I have learned so far almost all comes from school. It is very limited. Although I know most new ideas should be absorbed from society, I don't have time to participate in society.

Sincerely,

Su Wang

Su Wang
China

Mystery and Magic

When I first saw Toronto from the airplane, it seemed so green. I remember looking out at the blue sky and feeling happy, excited, and a little scared. We had come prepared with our coats handy, waiting to face the "frozen country" outside. Nobody had told us that Canada has summer too, and June is likely to be a hot month. We walked out on a June summer day with our coats on, swearing at every single person who had ever told us Canada was cold.

Since then, Canada has held many surprises. The frozen country in my old geography books has come to life. Recently, in my attempt to get a work permit and a student visa, the Immigration and Employment Centres have become ugly jokes. We have been at open war. In order to tutor at my school, I needed a social insurance number. To get permission to work, I had to go to the Immigration Centre at 7:30 in the morning. The line at the door was already circling the block. At 3:00 p.m. a woman looked at my letters of recommendation, my passport, and sent me to another line. At 4:25 p.m. I was heard again. A woman dressed in black looked at me and said, "You cannot work in Canada. You were misinformed." I tried to argue or explain. The woman turned around and left me speaking to myself. I looked at the empty counter, walked out of the building, and cried all the way home.

Then I went to another centre. A security guard, cold, proud, and very amused, advised me to get a number before 5:00 a.m. I arrived there the next day at 3:30 a.m. There were 26 people there already. By the time the door opened at 8:15, I got the pass number 180. Two lines and five hours later, I had my permit. Then I went to the Employment Centre and, after waiting half an hour, applied for my insurance number. Easy? I had spent 22 hours in line, three school days. Problem solved? No, my social insurance number got lost in the mail. I received it three months after my application, one month after my first pay day, after three more visits to the Employment Centre, and innumerable phone calls. Well, look at the bright side: my first pay check was huge—it was three months of salary!

Six months later I still had to get another work permit to work in a restaurant, renew my visa in Canada, and get a university student permit. I faced more than 100 hours in line and missed a week of school. I faced people who said, "You can't!" and others who told me my volunteer work in a hospital was illegal. One officer told me that with my experience in the immigration centres I could work in one. Five minutes later she told me I could not work in Canada at all.

The immigration officers disgust me. I've seen them mistreating people, making fun of old men who cannot speak English. I've seen a Japanese man who got a letter saying he owed money to the Canadian government for a loan he never got, being completely mistreated by a receptionist. The man did not speak English well, and the woman used every word she knew with more than ten letters. The last I heard of him he was thinking of going to Ottawa to solve the problem.

I know I am lucky. I can understand their jokes and fight back. I can read the rules. I can yell louder and make myself respected. They can also look at me and say, "You can't," then give me their best smile and wish me a nice day. I am "the girl with the cute brother," and some women think it's more fun to examine his passport picture than to talk business with me. I smile through all that and I try to keep myself sane. I don't want to strangle anybody and give them just what they need to kick me out.

Before this whole mess with the Canadian Immigration Centre, I used to think that Canada is the country where you are given every opportunity to make your dreams come true. Somehow my plans have not turned out the way I wanted them to. I feel very disappointed. I wonder why Canadians feel so threatened that they deny jobs to good workers. Such a policy brings stagnation and lack of inventiveness. Employers speak increasingly of lazy, undisciplined workers. I feel sad for immigrants and refugees who must depend on the Canadian Immigration Centres for their very lives, and who cannot even understand what is happening, much less defend themselves.

Some people think the only reason why a girl would live with a five-member family in a one-bedroom apartment, battle with immigration officers almost daily, stumble in the language, miss her friends desperately, and still remain in Canada is total craziness or water in the brain. I have a stable life back home, friends, financial security. Yet, I cannot help loving Canada. It is in the way the chocolate milk cartons have that "spout" that does not need scissors to open, the vivid blue of the sky in the summer, the sunset from my brother's window. It is cable TV, pop machines, parks, glass skyscrapers, the Big Dipper, and jazz concerts at noon free for everybody. It is the diversity of people, the intense cultural activity, and above all, the practical and beautiful English language.

There is a mystery here, a magic, that I think is related to my own dreams. I wanted adventure, and Toronto is still a city to be tamed. I don't want to go back yet, and I don't know why. In the Employment Centre at Front Street there is a poster that states Canada is the country of hope. Maybe that's just it. In each new friend or new experience there is a hope of adventure. Canada is no longer a paragraph in a geography book. I have learned to love this country.

Caroline Moraes
Brazil

Student Activities

Talking and Writing*

"Changes"

1. Describe the changes in Donna after her immigration to Canada. Describe the changes you see in your daily life and in yourself.

2. Form questions to find out about your partner. Ask about

   - native country
   - native language
   - length of time in Canada
   - hobbies and interests
   - favourite subject in school
   - most difficult subject in school
   - family members
   - changes in life since coming to Canada

   Interview your partner. Tell the class about your partner.

"Too Old?"

1. What do you learn about the writer from her description of her first years in Canada?

2. How have ideas been connected in this story? Connect each of the pairs of following sentences from the story and circle the subordinate conjunction (the connecting word) you choose. Refer to the story if you have difficulty.

   - The Cultural Revolution in China had interrupted my education in Grade 9. I had been out of school for several years.
   - I had to move away from home. We could not agree.
   - I studied at night. I could not understand a single word.
   - Sometimes I had copied the words incorrectly from the blackboard. I could not find them in the dictionary.

"Hamburgers and French Fries"

1. State four examples to show that Ted has adjusted to the Canadian life-style.

2. How does Ted try to keep his Chinese traditions?

3. What Canadian food do you like? Ask your partner to tell you his/her favourite Canadian food.

"Should I Change My Name?"

Why does the writer refuse to change his name even though some Canadians find it difficult to say?

"Names."

Describe the special meaning or importance of your name to your family. Would you ever consider changing your name? Why or why not?

"Don't Forget to Tip"

1. What is "tipping"? Why do Canadians tip in a restaurant?
2. In your native country do you tip food servers? Do you think tipping is a good custom? Give reasons to support your answer.

"My Father Looked Older"

1. Why was Steve surprised when he saw his father who had immigrated to Canada three years previously?
2. Why had his father changed so much? Why did Steve feel some guilt?
3. Do you think your parents find adjusting to Canada more difficult than you do? Why?
4. Connect the following sentences and circle the subordinate conjuctions you use. Refer to the story for help if necessary.
    - We arrived at the airport. My father greeted us. He had come to Canada three years previously.
    - It might have been our fault. We had immigrated to Canada.

"Fat or Thin?"

1. Compare the different attitudes towards physical appearance in India and Canada.
2. In your native country is physical fitness important? Is it important to you? How do you try to keep physically fit?

"Watching Television and Waiting for a Letter"

1. Why was William so bored at first?
2. Compare your feelings in your first months in Canada.

Talking and Writing**

"Challenges"

1. List the challenges Jodie faced when she first arrived in Canada.
2. What contrasts does Jodie make between Eastern and Western cultures?
3. What are the greatest challenges you have faced since arriving in Canada?
4. What kind of person do you have to be to overcome such challenges?

"Please Take Me Home"

1. The author feels a sense of helplessness when her parents bring her to Canada. Was your coming to Canada an independent choice or a choice made for you? Explain.
2. Snow says, "A deep bitterness swept over me." Did you feel some bitterness when you first arrived in Canada? Explain your answer.

3. How does the writer use repetition, parallel sentence structure, and short sentences to emphasize her feelings? Give examples from the story.

"Seeing People's Real Minds"

1. Describe Joseph's feelings when he first arrived in Canada. Give evidence to support your observations.

2. Give two reasons to explain why Joseph became depressed.

3. Describe two customs of Canadian teenagers that shocked Joseph.

4. Reading helps develop vocabulary because you can often guess the meaning of words from the context. What is the meaning of "unpredictable"?

5. Do you agree with Joseph's criticisms of how Canadian people relate to one another? Explain.

6. Each paragraph in this essay develops one main idea. Use the topic sentence (usually the opening sentence) to help you determine the theme of each paragraph. List the main ideas developed in the essay.

"Who Am I?"

1. Xuan feels lonely and confused after eight months in Canada. Why does he feel this way? Why do you think many young people who immigrate to Canada experience these same feelings?

2. How might parents and school help young people cope with these feelings?

"I Lost Myself"

1. Compare your dreams about Canada with Su's dreams. How did Su form his impressions about Canada before he came? How did you form yours?

2. What aspects of Canadian life does Su find it difficult to adjust to? Do you, like Su, feel that your future goals are limited because of your lack of English fluency?

3. Are you sometimes frustrated by the impressions Canadians have of your native country? Explain.

"Mystery and Magic"

1. Caroline says, "The frozen country in my geography books has come to life." List the pleasant and unpleasant surprises that Caroline has experienced in her first year in Canada. Compare your experiences with hers.

2. Examine the organization of this essay. Write a title for each paragraph.

Group Discussion

1. With the other members of your group, compare
   - the hopes and dreams you had before coming to Canada;
   - the surprises or shocks you experienced when you first arrived;
   - the changes in you since arriving.

2. Agree or disagree with each of the following statements. Compare your reasons with those of your partner or others in your group.

- There is little respect for age in Canada.
- I feel it is so hard really to be a full member of Canadian society.
- In Canada there is more chance for people to have a good future.

Writing Folder

1. Choose one of the ideas you have discussed in your group. Take a position and develop your opinion in a persuasive paragraph.

2. Keep a diary in which you describe your reactions to your daily experiences.

3. Write a letter to your closest friend in your native country. Describe some of your first experiences in Canada.

4. Write a letter to one of the student writers in this book responding to his/her ideas and describing your own experiences.

5. Describe an experience you had in your first year in Canada which gave you an understanding of Canadian society, values, customs, or family relationships.

6. Write a paragraph in which you develop one of the following topic sentences.*

    or

Write an essay to develop one of the following themes.**

- There are so many things I miss in my native country.
- I have changed a great deal since coming to Canada.
- A New Canadian can get rid of shyness in many ways.
- Who am I?
- Canada has held many surprises.

7. Interview your classmates. Write a report comparing the hopes and dreams of immigrants before they came to Canada, and their first experiences in Canada.

Laughter and Tears: Learning a New Language

Students who speak English as a second language feel acute embarrassment and self-consciousness in situations where they do not understand or cannot be understood. The constant struggle to communicate creates barriers of fear and frustration which are difficult to overcome. Everyday situations, such as answering the telephone, shopping, banking, taking the subway, ordering in a restaurant, visiting the doctor or dentist, or understanding instructions for homework assignments, can create problems of communication. Idioms and slang present special challenges. Expressions such as "I'm just pulling your leg," which means "I'm joking," or "You'll miss the boat," which means "You'll miss an important opportunity," can cause obvious confusion.

But as time passes and the students look back at their difficulties, they can see the humour in their early attempts and laugh at themselves. And as their English improves, most students begin to feel more comfortable in Canada.

If you have recently arrived in Canada and speak English as a second language, you will probably recognize many of the situations described in this section and will realize that you are not alone in having problems with English. If you can learn to laugh at yourself, then you will not be so afraid of making mistakes. The more you speak and the more you are willing to take risks with language, the faster your English will improve.

If you are not an immigrant, but have students in your classes who have recently arrived in Canada, the following stories will help you understand their feelings.

I Took a Taxi Everywhere

The first time I took the subway was terrible. There is no subway in Vietnam. I didn't know how to get through the gate. I tried to use ten-cent pieces, but the gate wouldn't work. I couldn't explain to the subway official what the matter was, or what I wanted. I didn't know whether I was going westbound or eastbound. The more I looked at the complicated map, the more of a headache I got. Finally, I decided to take a taxi. For the next two months I took a taxi everywhere rather than risk getting lost underground.

Cuong Vu
Vietnam

Loblaws or Dominion

Shopping at the supermarket was difficult in my first weeks in Canada. One day my father gave me a Coca-Cola coupon and said, "Bobby, take this and go to Loblaws to buy a case of Coca-Cola." I took the coupon and went to Loblaws. After a while, I found a case of Cokes and brought it to the cashier. There were many customers waiting at the cash register, and so I waited for a long time.

Finally the cashier came to me. I gave the Coke coupon to her. After she looked at it, she said, "The coupon is Dominion's. Do you have a Loblaws coupon?"

I said nothing. I didn't understand what "Dominion" was. I thought it was a pop like Coke. So I said, "I just want to buy Coke. I don't want to buy Dominion." Then she laughed and the other customers laughed too, but thank goodness, a man gave me a Loblaws coupon. So I was rescued. I said, "thank you," but I was very embarrassed.

Bobby Wang
China

Pronunciation Problem

Whenever I make a mistake in English, I am anxious that my English will improve quickly. A couple of months ago, maybe my second day in Canada, I went to Niagara Falls with my family.

After we had finished our sightseeing, we were waiting for my father to open the door of our car. When I stood beside the car, someone in a car approached me and asked, "Are you leaving?"

I was confused. I thought he said, "Are you living here?" So I confidently said, "No!"

But once we left there, the stranger looked at me strangely. I didn't know why he did, but my sister explained the reasons to me. I didn't know the man wanted to park in our spot. I was very embarrassed. It was the first time that I had tried to speak English with a Canadian.

Sung Ja Hong
Korea

Do You Have the Time?

The second day in Canada, I learned the sentence, "I'm just looking around." I wanted to say this to a Canadian. So I went to a store. I was looking around, but the shopkeeper didn't say, "May I help you?"

After about thirty minutes I gave up and went to another store. Suddenly a shop clerk said, "Can I help you?" Her voice was so loud, and I was so surprised that I forgot to say, "I'm just looking around." I could not say anything.

One day, on the way home, someone came to me and asked, "Do you have the time?"

I was very surprised because in Korea, if a boy wants to ask a girl for a date, he always asks, "Do you have the time?" I was confused. I thought, "Is this person crazy? Or just bold?" I said, "Pardon?"

The person repeated with a strange expression, "What time is it now?" I felt shame that I had so misunderstood.

So Yi Chung
Korea

Canadian Slang

My first job was in a submarine sandwich shop. I had just finished making a million submarines for the rush hour, putting tomatoes, cold meat, cheese, pickles, onions, lettuce on these ugly rolls. Suddenly, a man approached me and asked, "Excuse me, can you tell me where the can is?"

I was surprised because there were cans of different kinds of pop—orange, Sprite, ginger ale, Coke, Pepsi—you name it, right in front of him, and he didn't appear to see them. I asked him what kind he would prefer.

He laughed loudly, "I mean the bathroom, you idiot!"

Joey So
Hong Kong

A Different Accent

When I arrived in Canada, I was self-conscious about my odd accent—a Hong Kong accent. It was a kind of "Chinlish." When I wanted to express my feelings, I found it difficult to find the exact word. I still cannot distinguish between "can't" and "can." To me they sound the same.

I remember the first day in school. The teacher was a fast speaker with a kind of American accent. He talked as if he had a cold. All the students were concentrating on what he said, and I felt like an outsider because I couldn't catch a single word. Even now I sometimes hand in wrong assignments because I always misunderstand his meaning.

Margaret Chan
Hong Kong

Donuts

My first morning in Canada I woke up early and my family decided to go out to have a Canadian breakfast in order to understand more about Canadian customs. Down the street, a pleasant smell invited us into a shop. I went to the counter and ordered coffee for my family while they picked out their choices on the shelves. This was the first time I had used English to communicate with Canadians, but I was very confident.

"May I have five doo-nuts, please," I said to the girl with great confidence. "Do" and "nut" are very simple words in English.

The girl looked puzzled and she could not understand what I was saying. After some gestures, she said to me, "Do you mean those donuts on the shelves?"

I was very embarrassed at that moment since I knew that I had mispronounced "donut," and I felt shy and afraid to look at the girl again. I realized then I was far from fluent in English. The whole day was spoiled. From that moment on, I was self-conscious about my English.

Victor Chan
Hong Kong

Don't Always Answer "Yes"

Since I have been in Canada, I seem to have kept myself inside a stockade. I have never talked to my neighbours, besides greeting them sometimes in the morning when we happen to meet each other on our porches. Also I have been afraid to be a guest in my sponsors' houses or to be a host when my sponsors come to visit my family. In both situations, our conversations consist of their asking questions and my answering. When there are no more questions, the conversation stops, and both my sponsors and I keep silent until we realize the best way to conclude is to say good-bye.

At times, troubles result from phone conversations. It is my bad habit to answer yes at the end of every comment for it seems to me that it is more polite to answer yes than to remain quiet. In face-to-face conversation a person will realize I do not understand even when I say yes because I frown, but on the phone this is not the case. Once I received a phone call from a salesperson who spoke so fast that every time he halted his speech to take a short breath, I answered yes. I did not know what the man wanted. After several minutes, he asked my name and address. I was delighted that I had at least understood these two simple questions, and so I replied immediately. About two hours later, two men came to my door and displayed a big vacuum cleaner that their salesperson had talked to me about two hours previously.

Dan So Giang
Vietnam

Finding Myself

A lot of changes in myself began to occur after I had been in Canada a few months. My elder brother bought a phonograph and we spent time listening to rock music every day until late. My sister got to know some foreign friends who had a car and my sister and I would go out more often, neglecting working in the store. I looked for a job, as others did. I was busy involving myself in a lot of new things and new ways of living. Therefore, my parents started to restrict my unlimited behaviour, such as going outside often and coming in late and listening to music all day, but I ignored them, and attributed their actions to the fact that they could not understand my new circumstances and young people's minds. Our conversations became fewer and fewer.

As time went on, I slowly realized that I had a language problem. At first it did not seem serious because I thought it would solve itself as time passed, but it became more serious. I became afraid of communicating with other people, and at home there was a cold atmosphere. Conversations had dried up because my parents did not like the way we had acted.

Once I looked at some Korean magazines and I felt it had been a long time since I left and that I had changed a lot. I felt helpless and started asking myself who I was. I seemed to have lost my identity and I felt that I did not belong to any country. I had tried to accept every new thing and discard all the things I had learned in Korea. I decided to try to be myself.

I found that I could adapt to the new circumstances and could change my way of living, but that I could not change my ideas that I had brought from my country. It reminded me of an old Korean saying telling us that a fish always lives in the water he was brought up in, no matter how his life may have changed.

Joseph Park
Korea

Student Activities

Talking and Writing*

"I Took a Taxi Everywhere"

1. What problems did Cuong have when he tried to use the subway for the first time?
2. What was Cuong's solution to his terror of subways? Why was this not a good long-term solution?

"Loblaws or Dominion"

Explain why the other customers and the cashier laughed at Bobby.

"Pronunciation Problem"

1. What mistake did Sung-Ja make in pronunciation?
2. What are some English words that you find difficult to pronounce?

"Canadian Slang"

1. Explain why the man called Joey an "idiot."
2. What is the slang word for "washroom"? Do you know the meaning of the following slang words: "dough," "kid," "buck," "nerd," "jock," "broke"? Keep a personal list of slang words you hear.

Talking and Writing**

"A Different Accent"

1. What difficulties did Margaret have with English?
2. Guess the meaning of "self-conscious" and "distinguish" from the context.
3. Describe a situation where you have felt self-conscious about your English.
4. Combine the following sentences. Circle the subordinate conjunction. Use the story to help you if necessary.
   - I arrived in Canada. I was self-conscious.
   - He talked. It seemed he had a cold.
   - I felt like an outsider. I couldn't catch a single word.
   - Even now I sometimes hand in wrong assignments. I always misunderstand his meaning.

"Donuts"

1. Describe the situation which caused Victor to lose confidence in his ability to speak English fluently.
2. The English language often does not seem logical. Can you give another example of this?

"Don't Always Answer 'Yes'"

1. Give two examples of Dan So's fear of communicating with Canadians.

2. Why does Dan So have particular trouble with phone conversations? What example does he use to illustrate this trouble?

3. Combine the following ideas into one sentence. Circle the subordinate conjunction. Use the story to help you if necessary.

    • My sponsor and I kept silent. We realized the best way to conclude was to say good-bye.
    • Once I received a telephone call from a salesperson. The salesperson spoke so fast. Every time he halted his speech, I answered yes.
    • Two men came to my door and displayed a vacuum cleaner. Their salesperson had talked to me about it two hours previously.
    • I was delighted. I had at least understood these two simple questions.

"Finding Myself"

1. Explain why Joseph had a communication problem both inside and outside his home.

2. "I decided to try to be myself." Explain what Joseph means by this statement.

3. With your partner, role-play a conversation between Joseph and his father after Joseph comes home very late. Write the conversation in script form.

Group Discussion

With the other members of your group, compare specific activities which have helped you most in learning English. Look at your experiences in

    • classroom activities
    • jobs
    • watching television
    • activities with friends

Writing Folder

1. At the time, mistakes in English are embarrassing, but when you look back, sometimes you can laugh at your mistakes. Describe a mistake you made which now seems funny.

2. Describe a situation where you felt confusion because you could not understand or communicate.

3. Write a paragraph in which you develop one of the following topic sentences by referring to your own experience.

    • If you want to learn English quickly, you should follow this advice.
    • The following classroom activities have helped me the most in becoming confident in using English.

Making Friends

Many who come to this country as teenagers or young adults find it very difficult to make close friends in their first year in Canada. They feel like outsiders. This isolation of New Canadian students may result from language problems or cultural differences or may occur because close friendships within the school have already been formed. An additional reason is suggested by a student who points out that the emphasis on individualism in Canadian society can lead to self-centredness. Thus she believes that people are too busy to be open and welcoming to newcomers.

Achieving a balance between the family's culture and the new Canadian culture is difficult. Behaviour that might win and keep friends is often displeasing to parents. But, in order to be accepted, some students do give up their native customs and values. Making friends of the opposite sex is especially hard for young people from countries where schools are not co-educational and where dating is not encouraged. One young man from India says: "I think I am in love. I am not confident to tell her my feelings as she is Canadian. Will she like me? At a time like this I think that my Indian culture is a handicap."

One student believes that the first step towards friendship should be taken by native-born Canadians. He argues that if you visit a friend's home, you expect your friend's family to show interest in and warmth towards you. It is the responsibility of your friend to make you feel comfortable. Similarly, he thinks that the native-born Canadian should take the responsibility of making the newcomer feel welcome. But, another student believes that the newcomer should take the first step: "If you want people to be your friends, you should be friendly to them first."

What do you think? In a school where the ESL students are isolated, *who* is responsible for breaking down the barriers?

Finding Good Friends

I studied English in my country from the first grade, but I didn't learn it well because we didn't speak English in class, and so my speaking wasn't good. This made it difficult to find good friends. In my country I had many friends, but here I have only a few. I don't speak with students in class and that is because I'm afraid of making mistakes in English, but I'm getting more self-confident.

Keshavarez Golshani
Iran

Too Busy

Sometimes I miss what I had in Korea, especially friends with whom I talked, laughed, fought, and cried. I think probably they have forgotten about me, but I miss them very much because I do not have really good friends in Canada. Life in Canada is very, very busy, and people have to work hard; therefore, many people close their minds to other people. People become more selfish, including me.

Mi Suk Pong
Korea

Boyfriends

When I came to Canada, the big difficulty for me was how to get along with boys. Now after three years have passed, I feel much better with boys. I can talk to them as if they were girls, but only if they do not show any interest in me. However, I am still afraid to have a boyfriend because I still do not think that I'm mature enough to know a boy well on a one-to-one basis.

Laura Park
Korea

Good Advice

After being in Canada for two years, I have changed. I used to be very lonely, but now I have a lot of friends, even Canadian friends. They are friendly to me, not because my English has improved, but because of my own character. If you want people to be your friends, you should be friendly to them first, and not be shy to talk to them.

Kit Yin Tam
Hong Kong

Changes

When I first arrived, I really did not like Canada. I thought Canada would be nothing. The only thing it gave me was sadness and a feeling of being homesick. I felt all the people surrounding me were unfamiliar and unkind, and I felt upset and dull because I had no friends.

But now I feel I am going to like Canada, for it now begins to give me warmth and happiness. It is like a farmer who has forgotten to feed his plant, but he remembers to feed it now.

Joey So
Hong Kong

Valentine's Day

There was a Canadian girl who played an important role in my life. She was the one who raised my confidence. It was a wonderful feeling to have a Canadian friend. After many months of depression I was able to think positively that life was not that bad. She was friendly, but whenever she tried to communicate with me, I would tremble with fear. Because I couldn't reply to her, I felt angry with myself.

During school recesses, we would play games together and she would always make an effort to explain the rules to me carefully and slowly. I liked her, but I didn't think she liked me. Then on Valentine's Day she gave me a card which said, "I love you."

Tong Ang
Cambodia

Here We Go Again

My native language is Korean. When I moved to Bolivia, I had to learn Spanish, but my parents put me in an American school where we spoke English. Then we moved to Brazil where I continued going to an American school until my parents put me in a Portuguese school. I realized that I was in big trouble. The first year I had to go through hell. Every day after school I had private lessons in Portuguese. Most of the time at home I was doing my homework from school and from my private lessons.

In the second year it got worse because now I had school, private lessons, and swimming lessons. Because I had no time for fun, I became quite serious. Afterwards my parents bought me a computer for entertainment, which for me only meant more studying to do. The following year was even worse. Now I had school, private lessons, swimming lessons, an English course, and piano practice.

Gradually, as I learned Portuguese, my relationships with other kids got better. I wasn't so shy anymore, and I got out more. I took up guitar lessons and Tae-Kwon-Do. I was happy.

Then my parents told me we were going to Canada to start a new life. Now my life is really messed up. I can't speak English well. I can't speak Korean, my native language. I am forgetting Portuguese. I certainly don't feel comfortable living in Canada. I have no close friends.

In the Christmas holidays, I went back to Brazil. There I didn't feel like an outsider. The strangest feeling was that I went back in time, and I was twelve again. Everything had changed, but I couldn't admit that. However I had to face the truth and know that those golden years of my childhood would be only memories from now on.

On my way back from Brazil, in the airplane, I started to realize that those years of my childhood were the best years of my life and nobody could take that away.

Armando Cho
Brazil

I Want to Go Back

I have gone through many disagreements and conflicts with my parents through-out my life. But since coming to Canada these disagreements have intensified and become a habit. The reason for this is that since coming to Canada I have become closed into my own thoughts and shy because of lack of self-assurance in my knowledge of the English language. But my father does not want me to be sad and lonely and thus tries to persuade me to join various clubs and meet friends just as I did in Yugoslavia. The following is a typical conflict on this matter between my father and me:

"I'm so bored," I said. "I have nothing to do."

My father replied, "Well, why don't you call up some of your friends and go to the movies or something?"

"I don't have their telephone numbers," I said, trying to protect myself.

"Oh, I'm sure you do. It's just that you don't want to call them! What's the matter? You didn't behave like this in Yugoslavia. You were always surrounded by friends!"

"It is not the same as it was in Yugoslavia. I don't even know why we came to this country. We were perfectly happy before we came here. I can hardly wait to go back."

Trying to calm me, father spoke in a gentler tone: "This is an excellent opportunity to learn English perfectly and see some of the world."

"See some of the world! See some of the world! What can I see here? A bunch of skyscrapers. Besides, I would've seen it all sooner or later."

Seeing that it was not easy to convince me to enjoy life in Canada, father, now with anger in his voice, spoke: "Some day you'll be grateful I brought you here! You must live here and now. Life is as you make it."

I ran to my room, and slammed the door.

I continue to lead my "beautiful" life, counting off the months and years I still have to live in Canada.

Haris Blentich
Yugoslavia

Free to Be Me

At the age of ten I left Sri Lanka and went to Germany. I could not speak German. At that time I was very shy compared to the other German students who were in my class. They were all very friendly towards me, as I was the only student from a foreign country. Indeed they treated me as if I were a queen. Since I was very shy, I spoke very softly; this attracted my classmates. I hated wearing jeans, shorts, or mini-skirts to school and I hated sitting next to boys.

One day our teacher informed us that we would be going swimming. The following day everyone turned up in their swimming suits but me. However, I was eventually forced into wearing a swim suit by my friends. They admired my "golden tan" and encouraged me to leave the dressing room and go to the pool. I felt even worse when I told them, "I'm sorry. I can't swim."

They started laughing and said, "We are here to teach you. Get in the water." I was glad that I could hide my legs in the water. I jumped into the baby swimming-pool. After, everyone relaxed in the sun. They called, "Why don't you join us, Jeyanthy?"

I said, "No, my mom said not to go in the sun." They wondered why. I said, "Because if I go in the sun, I might get darker." So I just stayed under the tree and wished I had never opened my mouth to tell them about this. I felt so different from everyone else. This made me feel more shy.

Once I went to a birthday party of one of my girlfriends. I knew I had to eat with a fork and knife, and so I practised at home before going to the party since I was used to eating with my fingers at home. However, at the party, I felt my fingers going numb and could hardly cut the meat on my plate. My friend was very disappointed when she saw me leaving the meat behind, but she did not know that I couldn't use a fork and a knife. She asked, "Jeyanthy, don't you like our food? Is it very different from your own food?"

I didn't know how to tell her that I could not eat with a fork and knife. I just said, "Oh, I'm not very hungry. I ate at home before I came here, but I like your food. It tastes very good." For telling such a big lie, my stomach started crying and I wished I had eaten something at home.

Later my parents asked me what had happened and why I was upset. I started telling them that the European culture was very hard to adapt to and that I could not do it. I explained to them that if I wanted to be accepted I would have to dress in the latest fashions and take up smoking in order to show others that I was not a child. I would have to get a boyfriend and show lack of respect for my parents in order to prove my freedom. I would have to eat with a fork and knife. I would have to learn to swim and lie in the sun to get a suntan.

My parents looked at one another with surprise. My father paused a moment. "Jeyanthy, the creature who adapts to nature survives, but don't feel you have to adopt European culture totally. Only take the good customs and leave the bad behind."

From that day on, I felt more at home in school and less shy. I felt very free and just did what I felt like. I didn't dress fashionably. I thought people who liked me the way I was could be my friends, and those who thought I should change myself didn't need to be my friends. I did not need to smoke or dress like a model in order to be popular. With plaited hair and Indian dress, I could still do my best in school and make friends.

Jeyanthy Thurairajah
Sri Lanka

Leadership in a Multicultural School

Let's suppose that you visit your new friend's home. If you are surrounded by his family, you will certainly feel quite uncomfortable at first. In this situation, whom do you think is more responsible for opening his mind first, you or his family members?

Obviously his family. Since it's his home and his family is the majority, they should try to make you feel comfortable. If all of them show indifference to you, how can you start a conversation? You will definitely expect his family to show some interest and friendliness toward you when you meet them for the first time.

Now let's think about students who speak English as a second language. Their problem is much bigger than the example that I mentioned. They are surrounded by people whom they not only don't know, but also whose language, culture, and appearance are different. In order to understand their problem, you need to put yourself in their place. Suppose that you were thrown into the middle of Korean society because your family had to move to Korea. Unfortunately, they do not speak English in Korea. Instead, they speak Korean. Suddenly you become a fool who cannot express an idea in your mind. Even if you have some explosive feelings and erudite knowledge, you cannot express them in Korean. Tearfully, you take all science subjects at school and you are branded as "a guy who is good at science but dumb at humanities."

On the street, let's suppose you want to ask the time of a stranger. Instead of saying, "excuse me," you might say "execute me," in Korean since you are not good in Korean pronunciation, and everybody will laugh at you. Even the sense of humour is different. When you laugh at something, nobody else will, and when everybody laughs at something, you won't. When you are lonely, when you are harried by day and haunted by night by the fact that you are a marginal person who can never get along with the Korean people around, you will definitely need somebody—somebody who can help you and understand you.

Each of you should be this kind of somebody in Canada for New Canadian students. You can show true leadership. How can you do this? If you know ESL students who cannot speak English properly, just approach them and ask if there is any way that you may help. You may say, "Do you want to know how to join clubs in school?" or "Do you want to play tennis with me after school?" or "Do you have any problems in your school work?" or "Is there anything about school that you want to know?" Students who have just arrived in Canada will be radiantly happy, since they will get not only practical knowledge about the school and subjects, but also friendliness, warmth, and caring from you. They will feel that they are not alone, that there are many people who will help, and they will gain more confidence.

A leader is like a conductor. When we listen to an orchestra, we feel a unity of sounds, and at the same time a variety of harmonies. The difference between the violin and the cello is not condemned, but respected. Therefore, when people from different cultures are well led and united, the harmony that they make cannot even be compared to one monotonous sound. That's why I believe that Canada has the greatest potential in the world.

Let's suppose that a conductor is also a violinist and says to the orchestra, "I am a violinist; therefore, I will only care about violins in our orchestra. I don't like other instruments. Get lost!" He is clearly forgetting his role as a conductor of the orchestra.

Native-born Canadian students! You are violinists; however, you should not forget that you are the leaders of the orchestra at the same time. You are Canadian students; however, you should not forget that you are also responsible for leading and understanding Chinese, Korean, Vietnamese, Indian, Iranian, and Japanese students since they have limited knowledge in your language and culture, since they have come here to be Canadians, and since they are going to live with you. Only the true leader can make the fantastic sound of an orchestra filled with variety and unity. If you do that, each of you is a true leader.

Hwan Lee
Korea

In Love

I spent a very quiet Saturday. I did a little cleaning and went to work. When I look back on my day, I really spent it very differently from most Canadian teenagers. I did not talk on the phone to a friend or go on a date or hang out at a mall. I stayed home for most of the day. I am a loner, an island who keeps to himself. I felt lonely in a way. I wonder why I don't have a really close friend. Maybe it's because I am Indian and very emotional. I take even small jokes to heart and so not very many people want to be with me.

When I say that I did not do the fun things that Canadian teenagers do, do I know what Canadians teenagers do? I guess I don't know. So did I miss any fun? I guess not.

Today in the library during lunch break I got up my courage to go and talk to a girl whom I like. She's in Grade 12 and is a very nice person. I like her, but am shy to tell her so. I just talked to her about studies for some time. I have known her for quite some time now—about a year, I think. I wonder whether I should tell her I like her. It is against my culture in a way to fall in love. Am I in love? Isn't it funny that I am already thinking about marriage when I haven't even told the girl that I like her. Probably Canadians would have easily had the guts to tell a girl so.

Today I had the courage to walk the girl home part of the way. I think I am in love. In a way I am not confident to tell her my feelings, as she is Canadian. Will she like me? If I asked her, would it spoil our friendship? At a time like this I think that my Indian culture is a handicap as it has not provided me with an answer to these teenage questions of love. At this time I wish I were Canadian just so I could fall in love.

Ranjit Ebenezer
India

Human Relations and Political Systems

There are big differences in attitudes towards others that I noticed between the people here in Canada and the people in Romania. When I came here from Romania, I had a very lonely feeling inside me because I left behind all my friends, and I missed them. I truly believed that as time passed I would make new friends and that this would make me feel better. However, I didn't count on the fact that it would take three years of my life to have new friends.

About four months after my arrival in Canada, I started Grade 9. Most of the courses that I took were in the ESL section, because I didn't speak English well. I didn't feel any pressure when I was in my ESL classes, and I felt free to put up my hand whenever I wanted to make comments. But in my regular classes I never dared to speak up in front of everyone, since I felt shy because of my poor English. Very few people from my regular classes talked to me. Maybe one or two. But even the ones who did talk to me only chose to do so because I was sitting next to them, and sometimes they needed to ask me about what was written on the blackboard, because they couldn't read it or they needed to ask me if I understood the homework. But to be interested in me as a person? No, they never were. The most personal question I've ever been asked in these classes was, "How are you?" And even when these questions got as personal as that, they wouldn't wait for me to answer. At first I didn't realize that they didn't really want to know how I was. Back home in Romania if someone asked how you were, it meant that they expected you to tell them the whole story of your life. So anyway, at the beginning I answered people with "I'm fine," and after that I thought that they would ask me something else about myself. But no one did.

Just to make sure that my thinking was right, to make sure that it was true that these people didn't really want to hear an answer to "How are you?" once I decided to test it. What I did proved my thinking right. The next time a girl asked me the same question, I answered, "I feel terrible." I thought maybe if I said that she would ask me what was wrong and finally we would start communicating. But not only was this girl not interested in me, she was not even curious. From my point of view, when someone is feeling terrible, there must be a whole story behind how they feel. Even if someone doesn't care for you, they could still ask why you are feeling terrible, just out of curiosity.

I was very disappointed as I realized how indifferent to each other people in Canada are. In Romania I was used to seeing everyone caring for each other and cooperating. The attitude of Canadian people was very new to me. I realized, with time, that these attitudes have to do with the system. In Canada we have a capitalistic system that allows and at the same time forces people to be individualistic. In Canada, if you don't want to do something, then you don't have to do it. But if you really want to do something, you have to do it all by yourself. And since here everyone is independent about what they want and can do, people must be self-centred to be able to get where they want.

In contrast, in the socialist system of Romania, people are not exactly free to do what they want. There is much that the system forces everyone to do. No one can be indifferent to another person because people must be doing some of the same things together. They naturally cooperate. And when there is cooperation, there is also caring about each other.

I am not going to judge or tell anyone that I like one system better than the other. What I have tried to emphasize is that, in my opinion, the big difference in the attitudes of people toward others in different countries has to do with the different political systems of these countries.

Agnes Dombi
Romania

Student Activities

Talking and Writing*

Work with someone in the class you do not know well. With your new partner take turns reading each paragraph on pages 40 and 41. Then discuss the following questions.

- Why does each of these students have difficulties forming close friendships in their first year in Canada?
- Compare your experience by describing a situation you have experienced.
- What advice would you give to students who feel lonely?
- What quality do you look for in a friend? Describe a situation where your friend showed this quality.
- Find out about your new partner. Ask about interests or hobbies, best subject at school, most difficult subject at school, family, and future plans.

Talking and Writing**

"Here We Go Again"

1. Armando speaks of the "golden years" when he was a child. Why does he refer to his childhood in this way?

2. Do you feel that Armando exaggerates when he speaks of the first year in a new country as "hell"? Compare your experience.

"I Want to Go Back"

1. Haris has the option of going back to Yugoslavia after four years in Canada. If you were able to go back to your native country, would this make it easier or more difficult for you to adjust to Canada?

2. In your opinion, does the father give good advice to Haris?

"Free to Be Me"

1. Jeyanthy feels different from everyone else. Describe three occasions when she feels very different.

2. Describe the change in Jeyanthy which occurs after her conversation with her father.

"Leadership in a Multicultural School"

1. To whom does Hwan address his speech?

2. State the main idea of the speech and his supporting arguments.

3. Why does he introduce the examples of the family and the orchestra?

4. Do you agree that it is the responsibility of native-born Canadians to take the first step in making friends with newcomers? Explain.

"In Love"

Ranjit feels that his Indian background makes it difficult for him to relate to people. Describe a situation when you have felt that your cultural background prevents you from understanding and connecting with Canadians.

"Human Relations and Political Systems"

1. In your own words describe the incidents which lead Agnes to conclude that people in Canada do not care for others.
2. Agree or disagree with each of the following statements. Support your opinion by referring to this essay and to your own experience.
   - Agnes is too critical of Canadian students.
   - Agnes's conclusion that people are not interested in her as a person is wrong.
   - Political systems do influence how people relate to one another.

Group Discussion

With the other members of your group, debate the following issues. Give strong arguments to support your point of view.

   - In school ESL students should always talk English.
   - ESL students are responsible for their isolation.
   - To become Canadian you must give up many of your family's values and customs.
   - Dating many people before marriage is important.

Writing Folder

1. Write a paragraph outlining specific ways a New Canadian student can make friends.
2. Write a paragraph describing your best friend, her/his personality, and the activities you have shared.
3. Work with a partner and interview each other. Get as much background information as you can about your partner. Ask about interests, hobbies, and future plans. Write a short biography of the person you interviewed.
4. Write a persuasive essay on one of the topics discussed in your group. Develop arguments to support your point of view.
5. In diary form (like Ranjit in "In Love") describe incidents in your life over a period of a week.
6. Describe how a Multicultural Club or any other specific group might operate in your school to bring together students of different ethnic backgrounds. Show how specific activities could help students who speak English as a second language make friends with Canadian students.

School

It is never easy to come into a new school where everyone already seems to have friends, know the teachers, and understand the routines. But when that new school is in a new country, then the problems can be even more formidable.

For most New Canadians, adjusting to a new school system is the greatest challenge they have ever faced. They are unfamiliar with the language, the programs, the rules, the classes, the students, and the customs. They are often overwhelmed by the strangeness and afraid that they can never learn all that needs to be learned. In this section students share their initial anxieties, disappointments, and concerns, and their later satisfactions and achievements. At first they feel tongue-tied, deaf, and dumb. In her first months at school one student says, "My dictionary has become my best friend." Another feels like a "stone" when students laugh at a joke in class and she cannot understand the humour.

As the months go by, students may begin to feel like outsiders both at school and at home. The changes that inevitably occur when living in a new culture may not be enough to gain acceptance of native-born students, but are dramatic to parents and relatives. A student writes: "I felt as if I had a split personality. My family noticed the changes in me. They said that I was acting weird, and I was no longer the person I had been."

One student who has been in Canada for five years worries about losing her native culture and first language skills; she wishes to preserve her heritage language in order to communicate with parents and grandparents. However, another believes that teaching heritage languages in the school "would cause a deeper division of students by language and finally separate the school into small groups."

The following stories discuss frankly the problems faced by ESL students in school, but, more importantly, reveal their courage and determination to overcome these problems.

Like a Stone

The most difficult problem to overcome is language. Although in Hong Kong some subjects are taken in English, sometimes when teachers explain to the class they use Cantonese instead of English. Here, everything is taught in English, and when the teachers speak fast, I cannot understand. Sometimes a teacher makes jokes and students laugh a lot, but I just sit on my seat like a stone. How embarrassed I am.

Hau Yu Wong
Hong Kong

Do You Want to Dance?

After a while Joe became my best friend, and he asked me why I never went to the school dances. I told him that I didn't even know there were any. As soon as I got to the gymnasium, I recognized the same songs they had played in Hungary. I asked Joe, "What do you say to a girl to ask her to dance?"

He replied, "Do you want to dance?"

It took me one hour to get up my courage and ask a girl to dance. Hey, it was not bad, not bad at all!

Joeseph Csermak
Hungary

My Dictionary is My Best Friend

In my first week at school a strange thing happened. The teacher asked me a question and I stood up to answer it, but some classmates laughed at me. After that, one of my classmates who was sitting beside me told me that when you answer questions, you always keep sitting down.

The most difficult subject is English. Because I didn't understand, and the teachers spoke so fast, I couldn't follow them. I always looked up words in my dictionary. My dictionary has become my best friend.

Lin Wang
China

Afraid of Everything

When I registered at school, I felt like an alien. I was afraid of everything. I was afraid the principal wouldn't let me study in Grade 9, afraid that my terrible speaking of English would make the teachers laugh, afraid of possible racial tension in the school. My friends had told me that white people didn't like yellow and black people.

Fortunately, I was put in a special class for new immigrants learning English. There I met many Chinese friends, and if I had problems in homework, I could ask them. At first I felt embarrassed to see the different colour of people around me, but later I got used to it.

Now my English is better, but sometimes I still don't understand what the teachers say. I always ask the teachers for extra help after school. I am glad that my teachers are very kind, and they don't look down on me or laugh at me. Now I like my teachers, my classmates, and my school.

Amy Tam
Hong Kong

Bad Marks

When I got my exams back, I was disappointed. Although I had done my best, I had not done well. As the exams came back one by one, my heart beat faster and my hands became colder. One by one the bad marks appeared. When I looked at the physics exam, I could not believe it was mine. I looked at the name again and again. But it *did* belong to me.

Of course, I realize that it is not easy to learn English and study in a Canadian school. I can still remember the day when I quit my job and decided to go back to school. I was twenty-one. The sun was shining warmly, and the birds seemed to be singing their congratulations to me. I dreamed of my new life. I dreamed I would become a good student and go to university after a few years. I would get a good job. Although I knew that I would confront some difficulties, I did not think they would get me down. I did not think I was more stupid than others because I had been very good at school. That is why I had courage to go back to school.

However, since the Christmas exams, my courage has left me. When I look at those exam papers, I ask myself why I can not get higher marks. Is it because someone bothers me at home? No, there are neither sisters nor brothers to bother me. Is it because I do not have enough time to do the homework? No, I have not done any housework since going back to school. My mother has done all the housework. Is it because I am stupid? I do not know if this is true or not, but I was a good student in my Chinese school before coming to Canada. Why can I not do the same as before? Why do I get lower marks than other students when I am older than they? I do not know whether I can catch up or not.

How can I show my report card to my father? How can I talk to him about my problem at school? He not only supported my decision to go to school but has based his hopes and dreams on me. He expects me to finish high school and go to university. I can not disappoint my father. When I fail an exam, it breaks my father's heart. If I quit school, my uncles will jeer at me and say, "I told you so," because they felt I was too old to go back to school.

I do not know what to do. The wind seems ready to swallow me. Steadily the snow falls.

Hsia Ying Fang
China

The First Day

Although I had studied English for three years in Hong Kong, I had many difficulties understanding English when I first came to Canada because in Hong

Kong teachers speak Chinese when teaching English, and the students speak Chinese in English classes too. Since I hardly had any chance to hear or to speak English, I had an extremely hard time studying in a Canadian school at first, an extremely hard time that made me afraid of school.

It was May. The weather was very pleasant. It was not cold, but I was shivering all over; it was not hot, but I was sweating as if it were raining. It was not because I was sick or anything. It was my first day going to a Canadian school!

What will a Canadian school be like? Are the teachers kind or harsh? Do they use hard punishments? And the students? Will they like me or look down on me because of the colour of my skin? Will they laugh at me because of my terrible English? Will the courses be beyond my understanding? Numerous questions were waiting desperately to be answered. Thousands of different feelings—worry, bitterness, terror, curiosity, excitement, hatred—were like a fierce fire burning in me endlessly. I felt hot. I could not breathe.

"Oh, Pa, I want to go home. I am afraid of that school, afraid of those blue-eyed, yellow-haired strangers, afraid of the funny pronunciation of English, afraid of everything. Oh, Father, please take me home," I said to my father, with tears filling my eyes.

"Snow, If you really don't want to go to school, I will take you home, but Snow, you can escape from school for one day or more, but you can't escape it forever. So stand up and face the challenge. Don't let the difficulties get you down. You must get over them. And don't be afraid of failure because success doesn't come naturally. It comes after failure. Also, don't be afraid of your terrible English because practice makes perfect. So you see, there is nothing you should be afraid of. All you have to do is to try your best and do what you can do."

My father's lecture was like a light in the darkness. It lightened my heart. I was like a fish on the bank suddenly free—free to escape back to the sea. Yes, why should I be afraid? There are millions of immigrants who have succeeded in learning English. If they can do it, why can't I? Yes, father, thanks for giving me the willpower and courage. I will try my best to study. I will not disappoint you. I will do as well as other Canadians so that you can be proud of me.

I looked into my father's eyes bravely and said firmly, "Yes, Father, I want to go to school." We both laughed. A feeling of understanding shot through us. My father put out his hand. I held it tightly. The sun was shining brightly.

Snow Hsiung
China

Different Writing Styles

English is very different from my style. English people do not like sentences to go around and around and the idea must be clear, but in our tradition we tend to go around and around and then at last the focus becomes narrower and narrower.

Henry Ma
Hong Kong

Deaf and Dumb

After arriving in Canada, it seemed to me that the most important challenge for me was the new language, English. I had no English background in my native country except that I had tried to learn how to say and write the twenty-six English letters of the alphabet and some simple everyday vocabulary, but since I had never used these words, I forgot them quickly.

The first step in learning English was to learn the alphabet. The order of the letters was important because I had to look up words in the dictionary. At the same time, I practised my English handwriting. In the beginning, I wrote very slowly and my handwriting was awful. I was sure that it would make an English-speaking person laugh, but it got better later.

Grammar was a problem for me. The tenses especially confused me, and even today I still have trouble with them. Besides the grammar which bothered me, there was also pronunciation. I was not used to the multisyllables and tones in an English word because every Chinese word is a monosyllable. To learn an English word I had to know three things: the meaning, pronunciation, and spelling of the word.

I went to an elementary school in a special class which was for students from other countries to learn English. But all the other students were better than I in English, and I was the only one who spoke no English. This made me nervous and lonely. Fortunately, there were some Chinese students in the class. I did not know what to do when the other students spoke to me because I did not understand them. I was forced to use signs with my hands in order to communicate with people, just as if I were deaf and dumb. I hated the students who spoke to me. When the teacher wanted to speak to me, he had to get the other Chinese students to translate. Sometimes there was a joke, and I had to laugh with the others even though I did not know what the joke was, because I was afraid of being laughed at. I hated myself for being in such a situation, and I wondered when I would be able to understand what the people were talking about!

Gary Oue
China

Success Comes After Failure

When I first arrived in Canada, I could not understand a single word and I did not know what was going on in classes at all. I never asked questions nor answered questions in classes. The only thing I did was copy the notes from the board. When I studied at night, I did not understand 90 percent of the vocabulary; therefore, my notebooks were almost covered with Chinese. Besides, everything made me confused—the grammar, verb tenses, spelling, and pronunciation.

I always complained to my father when I got upset after failing tests. I told him that I did not want to go to school and I could find a job in Chinatown. It would not be difficult. My father always said: "You will never succeed if you are afraid of difficulties, but if you are not afraid of them, they will be afraid of you, and at last you will win. Success comes after failures. You fail this test; you will pass the next one. But do not give up whenever you have difficulties."

He also said to me and my brother, "I want you to finish high school, go to university, and gain as much knowledge as possible. This is the main reason we have come to Canada."

My parents influence me a lot. They give me willpower and courage. They expect a great deal from me. I cannot let them be disappointed; therefore, I face the challenge. I study hard, I do my best in everything, and I feel I am getting better and better.

Nora Chao
China

Big Man

When I first came to school I had the most terrible time because of the language problem. I was surprised and happy to see how each teacher was nice to me whenever I asked something. However, I noticed that many ignorant students discriminated against me because of the colour of my skin and my poor English. I felt miserable and began to miss my country very much.

My classmates would take a quick glance at me and never give attention to me from then on. Since no one talked to me, I tried to talk to them. But it was all in vain, because when I spoke to them, they didn't seem to understand what I was saying and continued to mind their business.

I went half crazy as I hardly said a word in school and understood none of what the teachers were saying. I didn't dare ask questions of the teachers because I was scared I would make mistakes. I began to hate our immigration to Canada. I hated my poor English. I hated school and I hated myself. It was much like living in hell.

After spending about a year feeling weak and grieving, I decided to console myself by studying hard and getting good marks. This made my classmates and the teachers aware of my vivid existence in the class. I began to feel self-confident and become vivacious. My family was really delighted to see me doing fine in school and I became their hope. Now, all I had to do was keep studying hard, go to university, and become a "big" man, so that my family would think that, after all, our immigration to Canada had been worthwhile.

Steve Lee
Korea

Lost Opportunities

It is difficult to practise English when you cannot find a friend with whom you can communicate. A boy in my chemistry class, who is Chinese but born in Canada, spoke English with me at first. Our conversation usually ceased in the middle when I could not express my ideas correctly. One day I asked him whether he could speak Chinese. When he answered proudly in Cantonese, my voice turned to Cantonese naturally. I was so comfortable talking to him in my native language that from then on we spoke only in Cantonese. I had lost another opportunity to speak English.

My awkward English causes me many problems in class. In my physics class, whenever we discuss problems or do experiments, instead of speaking English, I keep close to other Chinese students and we speak Cantonese. When we express our thoughts in our native language, we feel more secure. At the same time we are isolated from the rest of the class. I realize that I should be practising my English

Although my English teachers are familiar with my awkward English and can guess my thoughts before I finish speaking sentences which are full of mistakes in grammar and pronunciation, I feel teachers in other subjects may not be so felicitous. Sometimes I prepare a question well and correct it several times for sentence structure before I dare to speak it. Then, because I have attempted to memorize it too well, I speak it too fast. When I am required to repeat what I have said, my voice trembles.

Once in a mathematics class the teacher asked me to solve the problem on the board. He suddenly pointed at me and asked a simple question about the perfect square. He expected his students not to be so slow-witted that they could not answer it. He must have been surprised when I said nothing. He stared at me and the class gave me a strange look. Much to my embarrassment, I stared back intending to say that the answer was "open blanket." I knew the answer, but I was so nervous that the words would not come out. That was the first impression I gave to my mathematics teacher. I knew he would not ask me another question for a very long time.

Dan So Giang
Vietnam

Tongue-tied

The thick snow covered the front yard of my aunt's house. It was a quiet place in Mississauga where I spent the first month in Canada. It bored me to death because it was impossible to see and talk to anybody outside of the family. I had enjoyed watching movies and TV programmes in my country, but here I could only guess at the meanings by watching the pictures because I could understand only the words "How do you do!" and "How are you?"

My special pleasure was to go shopping with my aunt. One day my aunt said that we needed coats, mittens, and hats because it was too cold to walk outside. She took us to Simpson's and said, "Go, find what you like."

While I was selecting a coat, a lady asked, "May I help you?" I could not remember the simple responses my aunt had taught me. Then I felt myself blushing. What a shame I didn't understand English and couldn't express my feelings, for I was living in the country where English is the native language. I had made up my mind: I had to learn English.

My first day at a special school for New Canadians was awkward. My teacher spoke very kindly and slowly to me. I tried desperately to understand and even to guess what she was asking, but it didn't help much. I was so nervous that my whole body seemed to be on fire. The class went on and on and I almost fell asleep at the desk because I did not understand anything.

Day by day I learned more, but I still felt that English sounded strange to me, unlike my own language. When my English had improved, I was ready to go to high school. As soon as I got into the school, I knew it was going to be a very difficult time for me. With all those strange faces and voices around, I was tongue-tied. The teachers spoke so fast that I could not catch a word. One of my English teachers always wanted the students to look up from the book, but I was afraid that she was going to ask me questions which I did not understand. I started to hate myself. Why couldn't I be as good as others?

English classes were, however, not the biggest challenge for me. In the chemistry class everything was totally new, just like the first time I heard of the alphabet. The first test came as a shock; I had barely passed the test. I was so depressed because I used to be very good in chemistry, but because of the language, I could not use my talent. Once the teacher asked me a question which I understood, but I could not find the English to express the answer, and so I had to tell the teacher, "I'm sorry, I don't know how to explain it in English."

I always had difficulty understanding the daily announcements. One day my home form teacher gave me the announcements to read in the class because I sat in the front row. I was afraid that my classmates would laugh at me, and so I passed it to a girl behind me.

Facing all these problems, I didn't give up. I listened to the teachers very carefully in class and tried to learn the way Canadians spoke. I worked very hard on chemistry. English sounded more and more familiar to me. Finally came the achievement. I did a good job on the Christmas exams. I love this school where I have learned so many things, especially English. I'm going to be here for one more year. For the rest of my life, I must learn more English.

Binhua Wang
China

Too Much Pressure

In the last year of high school we suffer under much pressure. We must pass our exams and try to get into the university of our choice so that we can get a good job and have a secure future.

Where does this pressure come from? First, we hear stories from students who have graduated from school and who are now studying in universities. They keep telling us how difficult it was for them while they were studying at high school and how it is even more difficult at university. This makes us totally depressed.

Also teachers give us pressure. They give us piles and piles of homework, expecting the Great Wall of China to be built in a day. In addition, they give us too many tests. I have had a test almost every day and essays to hand in within a short period of time. As a result, because of studying for these tests, I have had to give up my study for exams. Since I can not catch up with the work, I have begun to worry about getting good marks on the exams.

Lastly, our parents push us too hard to get good marks. They want us to obtain the finest education. This means getting into university. Since parents give us pressure at home and teachers give us pressure at school simultaneously, we have no time to relax.

Perhaps this pressure keeps us studying hard and is good for us because it helps to shape our characters. On the other hand, it just might lead us to a nervous breakdown.

Sung Hoon Kim
Korea

Split Personality

It was four years ago when I suddenly became a different person. I don't mean that I physically changed or anything, but my personality changed because I had been known as Khanh and then I became Chris.

The name Chris came to me during summer school when my friends and I were walking along and talking about careers in the future. I said I wanted to be a fashion designer, not a doctor, as my parents had been dying for. Anyway, while we were talking, I had the idea of changing my name to Chris because I wanted be to a successful designer like Christian Dior. I like Christian because he designs women's clothes with a simple, casual look. I know the life-style today mainly focuses on clothes. I have a dream of opening a franchise all over the world, that is, if my parents approve.

My new name Chris created a few problems for me at home and at school. When I came to school, I wanted the teacher to call me Chris because it was easy for them and my friends as well. When I changed my name, I was not aware that I was no longer Khanh. I felt as if I had a split personality. My family noticed the changes in me. They said that I was acting weird, and I was no longer the person I had been. My parents told me that I should never have adopted any name other than the one I was born with. They said personality depends on the name you are born with. "Chris is not you," said my father. "It is somebody else, and you're being a part of that person's soul, not yourself."

At school my friends all knew me as Chris, not Khanh. If a teacher called me Khanh, I got embarrassed. However, on the first day of school this year when I came to home form to pick up my timetable, the teacher called Chris to come up. Since I had just taken my new name, I didn't think he meant me. There were three boys named Chris in my home form. In a way I am neither Chris nor Khanh.

I did not tell my parents about my desire to be a designer, not a doctor, because I didn't want to hurt them. I will find a way to tell them later in life. As Chris, I will try my best to deal with school and become a successful designer. This is my dream.

Chris Truong
Vietnam

Heritage Languages

Heritage Language Programs Should Be Taught At School

Heritage languages should be taught during the regular school day so that we can preserve our first language skills, our culture, and our identity.

I have been immersed in Chinese culture since I was born, but now I have been in Canada for four years, and it seems as if Canadian culture and the English language are dominating, while the Chinese culture and language I have learned are vanishing. For example, the concept of extended families was a very strong influence on me when I was growing up, and it disappeared completely when I came to Canada. I feel the loss of my identity because I cannot communicate very well in my own language. For example, it is difficult for me to translate a news report for my grandfather. I feel so helpless when my grandfather says something to me in Chinese and I cannot understand him.

Learning English is important, but the development and constant use of the heritage language is also important and necessary. Chinese should be taught at school. Although I have spoken Chinese since I was born, I have forgotten most of it, because for the past four years, I have not continued my lessons in Chinese and have been studying English very intensely. Presently, I can read only very simple Chinese characters and I do not know their meaning. Also I write very poorly—in contrast, I can write an English composition and understand novels without much trouble.

Some people argue that heritage languages should be taught on Saturday or after school. The problem with this is that many people like me would not be able to get involved in some of the extracurricular activities after school. Also, Saturday morning classes are not convenient for me because I work on Saturdays. This work is important to me because I need to save money for university.

Chinese is not only important to me so that I can communicate with my family, but it may also be important to me in the future when I apply for a job. Since so many businesses are making links with China, fluency in Chinese will be an important asset in the business world.

While learning English and the Canadian culture in Canada is most important, our own cultures and languages must not be forgotten. We need to pass them on to later generations. Thus, heritage languages should be taught at school.

Fee Mei Yeh
India

Heritage Language Programs
Should *Not* Be Taught at School

Now, there is a lot of debate about whether heritage languages should be put into the regular school day. I know that all people love their native country, want to speak the native language, and are glad if other people speak this language. This is quite understandable, but there are reasons why I think we should not teach heritage languages in the regular school day.

Canada is a country made up of people from all over the world. People from everywhere come here to find peace, love, and an opportunity for a good life. We come here to build a new country and a new life. When we are here, our lives are tied to this new country. If it is strong, we are strong; if it is prosperous, we are prosperous. That's why we should do our best to make it become better and better. That's why we should understand what Canadians are thinking and doing.

There are many differences between Asians and Canadians because of language, customs, and history. If we keep on making these differences bigger and bigger, they will separate this united community and make the life harsh for every one of us.

Think about how students of different backgrounds are already separate from each other. If heritage languages were put into the regular school day, they would cause a deeper division of students by language and finally separate the school into small groups. I don't think anyone of us would be glad to see that.

Also, teaching heritage languages would cost a lot of money. Last year the Toronto Board of Education spent $11,000,000 on heritage language education. If we keep on doing this, we will not have enough money for other regular school programs and new equipment; I think these are much more important.

If we put a heritage language program into our school, a lot of new students will choose the native language for one credit. This will impede their progress in English. Even though their native languages are very important to their future, students should put first things first. They have to live in Canadian society. Without English, they can do nothing. Without English, they will not succeed. For example, if students want to go to business at university or college, they must have strong English fluency and pass English tests. If they want to find a job, they have to communicate with people in English. That's why everyone should learn English as fast as possible.

Some parents want their children, especially the second and third generation, to learn their native language. But even if their children know how to speak the native language, they will still think of Canada as their home. They do not care about where they come from; they care about what they are going to face, how they are going to live, and what contribution they will make. They do not need to forget about their native country and their native language. They can learn their native language on Saturday morning or at night school.

We should not always think about our past. We should face our life which is in front of us, and build a great country and a new world. If we put our effort into Canada, we will think it as beautiful as our native country.

In order to have enough money for regular school programs, keep a united community, and make life more harmonious for New Canadians and native Canadians, we should *not* put heritage language programs into the regular school day.

Rei Zhong (Ray) Wu
China

Freedom to Speak

One of the most common comments on my reports has always been "ambitious." Yes, I am. I want to be a useful person in society for the rest of my life. A traditional Chinese proverb says that if you do not study hard in your youth, your life will bring you difficulties when you get older. I heard that proverb often from my mother's teaching before I went to school.

From the first day of school, I thought of becoming a scholar. Besides finishing the required assignments, I did a lot of extra exercises at home. That improved my problem-solving skills. I made a rule for myself in learning English to memorize ten new words per day so that when I graduated from high school, I would be able to read some simple stories in English.

My goal became higher as I grew up. I thought teachers were respectable persons who would bring knowledge into young minds by their industriousness and devotion. I wanted to become a good teacher; therefore, I studied as hard as I could, even on weekends and holidays.

Many Canadian teachers have the impression that Chinese students are mostly introverted. One of my teachers says that Chinese students may have a special talent but will hide it, or they may have a good idea but will hesitate to express it in class discussion. Being introverted is not an innate quality of ours. It is rather a result of the society of China. There has always been some successful person imprisoned in each revolution because of being too outspoken and critical of the government. The more revolutions that passed, the more people learned to speak less.

People who used to know me considered me an extroverted and curious girl. Besides studying, there were so many activities which interested me: swimming, table-tennis, dancing, singing. When I was in elementary school, everything seemed so sweet and simple, and I dreamed optimistically of a happy life in the future.

When I went to high school, I realized that society was more complicated than I had thought, and people who lived in our society had to pretend to support socialism or be thrown in jail. I did not see that Chairman Mao had done anything very worthwhile, but I did not dare criticize him in public. At that time, every word had to be carefully considered before you said it because there were always some students who were jealous of another's academic achievements and who would, therefore, spread rumours. I was bored at the long and silent meetings we were forced to attend. I loved to share my opinions with others, but I was afraid of those students who would see weaknesses in me. For my own safety, I disciplined myself not to speak too much. From then on, I forced myself to become a quiet, reserved person. I hated to live in that kind of closed society. It was like being locked in a silent world where I could only speak to my own heart.

I was lucky to come to Canada—a democratic world where a person can express his or her thoughts. Now at school, I hear straightforward and friendly talk every day. The teachers always want the experiences of talking with students; therefore, I have started to speak out without hesitation.

Immigrating to Canada has changed my personality in other ways. I am used to western life-style and I have grown a little impatient with people around me. Sometimes my sister wants to discuss some questions with me while I am troubled by my own assignments. I shout at her not to ask me anymore. I hate myself for this.

No matter where I live, I want to be myself—a studious, thoughtful, and self-controlled person.

Binhua Wang
China

Women Are Equal

Since I have been in a Canadian high school, I have begun to question some of the beliefs I had in Japan. In Canada, it is generally thought that women should have the same rights as men and should be treated equally. However, in my native country, Japan, the tradition is that women should be devoted and obedient to men. This idea still persists today.

In the high school I used to go to in Japan, sports clubs were very popular. When I was in Grade 10, I was asked to be a manager of a boys' volleyball club. In sports clubs "manager" means a person who does all the odd jobs for the members of the team, and usually the manager is supposed to be a girl. I am sure that this job looks absolutely ridiculous to independent-minded girls in Canada, but among Japanese girls, to be a manager of a sports club was almost a prize.

Soon after starting as manager, I was amazed to realize what a stupid and boring job I had. In our club the manager's jobs were to wipe the balls, write in the score book, time each exercise, fold up the members' uniforms, and prepare tea. In short, being a manager was just like being a maid, except the manager did not get paid.

At the beginning, I enjoyed watching the boys and helping them. But as time went on, the boys became more demanding and rude to me. They were the same way to all the other managers too. When we got on the subway on the way to a volleyball meet, the boys would sit down first, not offering a seat to us managers. When we gave handmade presents to all the members, there were only a few boys who said thank you. None of them seemed to really appreciate our work or even to think of how hard we were trying to help them. I bet they never considered how much it hurt when the balls spiked us on the face.

One day some of the seniors, the graduates from the volleyball team, invited me and the other managers to have dinner with them. They seemed to be much more friendly to us than the present members. So we accepted the invitation. They took us to a Japanese bar where businessmen drank and laughed loudly. What made me even more angry and surprised was that one of the seniors said to me with a smile on his face, "Can you fill my glass?"

I felt very insulted and was about to say, "I'm neither your wife nor a barmaid," but I knew it was too impolite to say to a senior student. I filled his glass, but I felt bitter.

Although I knew it was not worthwhile to stay in the club, I still could not quit. Somewhere in my mind, I must have still believed in the virtue of obedience and self-sacrifice. I stayed in the club until I left Japan.

Now, living in Canada and being affected by the girls around me, I realize how urgent it is for Japanese girls to fight against the inequality that exists even in high schools. I would not say that the traditional ideas of women's obedience and devotion are totally unworthy, but we should know when and to whom to apply them. It is very frightening to be surrounded by old traditions which everybody follows. Unconsciously, we start believing in their value, without even questioning them.

Reiko Kawamoto
Japan

Student Activities

Talking and Writing*

With your partner, take turns reading the stories on pages 52 to 54. Then answer the following questions.

1. Explain why:
   - The writer compares herself to a stone. ("Like a Stone")
   - Joe feels very pleased with himself. ("Do You Want to Dance?")
   - Lin's classmates laugh at her in the first week of school. ("My Dictionary Is My Best Friend")
   - Amy is afraid when she first registers at school. ("Afraid of Everything")
   - Hsia Ying hates to take home her report card. ("Bad Marks")

2. Tell what subjects you are finding most difficult now at school.

3. Tell about a funny or embarrassing experience you had when you first arrived at your school.

Talking and Writing**

"First Day"

1. Why was Snow so frightened on the first day of school? On your first day did you have similar thoughts?

2. What three pieces of advice did Snow's father give her? In your opinion, is this good advice? Explain.

3. Describe the relationship between Snow and her father. Support your answer by referring to details in the story.

"Different Writing Styles" and "Deaf and Dumb"

1. Why is the phrase "deaf and dumb" a good way to describe the situation of a New Canadian?

2. State clearly three differences between your native language and English and explain why these differences cause you problems.

"Success Comes After Failure"

1. Here is another girl who received great strength from her father. How did her father help her?

2. Vocabulary is a great problem for anyone learning a new language. With a partner discuss the methods that have worked best for you in learning new words.

"Big Man"

1. Explain, by referring to Steve's story, why he went "half crazy" at school and why it was like "living in hell."

2. How does Steve overcome his isolation and anger?

3. Steve meets discrimination and disinterest at school. Is his experience unique? Compare his experience to a situation in which you have been involved.

"Tongue-Tied"

The personality of this writer becomes clear through her story. State two qualities of her character that are revealed here. Support your answer by references to her narrative.

"Too Much Pressure"

The style of this essay is clear and persuasive. Give examples of each of the following:

- clear topic sentences which emphasize main ideas;
- transition words to show connections between ideas;
- repetition to emphasize important ideas;
- rhetorical questions to catch reader's interest.

"Split Personality"

1. Chris and his parents have different opinions about his name change and his future. With a partner, role-play a discussion between father and son about his name change and his future plans.

2. With whose point of view are you most in sympathy? Explain.

"Heritage Language Programs"

1. Summarize in point form the arguments on both sides of this issue.

2. Find examples of parallel sentence structure.

3. With a partner evaluate which essay seems to be the most persuasive.

"Women Are Equal"

1. How has a year in Canada changed Reiko's values?

2. What evidence does Reiko give to show the inequality of females in Japan?

3. In your native culture are men and women equal? Give examples to support your opinion.

Group Discussion

1. Read "Lost Opportunities." In a small group discuss each of the following statements. Refer to your reading and to incidents from your own experience to support your opinions.

   - Students should never speak their native language in the classroom.
   - Teachers should put ESL students with partners who do not speak their native language.
   - Teachers should ask ESL students direct questions to force them to speak in front of the class.

2. Ask the other members of your group about education in their native countries. What are important differences between education in Canada and in other countries?

3. Do you agree or disagree with each of the following statements? Give reasons to support your opinion.

   - Canadian teachers should be more strict.
   - Computers should replace teachers.
   - Heritage languages should be taught in the school.
   - Formal exams should be abolished.
   - ESL students should be given more time and the use of a dictionary for formal exams.
   - Schools should be co-educational.

Writing Folder

1. Describe a funny or embarrassing experience you had when you first arrived at your school.

2. Write a letter to a good friend in your native country describing your new school in Canada.

3. Choose one of the topics you enjoyed discussing in your group. State your opinion clearly, and develop three arguments to support your opinion.

4. After discussing the essays on Heritage Language Programs, write a persuasive paragraph in which you give arguments in support of your opinion on this issue or another controversial issue of interest to you.

5. In a persuasive paragraph explain how your school might do more to help New Canadians.

6. Compare your school in Canada and your school in your native country. You might discuss evaluation, teaching methods, relationship between teachers and students, extracurricular activities, and course content.

7. Many students in their first years in a Canadian school feel isolated. Interview some classmates. In an essay explain the causes and effects of the isolation of New Canadians. Refer to your own experiences, your reading, and your interviews with classmates.

Jobs

Students work at part-time jobs for many different reasons. They may need to earn money to give to their families or to use for their own activities; they may want to learn new skills; they may find a job a good way to meet other young people; or they may wish to become more independent.

The kinds of jobs they are able to get are usually unskilled and low paying, such as working in grocery stores, serving food in fast-food restaurants, or pumping gas in gas stations. Some are fortunate to have helpful employers, kind co-workers, and enjoyable tasks, while others encounter coldness, prejudice, and unpleasant duties. But all find that, regardless of the circumstances and conditions, working at a job outside of school has many advantages. A job brings independence, social confidence, and increased fluency in English. Above all, a job results in greater understanding of and participation in Canadian society.

As you read the following stories, think of the benefits and disadvantages of a part-time job for yourself. If you already have a job, compare your own experiences to those of the writers.

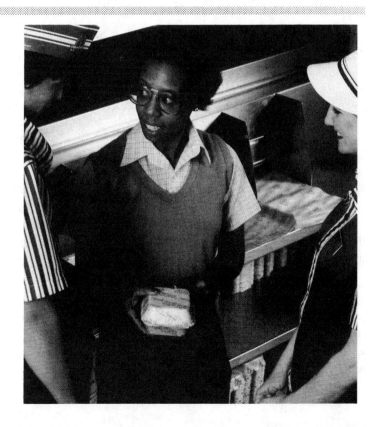

McDonald's

I applied for a job in McDonald's at the end of July because I was getting bored with the summer holidays. On the first day of training, I was so nervous that I almost lost my voice. My trainer, Paula, is the host and also the head of the crew. She likes to joke around and make us do lots of extra work, but she's really pleasant. She designed everything in McDonald's, our activity calendar and the decorations in the lobby during holidays like Halloween or Christmas.

Working there, I have learned a lot of things that I cannot get from school: how to be a leader and how to relate to a boss. My managers treat me well. Now I can work on any station: cook, cashier, lobby.

In McDonald's there is a crew activity every month like skiing, skating, dancing, and in the summertime we go to the Canadian National Exhibition or Canada's Wonderland. It is very exciting to take part in these activities, and all you have to do is just sign up.

Wayne Cheng
Taiwan

Two Managers

Three years ago, I got my first job at McDonald's as a cashier. All I had to do was to take the customer's order and to collect the money. Maybe you think that it was an easy job. What was difficult for me was not the sore back or strained face muscles from smiling. What was really difficult was to work with two managers at my back.

In a situation where one manager told me to fill up the ice while the other manager told me to sweep the floor, it was always hard to decide what to do first. Sometimes I planned to fill up the ice first and then sweep the floor, but the manager who told me to sweep the floor always got angry because he thought that I was not doing what he told me to do. One manager told me to fill the soft drink cup right up to the yellow line of the cup. Another manager told me to fill it up above the yellow line. Therefore, I was always being blamed for not doing the "right" thing!

Once I was really frustrated. One day when it was not very busy, there was a customer in my line who ordered two hamburgers and two large fries. The hamburgers were not ready at the time he ordered and they took about fifteen minutes instead of the usual five minutes. At the same time, I was making the fries. I had the fries ready just before the two hamburgers were up. While I was filling up the fries, the manager said to me, "You should have the fries prepared ahead of time because the man has been waiting for almost 15 minutes." I was really angry and said, "The fries only take two or three minutes to cook and I am already filling them up." I thought, "What takes 15 minutes is your hamburgers!"

Although I did not seem to have a very good time at McDonald's, it was a worthwhile experience. I learned a lot from my job. For example, I learned how to work and communicate with people. I also learned some slang words even though sometimes the slang words "screwed me up" a little. Furthermore, I think my English improved.

John Wong
Hong Kong

Family Pride

I had a very busy day today. I sold three magazine subscriptions and got a bonus at work. My aunt and my father were waiting for me when I got back from work. They are very much against my working after school. However, we need the money. My aunt says that my grades are more important. My dad is also worried and is feeling bad that I am working when he is not. For him it is a question of family pride.

Ranjit Ebenezer
India

One Step Forward, One Step Back

I feel as if every time I step forward, I also step back.

When I was younger I didn't like to communicate with others, but since coming to Canada I have overcome this problem. Now I talk a lot, and I like to have friends to hang around with.

Although I am happy about overcoming that problem, I also feel very disappointed with myself because sometimes I talk too much and hurt people without even noticing it. For instance, now that I am more extroverted, I sometimes judge people too quickly and express my opinion too impulsively. Then I hurt people.

Even my family says that coming to Canada has made a big change in me. For instance, my aunt says that I spend too much time talking on the phone. She also says that I spend all my money buying things like clothes, shoes, posters, tapes, records, and I don't really need them. Well, I think she is right. The Canadian life-style has affected my behaviour a lot, but I feel she does not understand that in order for a teenager to learn to be responsible and grow up to be an important member of society, that teenager has to learn from mistakes, and the only way to learn from mistakes is to make them.

Every time I wanted money, I almost had to beg my aunt for it. At first my aunt didn't want me to work because she said that if I work and study at the same time, it can affect my marks at school. Besides, she said that in Costa Rica teenagers at school don't work and that's why the majority do well in school. Finally, I convinced her to let me work.

I have to work to feel independent.

Karla Ramirez
Costa Rica

So Much to Do

Because I have so much work to do every day, I always go home immediately after school. Sometimes my friends want me to stay at school to finish our homework together or join some club. I really want to, but I can't because I have to look after my sister.

When I get home, I have to wash the breakfast dishes which have been left from 5 o'clock. My mother comes back home at 5:30. When we have finished dinner, I have to wash the dishes again.

After this, I take a bath and then begin to do my homework. When I sit on the chair, I always feel there is so much homework that I will not be able to finish it. At first, I cannot concentrate, but if I have already started it, I am able to concentrate without letting anyone interrupt me. When I finish my homework, I feel it has not been too bad and I am glad I have done it.

Shirley Kwong
Hong Kong

Busboy

Son: Hi, Mum.

Mother: You're late for supper. Where have you been?

Son: I had an interview for a job. At a restaurant. I got the job and I'm starting work this weekend.

Mother: You didn't ask me about that. I don't want you working in a restaurant. What will you be doing?

Son: I'll be working as a busboy. What's wrong with that?

Mother: What will our friends say?

Son: I don't care what they say. Don't tell them. Look, I'll be making $7.00 an hour, plus tips. I can use the money!

Mother: Why do you need money? I don't like my friends laughing at me when they hear you're working in a restaurant. We didn't come to Canada so that you could work in a restaurant!

Son: It's only a part-time job. Lots of my friends have jobs like this. I know that you don't need money but...

Mother: No! I don't want to hear anymore. Quit the job and study hard. That's the only thing I want you to do. Do you understand?

Son: Look, I'm 16 years old. Everyone at school has a part-time job! My friends have their own money to spend. They don't have to ask their parents for money. I want to be like them.

Mother: If you need more money, we can give you some.

Son: No, Mum. What I'm saying is that I want my own money so that I can buy what I like. I want my own stereo in my bedroom.

Mother: What's wrong with the stereo we have in the living room?

Son: The sound is terrible. There are sales on now of terrific new equipment. What I want costs about eight hundred dollars.

Mother: Eight hundred dollars! Are you crazy?

Son: You see, I said you wouldn't understand. I don't want to have to justify everything to you.

Mother: My friends will think I don't care about you. My friends will think you are going to work in a restaurant for the rest of your life, and that you don't care about your studies or going to university.

Son: We'll never agree.

Cuong Vu
Vietnam

Independence

The way girls are treated in the family is different in every country. In my country a girl is not allowed to go out alone. Some families allow the girl to go out with a boy who is well known by the entire family, but only in the afternoon. If a girl wants to go out with a boy at night, she has to be accompanied by a sister or another relative. I find these restrictions very old-fashioned.

My problem began when I got fed up. I got the courage to stand up and express my feelings about being pushed around by my family. "Listen," I said, "you don't have to worry about me so much. Just because I'm a girl doesn't mean I can't take care of myself."

After I finished my speech, they were very surprised, and I was even more surprised than they were. I never speak up, and I do not know how I got the courage to do it.

My uncle was very upset. "We all have rights and we have obligations too. This you have to understand," my uncle said angrily.

"Yes, I seem to have obligations, but my rights are very limited," I replied.

"Don't talk back to me, little girl," was his answer.

I did not want to hear another word about it. I wanted to finish the discussion. "I'm not a little girl anymore," I said. "This is what all of you don't understand, but from now on you will have to understand." I went to my bedroom before my uncle could say anything more.

I was determined to get a job and be more independent. I had never worked before in my whole life because they would not let me, and I knew they would be very disappointed if I got a job, but I didn't care. This is how I got a job against their will. I knew this was the first thing I should do, and I know it was the right thing to do.

Annelise Monroy
Columbia

Factory Worker

You can imagine that anyone who comes to a foreign country knowing nothing, not even its language, finds it hard to live there! You are always classified as a stupid person because you cannot speak. How can I describe my feelings when I arrived in Canada. How cold and hopeless I felt at that time! Immigrating to Canada was the end of my innocent childhood and the beginning of my grown-up life. There were so many pressures: language problems, family problems, and personal problems. Because I was forced to solve these, I became more mature.

In order to help my family pay a heavy debt, I had to work. Working in a factory! I had never thought of it before in my life, but I had to do it. The day my uncle brought me to see the boss, I was so frightened. After passing through a huge and noisy room, we arrived in the boss's office. A tall, fat man greeted us. From his expression I knew he must be the boss. While he was talking to my uncle, I saw his sharp, cold eyes judging me as if they asked, "Is she really able to work here?" To my surprise, my uncle told me that I was hired. Convincing a boss must not have been so difficult for my sharp-tongued uncle. Now I was a worker, not a child anymore, I thought.

Although I had been taught a hundred times that working people were different from children and well-educated people were different from non-educated people, when I really understood this was the day I started working in the factory in Montreal. My master builder was a kind, cultured, and gentle person who knew that I could not speak French; therefore, she always showed me slowly and clearly each step of the work. I appreciated her because she was the first kind Canadian I had met since arriving in Canada about two weeks before. But when some non-educated workers learned that I could not speak French, they were very nasty to me. They picked on me and laughed at me as if I were born more stupid than they. When I considered those kind of people, I thought of a proverb: "Big fish eats small fish. Small fish eats shrimp!" Sometimes I tried to be friendly to them. The only way I could show it was by smiling, but they seemed to find my smiling stupid and unkind.

"No hard time can stay forever." This is my philosophy of life. Although immigrating to Canada has made my life very hard, I have learned quite a lot from working people and the world of work. Because I have gone through difficult experiences, I appreciate my studies now and I am glad to be at school.

Li Yuin Tam
China

Not a Princess

When I was 15 years old, I had my first part-time job. My experience might be very common to many people, but it was really an unusual experience for me.

When the manager of Harvey's restaurant phoned and told me that I could work in his restaurant, I was very excited. At first I thought I should tell my family about this news, but I changed my mind after a few seconds. It was because I knew that they would look down on me. I don't mean they would feel my job was bad. I just mean they would think I did not have any ability to do this job because they thought I was very careless. In my family's eyes, I was weak, afraid of everything, and shy, just like a princess.

In fact, I do not believe I am this kind of person. Therefore, I changed my mind again. I decided to tell my family about working at Harvey's, because I wanted to show them my ability and courage to do this job.

When I was working at Harvey's Restaurant, I often met terrible customers. One time a lady came in. "Hi, can I help you?" I said politely.

"Yes, I want to buy a coffee. How much is it?" The lady's voice was very sharp.

"Fifty cents," I replied.

After I finished making the coffee, I gave it to her and took the change.

"Oh, sorry. You just gave me thirty cents. The coffee costs fifty cents," I said.

"What? I only gave you thirty cents! You're wrong. I'm sure I gave you fifty cents," the old lady said loudly and angrily. All the customers in the restaurant began to look at us.

"No, you"… At that time the manager came out from the kitchen.

"What's wrong?" the manager said.

"She just paid thirty cents. It's supposed to be fifty cents," I said.

"No, I've already given her fifty cents," the lady spoke more loudly.

"Okay, I don't think it's your mistake. I'm sorry," the manager said to the lady.

I was very angry and choked back my reply. At this point I could see the manager did not believe me. I was insulted. Everyone really thought it was my fault.

I worked at Harvey's only one month. At the beginning I thought that working was easier than studying in school. We did not have any tests or homework. In fact, I was wrong. It was not easy at all. Also I understood that school and society are two different worlds. In school, people are simple and honest, but in society, there are many dishonest people. This was really a good lesson to learn.

Lois Chan
Hong Kong

Picking Worms

Last summer I tried to find a job as other students did. It was really hard for me to find a good job because my English was not good enough, and I didn't have any experience for a job in a factory. At last I found a job which anyone could do without experience. Picking worms!

During the summer I had to take an English course to improve my English at the same time as I worked to make money. Trying to do both at once was very difficult. My job started at eleven o'clock at night and stopped when the sun rose. Then I had to be present at school at 8:30 a.m. The trouble was that I didn't have much time for sleeping and studying; however, I had no choice.

Picking worms had to be done at night, especially in the rainy weather when the ground was soft. I had to wear a light on my head, a battery on my back, and two cans tied to my legs. In one can I put the sawdust and in the other one I put the worms. Also, I had to wear heavy waterproof boots, a rain coat, and warm clothes.

I always worked on farms outside the city. In the evening at seven or eight o'clock, a truck came to my house and picked me and other people up to go to the country. There were usually about 15 people in the truck.

My salary depended on how many worms I picked. Consequently, I had to pick the worms alive, pick them carefully and quickly. The boss gave $25 for each thousand worms. If you had a good hand and the weather was good so that the worms came out, you could get from $100 to $150 a night. It was a very good payment.

The job was especially difficult the first time. I had to bend my back and walk slowly to see the worms easily by the light attached to my head. I remember the first morning after I finished the job I could hardly stand and walk. My back and my legs hurt so much that I couldn't walk up the stairs, and when I changed my trousers, I had to lie on my bed to change them.

Since the job was so difficult and interfered with my studying, you might wonder why I had to take it. There were two reasons. First, I have to help my family in Vietnam since I am the only member of my family who escaped. The rest of my family suffers a great deal since they do not have enough food and money. I hope with the money I send them their life will be better. Second, I need money for my studying this year. I need to pay my rent, buy my food, and buy my books.

I know I won't keep this job all my life, but I think temporarily it will help me keep on studying and also help my family survive. At this time, picking worms is the best job for me.

Long Bui
Vietnam

Student Activities

Talking and Writing*

"McDonald's" and "Two Managers"

Compare the feelings of Wayne and John about their first jobs. Refer to incidents in their stories to illustrate their feelings.

"So Much to Do"

1. What jobs must Shirley do at home? What jobs at home are you responsible for?

2. Do you think a high school student should have to do jobs at home? Explain.

"Busboy"

1. With a partner read this story. Now change roles and read the script again. Discuss the following questions:

   - Cuong and his mother do not agree about his working. What arguments do they use to support their positions?
   - With whom do you feel the most sympathy? Why?

2. In pairs, develop and role-play a dialogue between a parent and a teenager about jobs.

Group Discussion

1. Read independently all the stories about jobs. In a group of four or five, discuss the following questions. Refer to these stories, your own experiences, and those of others in the group in your discussion.

   - What are the reasons many teenagers get jobs?
   - What might be some arguments against taking a part-time job?

2. Find out if members of your group have had jobs in Canada. Find out how they got the jobs and whether or not they would recommend these jobs to you. What advice would you give to a friend who wants a job?

3. Debate one of the following topics.

   - Girls should have less freedom and independence than boys.
   - A teenager has the right to get a part-time job even if parents disagree.
   - Long Bui should forget about picking worms and concentrate on summer school.
   - Every teenager should have a part-time job.

Writing Folder

1. Role-play and then write a script on one of the following situations.

   - The manager of Mcdonald's interviews you for a job.

- Your father and you debate whether or not you should take a part-time job.
- You and another worker come into conflict.

2. Write five questions you should ask when you apply for a job.

3. Write five questions you might be asked if you were applying for a job at McDonald's.

4. You are applying for a job. Write a description of yourself to convince the boss to hire you.

5. Interview at least three of your classmates about their part-time or summer jobs. Write a persuasive essay about jobs. Choose a theme, state your theme in the opening paragraph, and develop at least three arguments to support your theme. (Refer to your reading, your own experience, and your interviews.)

6. After discussion with your partner or in a group, write a short response to three of the following situations. What would you do if

- your parents refuse to allow you to work?
- a co-worker is stealing?
- the boss makes unreasonable complaints against you?
- you get overpaid?
- you get underpaid?
- you think you are being discriminated against because you are an immigrant?

7. Choose the topic you were most interested in discussing. Write a persuasive essay in which you support your position by developing three strong arguments.

Parents: Newcomers to Canada

Young people are keenly aware of the problems facing their parents when they come to Canada. Often parents have left behind homes, possessions, jobs, and, above all, family and friends in order to shape a better future for their children.

In these stories, students observe life from the point of view of their parents, or they describe what they see of their parents' experiences and reactions. The students reveal worries about the hard work, financial insecurity, and isolation their parents face, and express appreciation of their parents' sacrifice. When parents have come to Canada to ensure a better life for their children, students sometimes feel intense pressure to live up to the high expectations of their parents and experience guilt if they do not fulfill their parents' dreams.

As you read these stories you might examine the problems your parents faced in their first years in Canada and consider the changes in your parents and in your relationship with them.

We Imagine How Our Parents Feel About Life in Canada

Always Alone

I have been here now for three months and I haven't yet adapted to the surroundings and people. I don't know a single sentence of English except for a few words my daughter taught me. I have lost my way twice downtown and I don't know how to ask my way back until I meet a Chinese person. That's why I don't dare to go far. Even though I know how to get on a subway, I don't know which stop to get off at because I can't read a word of English. I have to force myself to memorize a word letter by letter. There are only four stops I am familiar with in three months' time. I'm always alone in the house, pacing and sleeping. I feel old and tired.

Maria Mok
Hong Kong

Opening an Account

I remember when I came to Canada, I could not read, speak, understand, or write English. I could only write my name in English. Two weeks after arriving in Canada, I went to a bank to open a savings account. Before I went there, my daughter told me that the cashier would take care of me.

So I went to the bank and there was a long lineup. I got into the line and waited for my turn. When my turn came, I went to the cashier and told her exactly what my daughter had taught me: "I want to open an account." I repeated the words carefully and slowly three times before she understood me. Then she pointed to another counter.

Then I went there and told another lady the same words I had said before. That time the lady asked me, "What kind of account would you like to open?" I could not find the words to reply. I was so embarrassed that I left the bank as fast as I could.

Robert Queh
Burma

Like a Child

Coming to Canada was the biggest change in my life because I had to go out to make a living for my family. When I was in India, I had my own business, but here I can't work in business because I can't speak English. I had to ask my son or daughter to come with me to look for a job. It made me feel like a child when I looked for jobs in factories. Luckily, after weeks of searching, I found a job.

When I started the first day, one of the workers was assigned to show me what I had to do. It took me a very long time to understand what she was trying to say. At last, I was able to understand her by her actions and a few simple words. I felt so stupid and helpless.

Fa Jung Li
India

Too Old to Start Again

I have decided to go back to Hong Kong next month. Don't persuade me against this because you will never understand. Don't tell me that I can learn English from "A" to "Z" as my grandchild does. Don't forget that I am already sixty-eight—too old to start again. I feel that I and dad are like "cabbages" here. We are handicapped. Don't tell me that we can go shopping, sightseeing, visiting, as you can do, because we can't read the street names, ask directions, or answer the phone.

Margaret Chan
Hong Kong

Nothing to Do

How lonely I am! My wife and daughter go to work. My son goes to school. I am alone at home with nothing to do. I can't go out because I have to baby-sit my grandchildren. In India I managed a large business.

Most Chinese in Toronto don't speak Fukienese. The other day on a streetcar, I heard two Chinese talking in Fukienese. Oh, how glad I was! I went to them and introduced myself. I asked them where they came from, and made friends with them. I got their phone numbers, and now I phone them every now and then. My wife reminds me I may be annoying them, but I am just glad at least I have some friends.

I was on the subway train one day. At one subway station all the people on the train got off after some announcement was mumbled through the speakers in the train. I didn't understand what was said; therefore, I stayed on the train, alone and puzzled. The train left and went on to the next station. I was alone and frightened. Fortunately, a subway worker saw me and spoke to me in English. I did not understand. Finally, the subway train returned to the station it had just left and let me get off.

Tze Kan Yeo
Burma

Superman

Faced with a different environment in Canada and the language problems, my father has a feeling of being "a dragon in shallow water which has become the butt of shrimps." He could not find a job which was suitable for him. But at last, he found a job in the Computer Bar System Corporation where he deals with machines all the time. He says he is pleased with this job although the wage is not high.

My father is an industrious person too. Now he is studying at night school every night to learn more English. After the whole day's work he still has energy to listen to the teacher. I wonder if he is a superman.

I asked my father what he expects us to do in the future. He answered me with a smile that he wants us to marry good husbands and have good families. I doubt it. I know he would like me and my sister to be famous persons, doctors or something that would make us more useful.

I know my father's thoughts as he knows mine.

Amy Tam
Hong Kong

A Cruel Joke

My parents have changed a great deal since they came to Canada. My father used to be the manager of a company. He did not have to work at all because he hired many employees to work for him. Now he is a workman doing a labouring job in a factory. My mother did not have to do any housework because we had maids and cooks. Now she goes to work in the daytime and at night she does all the housework. Every morning, she gets up at five because my father goes to work at six. She has to make breakfast and lunch for my father and for us. It seems that fate has played a cruel joke on my parents.

I feel very sorry for them. Sometimes when I try to help my mother she just says, "It doesn't matter. Let me do the housework and you go do your homework." She continues in a determined voice, "No matter how difficult it is and how hard I work, I can tolerate it, but there is one thing I want and that is that you go to university. I know you can do it." I never forget what she says, and now I am trying my best not to disappoint her.

The most difficult thing for my parents is to learn English. At first, wherever they went, they had to bring one of their children with them unless they were going to Chinatown. But now they do not have to do that anymore. I think perhaps since they work in a Canadian factory and they always watch television on the weekends or whenever they have free time, they can understand English. I am very proud of them because most of the old Chinese people have not bothered to learn English!

Cam Thanh Tran
Vietnam

Guilt

Since my parents do not know English, they never step out on their own. I feel guilty about their being imprisoned in the house for years. I plan to take them out for a little tour downtown, but I just have no spare time. In fact, I hate to bring my old parents out with me. I don't know why. I feel guilty if I don't grant them this. I feel worse when they don't say anything. It would help me if they complained, but they never do. Are they taking revenge on me? They seem to know I care for them and try to hurt me this way.

Yu Chung Ko
Hong Kong

Phone Calls

When we arrived in Canada, we settled first in Drummondville, Quebec, because we had been sponsored by the Catholic Church there. The problem of language always created a disagreement in my family. Each time the telephone rang, no one dared to answer it. Everybody was afraid to have to try to speak French on the phone. Even though the phone call was supposed to be answered by my father, he did not want to respond to it. On the contrary, he insisted on my answering for him.

Sometimes it made me so angry that I said, "Papa, this call is for you. It's your responsibility to answer it. I can't substitute for you, for I know nothing about your business."

"But I can't understand French well enough to answer the phone!" he replied. He always refused in this seemingly logical manner.

"Papa, how will you learn French if you have no courage to speak with people? You can't always depend on me to do your talking! What will you do when I'm away? Please answer the phone and practise your French."

These words seemed to impress my father. He then understood what he had to do to adjust to life in a new situation.

Thuy Van Luong
Vietnam

She Survived and Changed

The day has finally come for her to leave. Much as she loves her husband and three very young daughters, she knows she has to go. Armed with one suitcase and the dream of a bright future for her three daughters, she walks away and boards the plane that will take her to a different country. It is then that her doubts come flying back to her mind. What if everything goes wrong and she doesn't have anyone to run to? And is her husband going to wait a very long time for her? Will her daughters remember the love and caring she gave them? Will everything work out the way she wants it?

Then the memories of her childhood came back—those memories that have haunted her for years: tilling the land, taking care of her six younger brothers and sisters, sharing what little food their family could afford with their meagre income, working her way through university to obtain a degree in nursing, and starting a career, cut short by her marriage.

Because of the worsening economic condition in her country, the salary of her husband as an engineer was just enough to cover their basic expenses. For her, it was not enough. She wanted more for her three daughters. She didn't want them to undergo the same hardships she had. She knew she was doing the right thing and prayed to God that her dream would come true.

It was an exhausting day—the day my Mom went away. "I'm going to a very far place," she said. "Always remember that I love you and I'm doing this for you. I'll give you everything you want, dolls as big as you are and many beautiful dresses." She said the same to my two sisters, but of course, they didn't understand it back then. I was the only one who knew what was really going on. I tried to keep her from going by crying out loud in front of her and embracing her very hard with all my might. But what can a little girl do as she watches her mother go away?

At first, it was very hard to forget somebody I really cared about. As time flew by, the pain healed. Anyway, I still had my father who was really loving, my two sisters, and, true to my mother's words, many toys and colourful dresses. We went back to our own life.

While we had one another, my mom had no one. Working day and night as a domestic helper, she had to learn to deal with different foreigners and endure hardships. She survived with the only weapon she had—her dream.

As the years went by, we even learned not to miss her anymore. Well, yes, she was still a part of our lives when she came home for a month or two every three years for the past twelve years. She told us every chance she got that she loved us very much, but it was not the same as having her near us.

Then, at last, her break came. She was able to enter Canada from Greece. She worked even harder in Canada and studied to be a nurse's aide. After being a nurse in the Philippines, this step down was a humiliation to her. She became a landed immigrant and eventually was able to sponsor us.

The day of our meeting at the airport was a day we all can't forget. It signified two things: for mother—the end of sacrifice, and for us, the start of silent suffering.

How would you feel if a complete stranger suddenly took charge of your household and your life? That's how we felt the very first day we came to live with my mother. The first few weeks were really different. There was somebody to take care of the family instead of me. My Mom did everything that a mother does. Everything! At first, it was relief I felt.

After a few months she began taking control of our lives. We even lost our independence and privacy. Now, she even has a plan about what we are going to take at university. Oh, we know that she really loves us and she's planning our future lives to ensure our happiness. She is a perfectionist. She wants everything in order. She's very demanding. She wants to know everything we do. We can't act as normal teenagers anymore. We can't be carefree or leave a mess in our rooms. We know we can't complain because she has done so much for us already.

One day my sister tried to explain to mother why she hadn't done her chores, but mother told her all the things she had endured from the start to the end. My sister ended up crying silently in our bedroom. So now you see why we can't complain. I can see that my father feels the same way. He feels that she is not the same woman he married twenty years ago. She has become very independent and very sure of herself.

I know, somehow, someday, I have to take a stand. But in the meantime, I know what I want to do—give in to her wishes and make her very happy.

Analyn Saupan
The Philippines

Sorry, Mom and Dad

In Canada I used to avoid answering questions such as "Where do you live?" "What are your parents doing?" When people asked me, I felt ashamed to tell them that I was living in a small apartment and my mother was a caretaker. What I mean is I felt ashamed to let people know that my family is poor.

It was not this way when we lived in China. My mother was a high school teacher and my father was a university teacher. Compared with other Chinese people, we were quite comfortable in our life-style. But compared with Canadians, like other recent immigrants, we are poor.

Before coming here, like so many other dreamers, I thought North America meant big houses, beautiful cars, and a luxurious life. But when I found out that I have to share room with my sister, I have to walk to school everyday, and I have to obey mother's tight fiscal policy, I felt dissatisfied.

One day after a fight with my sister about who was going to use the only desk in our room, I exploded. I rushed into the kitchen and shouted to my mother who was cutting vegetables, "Mom, I can't stand this anymore. Will you do something about it?"

"Why don't you go to the library? There are other places you can study. You don't have to stay in your room," said my mother impatiently.

"How can you say that? You're my mother. You're supposed to support me in what I want. Other parents aren't like you. They provide a good environment for their children. Look at what you give me—such a small room that I even feel embarrassed bringing friends here. You're just cheap!" As soon as I said this, I felt guilty.

Her hands stopped above the vegetables she was cutting. Her breathing came faster. I kept looking at her back, waiting for the fire.

"Do you feel ashamed to have this home and ashamed of your parents?" my father exploded before my mother could say anything. His eyes flashed with anger. "You are totally insensitive if you criticize us. I tell you, I have nothing to regret as a father. I came from a small city. I went to university, passed the English entrance tests, and came to Canada. What did my parents give me? Nothing! I achieved all this by myself. I never complained. I was the best among my friends. I am proud of my accomplishments."

I bowed my head as my father was speaking.

"I would have been a professor in China, but I am still a student here. And look at your mother. She is only a caretaker here. Do you think she feels better than if she were a teacher in China? Why do we stay here? It's because we have undergone so many hardships in China. We don't want you to suffer them again. How much sacrifice..."

My mother stopped him before he finished, and pushed him to the door: "Let's take a walk."

But she stopped at the door and turned her head to me: "I only want to tell you that rich parents do not necessarily love and care for their children more than the poor. In fact, poor parents sometimes care more for their children."

They left and I was alone with my thoughts. Am I really a kind person? I used to think I was. Because I feel pity for vagrants who sit on street corners, pity for the characters who suffer a tortured life in the movies, even pity for dogs and cats sometimes. But ironically, I never feel pity for my parents. My parents have made their best effort, but I am still greedy. My mother never buys good clothes for herself, but she buys good clothes for me and my sister. She never lets us feel we are short of anything. She ought to take a bus to go to work. But she walks everyday. Once I asked her why. She said: "I want to save money in order to buy a computer for you. You need it in university."

Now I realize it's not a shame at all to tell people that I am poor. The real shame is not to tell the truth and not to admit the truth.

The night was dark. It was late. I could not wait any longer. Honestly, I did not have courage to face my parents again. Instead, on a paper lying on the table I wrote: "Dad, Mom, I love you. Believe me. I understand everything now. I love this apartment. Although it is small, it is my home."

Fong Yuan
China

Student Activities

Talking and Writing*

Read the five stories under the heading "We Imagine How Our Parents Feel About Life in Canada" (pp. 83–84). In these stories students put themselves in the place of their parents and look at the world through their eyes.

1. List the problems these parents have in Canada.
2. Do you think life is more difficult for parents or small children or teenagers in the first year in Canada? Give reasons to support your opinion.
3. Put yourself in the place of your mother or father or grandparent. In a paragraph describe an incident through the eyes of this person.

Talking and Writing**

"Superman"

How typical is Amy's father of newcomers to Canada?

"A Cruel Joke"

1. Contrast the life of Cam Thanh's parents before and after arriving in Canada.
2. Explain the statement, "Fate has played a cruel joke on my parents."
3. Why does Cam Thanh feel both sympathy and pride towards her parents?

"Guilt"

Yu Chung's feelings towards his parents are complicated. Describe and explain his feelings. Compare your feelings towards your parents.

"Phone Calls"

1. How does Thuy Van try to help his father?
2. Do you feel he was right to refuse to answer the phone for his father? Why?

"She Survived and Changed"

1. What do you learn of the personalities of the writer and her mother from this story? Give examples from the story to explain your observations.
2. In this situation do you feel more sympathy for the mother or the daughter? Explain.

Group Discussion

"Sorry, Mom and Dad"

1. How does this story help us understand the difficulties faced by parents who are newcomers to Canada?

2. What are other difficulties faced by parents? Refer to the other stories and to your own family.

3. How do the problems of parents affect children in the family?

4. Find out from other members of the group why their parents immigrated to Canada.

5. Put yourself in the place of your parents. Would you have immigrated to Canada in their position?

Writing Folder

Interview one or two adults about their reasons for coming to Canada and their impressions of Canada.

1. Imagine yourself as one of these adults in a specific situation. Write your thoughts and feelings in the first person.

2. Use these interviews and your own observations to develop a short essay on the problems faced by adults who immigrate to Canada.

Family: Strangers

Most teenagers want more freedom and independence and believe that their parents try to restrict them unnecessarily. At this stage in their lives, they feel ready to make their own decisions as they forge their own separate identity. However, most parents still want to control their children, at least to some extent. They want their children to be secure and happy in the future, and worry about their dating, education, and career choices. These two attitudes inevitably clash as teenagers and their parents try to achieve opposing goals.

When the family recently has been transplanted into the new Canadian culture, the tensions between parents and their children may be even greater. The outcome of the desire for independence and freedom can result in behaviour that appears to reject parental values.

Even after many years in Canada the family tensions continue. Adolescents who have grown up in Canada are unable to communicate with parents. Often they feel lost between two cultures and angry at parents who force them to be what they are not. One student from Burma writes: "You have to let go, mom, because you lost me the minute I landed on Canadian ground. You can't have an obedient Chinese son because I have become deeply rooted in Canadian culture. Please, just let go. I don't belong to you anymore."

As you read the following stories, examine the causes of the conflicts between parents and teenagers. Some may be avoidable, others inevitable.

My Parents Do Not Understand

My parents are wage-earners who ask me to study hard. They do not want me to study so that I can improve my knowledge, but rather so that I can earn more money after I have graduated. They want me to be an outstanding person, to be a doctor or a lawyer. I hate this. I don't want to be a "money-slave." I like freedom. I would like to do a job that I am interested in, but my parents don't understand these things.

I think my birth must have brought my parents happiness because I was the first child they had after they had married. I saw some pictures which were taken in my childhood. At that time I looked like a boy and was carried by my mother. Some pictures were taken with my father and my relatives. I could see the smiles on my parents' faces. They were sweet and warm. But I can't find any smiles on them anymore. They worry about making a living all the time, and I feel they are very old. After my last sister was born, they seemed to forget me. Sometimes I feel jealous of my sisters and I want to be my parents' only child.

Amy Tam
Hong Kong

Counting the Stars

One day I decided to ask my parents about my future life in Canada. My father told me I should make money first and get married to someone. I was not surprised because everyone, including my father, did this. I thought I was fortunate to be in Canada because I could go to school without paying and learn English, but my father said I should work in a factory.

I decided to leave home. I slept in a park for about a month. In the park I was lonely and sad. I looked at the sky. I tried to count the stars in the sky, the buses on the road, the people on the sidewalk.

Since then I have gone to my father's home only three times. The last time my father said, "Don't come to my house. You are none of my business."

Kyung Ju La
Korea

Do As I Say

Father: If you speak one more word of English to your sisters in front of me, I will be really annoyed with you. Is this clear?

Son: But this is the best way to learn English.

Father: You can practise English outside if you want, but not here. You know I don't understand English.

Son: But you should learn English if you want to live happily in Canada. You're being unreasonable. Can't we speak English at home? We feel as comfortable in English as we do in Urdu.

Father: I'm afraid you will forget your own language.

Son: No, I could never forget my mother tongue. After all, I've been speaking it for 18 years.

Father: Many Pakistanis who have been living in Canada all their lives forget Urdu, and when their children are born, they never learn to speak Urdu properly.

Son: No, I can't see any reason for not speaking English at home.

Father: Will you stop arguing and do as I say!

Asif Khan
Pakistan

Too Old to Change

Son: Morning Dad! Where would you like to go today? I'd planned to take you out to see some of Toronto.

Father: I just want to go to Chinatown.

Son: How about going to Yonge Street and the Eaton Centre after we've had our morning tea in Chinatown? Wouldn't you like that?

Father: Morning tea in Chinatown is excellent, but Mom and I don't want to go to Yonge Street. Instead, we want to buy some fresh seafood in Chinatown. Then we'll come back and prepare our supper.

Son: You should try to go somewhere else besides Chinatown. You don't know anything else about the rest of Toronto.

Father: No, Yonge Street isn't suitable for us. We aren't interested in it. I'd rather stay home instead of going there.

Son: Don't stick to Chinatown only! Don't you feel bored always going to Chinatown?

Father: Of course we don't! We are Chinese, and it reminds us of home. Don't force us to change our ways. We feel more comfortable with our own language and our own people. We're too old to change.

Son: Won't you just try to experience something new for a change?

Father: Don't force us, son! We're quite satisfied with the life we lead. I hope you'll understand when you get older.

Victor Chan
Hong Kong

Just Average

Mother: Son, how was your day at school?

Son: Fine, mom. Can you come here for a second?

Mother: Yeah. What's the problem?

Son: Isn't life wonderful? I just want to say that, in spite of everything, I still love you.

Mother: Are you feeling all right, son?

Son: Very funny, Mom.

Mother: OK. Let me guess. How much do you want?

Son: Can you sign my report card? Please.

Mother: How come you have only three A's on your report card? As a matter of fact, you have more low marks than high grades.

Son: No problem, mom. I can pass this year easily.

Mother: Pass? I'm not talking about passing. I want you to be among the five best students in the class. In Korea, students of your age study all day because they want to be the best and have a good life.

Son: But this isn't Korea, Mom. You probably studied a lot there, but not here. Do you want me to study all day?

Mother: I didn't tell you that. I just expect better grades from you. I want you to study and have good grades so that you can have a good life in the future.

Son: I don't get it. A pass is a pass. What's the difference? This is the 90s. The world has changed. Besides, there's people worse than I in school.

Mother: I don't care how your friends are doing. I've always tried to give you the best of everything. Can't you at least study a bit harder?

Armando Cho
Brazil

Proverbs

I: Mom, I'm back.

Mom: Don't you have a watch?

I: Yes, I do.

Mom: Then tell me what time it is now.

I: Almost 11 o'clock. But, Mom, today is the weekend and I...

Mom: Listen! I don't like you to stay outside at night. I have told you a thousand times that there is more danger in North America than in China. You are too young to be out alone!

I: Oh! Don't always treat me like a child. I am already 17 years old and all my friends...

Mom: Seventeen is the most dangerous age. There are many things you can't quite understand. When I was your age, I never came home as late as you. There is a Chinese idiom...

I: But life has changed. Now we are in Canada, aren't we? Don't always use those Chinese idioms. It isn't suitable for Canadian culture. What we need now is to go outside to have more Canadian experience. This is called socialization. Our society teacher said that it is a very important process to learn from the society and to adapt to the society.

Mom: Don't try to teach me, my son. The salt I have tasted is more than the rice you have eaten. The bridge I have crossed is longer than the road you have walked. I have more experience than you. I know what I should do and what I must not do!

I: No! No! Both of us should learn from the very beginning. We should learn to adapt to change. I have read an article about the Chinese. It said we never have had the ability to adapt and change. We close the door and use ancient experience to cover weaknesses. We should not be so afraid of change. We must...

Mom: Since when do you talk to your mother so rudely!

I: I just want you to understand...

Mom: Listen! I don't want to hear anymore. Remember. Don't try to go out at night without my permission!

Xuan Cen
China

A Dangerous Age?

"Mom, can I go to a party tomorrow night?" I asked eagerly.

"What? Go to a party again? Who is this? Do I know him? How old is he? Is he working or studying? What kind of friends is he going to invite? Where will the party be held? Have you asked your Dad?" asked Mom reproachfully while she was making a cake.

"I say I have been invited to a party tomorrow night and it's only the first time, so please don't say 'again.' This is my schoolmate, a girl, not a boy. She is a year older than I and the party will be held in her house. I haven't asked Dad yet because he is reading a newspaper. Are you satisfied with all my answers?" I shouted out my words, for I hated to be questioned in a way that seemed like a judge questioning a criminal.

The worst thing in my life was to hear Mom's voice full of anger, yet not know exactly what she was saying. I turned on the radio in order to escape from her attack.

After cooling myself, I decided to talk to Dad hoping he would understand me. "Hi, Dad. I…" I said, pretending to be calm and carefree.

"Your Mom has told me everything Kit-Ping. Why aren't you satisfied with what you have? A big house, enough food, warm clothes, and a large weekly allowance. What is so good about going to a party? Don't you know that your age is a dangerous age? If you always go to parties, it will do you no good. When I was your age, I was out of school and working in a fruit market to help out my family."

I immediately burst into a rage and said, "Do you want me to go to work? I have heard enough about how hard you have worked and how much more I have than you had. I'll quit school tomorrow and find a job."

Suddenly he slapped my face with his hand. At that moment, my innocence evaporated. I stood still for a few minutes. Covering my painful face, biting my lips to stop the uninvited teardrops from rolling, staring at him with hatred in my eyes, I rushed to the door.

When I was putting my first foot out of the door, he shouted appealingly, "Maybe we can talk about it."

"There is really nothing we can talk about. You only know how to make money, but you understand nothing else!" I shouted to him as I stepped out the door.

Maggie Tam
Hong Kong

Boys Are More Precious Than Girls

In Chinese culture children are not allowed to question their parents' commands. They are trained to be obedient and must ask parents' permission for everything.

I attended the Valentine's Dance at my school, and my troubles came up the next day. At dinner my brother said, "Daddy, don't permit my sisters to go to the school dances. It's extremely dangerous for girls to go alone."

My father added, "Probably they are smoking secretly. If we searched their bags, we would probably find some cigarettes." I got so mad that I didn't finish my dinner and went upstairs. My mom stared at me, but didn't say a word.

The night after, my anger still remained. I ignored my brother. I yelled at my sister. Then my mom screamed, "I don't approve of your attitude. Shut up."

I thundered, "What about Isaac? He yelled at me for no reason. It isn't fair."

My mom stormed, "What your brother said was absolutely right. From now on, if you want to go out, you must have my permission first." I kept silent. Then I went upstairs.

In my opinion, children should not have to be one hundred percent obedient. They should be able to reason with their parents and stand up to them if disagreement occurs. I believe that I have been influenced by Canadian culture and that's why I dared to talk back when I wasn't supposed to.

To many Chinese, boys are more precious than girls. My parents tolerate me, but they love my brother the most, I believe. They think he speaks words of wisdom. They listen to whatever he says. Before the dance, I only had to inform my parents when I went out. Then with only one word, my brother could change my parents' attitude.

Two days ago, my mother announced, "You're not going out at night." She stopped me from going out for no reason, with no explanation. She is reluctant to accept the ideas and new living style of teenagers. I don't know how long I'll have to live through this phase. I know that I have to be tolerant and considerate towards my mom, but I wish my mother could be enlightened and would realize that we *are* growing up.

Iva Wat
Hong Kong

Nobody's Fault

It was nine o'clock when I arrived home after a long day's work in a fast-food restaurant. My knees were sore and my hands were aching. "I'm home," I called to my parents in an exhausted voice. Then I saw my mother's angry face. Suddenly I remembered that I had forgotten to phone her about being late. "Sorry, Mom," I whispered.

"What for?" she answered impatiently, without even looking up.

"I should have phoned you this afternoon to tell you that I would be late tonight so that you wouldn't have had to wait for me for dinner."

"Oh, so you grant I'm your mother," she said between sobs.

All of a sudden, I realized what had happened. My parents had just received a letter from my grandmother in China. Her letters always caused a storm in the house. My grandmother brought me up. Because of the Cultural Revolution my parents had been sent to the countryside just after graduating from university, and they felt I would be better off with my grandmother.

Without saying a word I went to my bedroom. When I heard my mother banging the dishes and sighing deeply, I wondered why I had come to Canada, why I had joined my parents whom I had never lived with before, and why I had left my grandmother behind.

For eighteen years I lived with my grandmother. I remember when I was a little kid, I felt very envious when I saw other children going to parks with their parents. I really wished I could live with my parents. But when my parents came to Canada and applied for a permanent residence visa for me and my brother, I hesitated because I did not want to leave my grandmother and was afraid to live with my parents. Finally my grandmother persuaded me to leave: "Don't be silly, my dear. You will have a good future if you go to Canada and you should live with your parents sooner or later. It will be ten times better than living with an old woman. And I still can come to see you." So I listened to my grandmother and came to Canada.

The long separation created an impassable chasm between me and my parents. Their own conflicts just made the tension worse. When my grandmother visited in the summer, the tensions between her and my parents increased. My parents, especially my mother, hates the way I am. She thinks I am too stubborn and too single-minded—just like my grandmother. Of course, she blames all my weaknesses on my grandmother. Also she blames my grandmother for our differences.

On the one side are my parents who always supported me financially while I was growing up. On the other side is my grandmother, who with all her love brought me up. Why do I have to be in the middle? It's nobody's fault, I guess.

I feel totally lost. But I am very clear about one thing. If I have children in the future, I will never leave them behind, even for one second. I don't want this tragedy to be repeated.

Anonymous

Ten Thousand Miles Apart

Though I did not grow up with you,
when we met at the airport,
half-strangers,
we tried to understand each other
and make up the years
that we were separated.

I loved you
but did not know
how to show it.

I was not the little boy
that you had expected
and you were not as loving
as I remembered.

Seeing each other every day,
but still ten thousand miles
apart
we were disappointed.

You went to see psychologists
and I closed my door
and gazed to the east with tears.

I loved you truly
but did not know
how to show it.

We had a lot of arguments.
Do not remember
any words I said.
I did not mean to hurt you.
Loneliness and anger over-powered me.

You were afraid.
I was spoiled and selfish.

You could not concentrate at work.
I could not concentrate at school.

I loved you truly
but did not know
how to show it.

Now we have changed.
Now we understand more.

You let me travel
and open my mind.
You become more and more
loving and patient.

And I have more and more
respect for you.

You begin to have more confidence
and my school average
goes up from C to B
and from B to A.

I love you truly
and will forever.

Shuang Zheng
China

My Double Life

When I immigrated to Canada, the hardest, but yet the most golden times, came in school where I learned not only English but the Canadian life-style; consequently, my own customs have changed a lot.

What affected me most was the relationship between boys and girls in the school. The first time I saw a boy holding a girl and kissing in the hall, my head turned away from them automatically. I felt ashamed inside. Although I lived in Canada, my mind still kept thinking as if I were in China, where a rule existed that a student could not have a close relationship with the opposite sex. If a girl and a boy spent time together, their reputations would be ruined in the school. In order to keep our reputations, we always kept our distance from boys. We didn't often make jokes with boys and we gave the same smile to every boy. The conversations between boys and girls concentrated on one and only one subject—studying. You may think it was strange that if a boy walked on one side of the sidewalk, I would walk on the other side.

After a year of student life in Canada, I got used to Canadian social life. I thought I should have the same individuality and freedom as other Canadian kids had. Why should I lock myself away from the society? Somehow I found that my parents' minds were too old to understand this. One day, a friend invited me to his cousin's birthday party at night. I was so excited about it, but my parents said, "It's too dangerous to go out at night, especially for girls." I told them that he would drive me home. "That's even worse," my mother said. "Remember, don't ever sit in a boy's car." From her face I knew mother was very upset with me. I got really mad, but I was too embarrassed to say anything more, for I was born to a Chinese family that couldn't do anything without my parents' permission.

As I read *Fifth Chinese Daughter* I had a deep feeling of empathy for Jade Snow, who was over-protected by her traditional parents, because I have had experiences of seeing the middle way between two totally different cultures. I cried many times in my heart. I always asked myself, "How long will it be for me to be independent? Will I have this kind of double life forever?"

Binhua Wang
China

No Freedom

It is said that Chinese culture is very strict and disciplined. As I grow older, I realize this more and more because I am living with someone who has old-fashioned ideas. My mom doesn't understand me and my situation. She forbids me to have a boyfriend, to go out with my girlfriends, to take part in school shows or school karate lessons. Everything I do without consulting her, she considers wrong.

I have discovered that as I grow older, my life becomes more complicated and strict. Not only have I had to face the confusion of a new world, but also I have to keep my culture and heritage alive as well. At school I am forced to face the pressures of friends and teachers, and when I get home, I have to act like a naive, innocent girl who never has grown up in my mom's eyes.

My friends had told me about their privileges and freedom. I was envious. So one night I decided to go out without permission and not to come back until very late at night. When I entered the house, I could feel the tension. I saw my mom was about to explode. She questioned me as if I were a victim, and I only gave her cryptic answers. She became furious. She didn't ground me like Canadian parents do, but she punished me with a stick.

I know the best solution is to talk to her. I did that. I tried to reach out and communicate with her, but before one soft word of compromise was out, she concluded the conversation by saying that she was the head of the family and I had to listen to her. Now we hardly communicate anymore because we both have different views of life, and unfortunately, I have no power to express an opinion.

I have tried another method with her. I encourage her to watch more TV so that she can compare our life with Canadians. Still her decisions remain the same. When I question her about it, she replies that Canadians are different from us and we cannot be compared to them.

According to Chinese culture, children should be dependent on their parents for financial and emotional support until they are married. Children should show their gratitude by eternal obedience. That means listening to every word their parents say. It is not likely that children will talk back to their parents even though their parents are wrong. Parents have so much power that they sometimes rule their children's lives forever, even after the children's marriage.

Whenever I come up with some idea, without even considering it, my mother has a negative response to the idea and tells me not to mention it again. That is how my life is going to be until I'm married. Only then can I hope for any freedom in my life. I hope the next generation of kids will have more freedom.

Le Trang Tran
Vietnam

Strangers

In *The Joy Luck Club,* Jing-Mei says about her mother: "We never really understood one another." This is exactly the way I feel about my mother. Every day I lose more and more of my Chinese thinking. It's getting harder and harder to live with my mother.

We cannot communicate with one another. We hardly talk because I have trouble expressing myself. I fully understand what she is saying to me, but I can't answer back. One time we were watching the news together, and she asked me what it was about. So I started explaining in Chinese, and then when she couldn't understand me, I switched to Burmese and still she couldn't understand; so I switched to English hoping she would understand, but I had no luck. Eventually I got so frustrated that I ignored her. Talking with her reminds me of the anger and frustration I felt the first year in Canada when I tried to talk English. Now I hardly ever start a conversation with her.

Sometimes I regret that my English is so fluent. Maybe I should have taken a Saturday morning class in Chinese so I wouldn't have this problem. My friends and I have been here almost the same time, and they don't have trouble speaking with their parents. Their English may be a bit weak, but they are in a better position than I am at home. The way I look at it is that you can't be good in English and your native language as well. It seems as if I had to give up my native language in order to be fluent in English.

As communication disintegrates between me and my mom, I feel more and more separated from her. She has no idea what I want and who I want to be. I'm like a mute trying to communicate and feeling only the loud laughter of humiliation. Sometimes I feel that we're just strangers living together and not a family. My mother, on the other hand, does not see it this way. She thinks that I'm just disobedient. She does not see that I have a problem communicating with her. She thinks that I just don't want to talk to her. Many times she complains that I am disrespectful. I

never do what she says and I'm not one of those typically good sons she sees in Chinese movies. She wants someone who is dependent, respectful, and caring— someone like one of my friends who has just arrived in Canada. At first I wanted to be like them—caring and respectful. I really tried, but I realized that I can't because I have grown up in Canada. I am influenced by Canadian culture to be independent and strong. Of course this is the opposite of what my mother wants.

Actually my mother is an old-fashioned woman. She is very superstitious. She still thinks that my two sisters, who died in a car accident, were cursed. So everyday, she makes my brother and me carry a bag containing God knows what that will protect us from evil. I refused at first to carry it because not only does the bag bulge out from my pants, but I don't believe in this superstition. However, she scolded me and said it was for my own good and so I had no choice. Often on special occasions we have religious ceremonies which require a lot of work and time. Often I don't bother to participate and again she scolds me, complaining that I'm insulting Chinese culture by not believing in Buddhism.

My mom and I have totally different thoughts. Sometimes I wonder why. Is it because of my personality or because of the Canadian environment I grew up in? My father died in Burma when I was eight years old. Two years later we came to Canada. So I practically grew up here, accepted the Canadian culture, and rejected my Chinese self because I wanted to fit in. Maybe this is the cause of our different values and beliefs. I was too busy trying to gain the benefits of being a Canadian so that I didn't know I was losing myself as a Chinese.

So as every day goes by, I feel ashamed—ashamed that I'm no longer Chinese. I remember one time when I was working, an old Chinese man asked me a question in weak English. When I couldn't understand him, he spoke in Chinese. Knowing I couldn't understand, I asked one of my friends to help him but he was busy so there I was with the old man who was getting more impatient by the minute. Then he finally said, "You are Chinese and you don't speak Chinese."

This really insulted me and I said, "You are in Canada and you don't speak English!" This offended him and he left. Though I was victorious, I felt defeated because what he said really hurt me. I felt ashamed and afraid.

Who am I? I'm Chinese. If so, why don't I think like one? I'm Canadian. But I don't look like one. Who am I? I feel lost—lost between two cultures. Increasingly I feel angry at my mother for forcing me to be what I'm not. You have to let go, mom, because you lost me the minute I landed on Canadian ground. The harder you try to force me to be what I'm not, the more I will reject my Chinese self. Using force will only make you unhappy and tear me apart. Just let go. You can't have an obedient Chinese son because I have become deeply rooted in Canadian culture. Please, just let go. I don't belong to you anymore.

Michael Ngo
Burma

Student Activities

Talking and Writing*

"My Parents Do Not Understand"

1. Why does Amy criticize her parents?
2. In what way does Amy feel her relationship with her parents has changed? Has your relationship with your parents changed since coming to Canada?

"Counting the Stars"

1. What conflict exists between father and son?
2. How does the son resolve the conflict? Do you agree with his decision? Explain.

"Do As I Say"

With your partner, read the script. Now change roles and read it again.

1. Explain why the father and son are arguing.
2. Do you agree with the son when he says his father is being "unreasonable"?

"Too Old to Change"

With your partner, read the script. Now change roles and read it again.

1. Describe the different points of view of father and son.
2. Why does the son want to take his father to see some of Toronto? Why does his father wish to go to Chinatown?
3. Do you believe the son should force his father to "experience something new"?

"Just Average"

With your partner, read the script. Now change roles and read it again.

1. What pressure does Armando feel from his mother? Why does she put this pressure on her son?
2. With whom do you feel most sympathy—Armando or his mother?

Talking and Writing**

"Boys Are More Precious Than Girls"

1. Iva finds it hard to get along with her parents. What problems does she have at home?
2. How typical is Iva's family situation? Compare families you know.

"Ten Thousand Miles Apart"

1. The speaker in this poem is addressing his parents. Why does he feel he must speak to them?

2. Why is the title of the poem appropriate?

"My Double Life" and "No Freedom"

1. What similarity is there in the family situation of the writers of these two stories?

2. What advice would you give these girls?

"Strangers"

1. Michael analyzes the reasons why he cannot communicate with his mother. What are these reasons?

2. Why does Michael think of himself as being "lost"?

Group Discussion

Read the stories in "Family: Strangers" for homework.

1. In these stories the writers express frustration because they do not have enough freedom. With your group, in point form

   • list the arguments the teenagers give to support their demands for more freedom;
   • list the arguments their parents give in answer to these demands.

2. Do you agree or disagree with the following statements? Support your opinion with as many reasons as you can.

   • Children should always obey their parents.
   • In the teenage years girls and boys should not have close relationships.
   • Boys get preferential treatment in families.
   • It is best to marry someone of the same ethnic background.

Writing Folder

1. With your partner, read aloud the dialogues in this section: "Do As I Say," "Too Old to Change," "Just Average," and "Proverbs."(pp. 95–98)

   • Role-play a situation which portrays a real disagreement or conflict between you and a parent.
   • With your partner, write your dialogue in play form. Rehearse it before acting it out in front of the class.

2. Read "A Dangerous Age?" again. In narrative form tell about an incident which created tension between you and your parent. Try to include some dialogue.

3. Imagine you are a parent with a child who seems to be rejecting your traditions or values. In diary form write your thoughts and feelings.

4. Write about one of the topics that you discussed in your group. Write three paragraphs in a persuasive style. (State your theme in your opening paragraph and develop your theme with examples from your reading and your experience.)

FAMILY
ROOTS

Traditions

When young people immigrate to a new country and are exposed to new customs, they frequently begin to question what they have learned from their parents and try to behave differently. Some decide to reject family traditions; others find that their belief in the values of their parents becomes stronger. In the search for identity, it is often a difficult struggle to find a balance between new and appealing Canadian customs and deep-rooted family traditions.

In the stories that follow, students examine the relationship between their parents and themselves. They think about duty and love, obedience and freedom. They consider the amount of control parents should have over children and the division of authority in the home. They point out the importance of their first language in communicating with parents and grandparents.

In the process of becoming Canadian these young people often discover their roots and develop a strong interest in and appreciation of family traditions and their cultural heritage.

You Can Ask Me

In my opinion, my father is the most learned person in the world. I admire him very much.

My father is a doctor. He worked very hard in China. Also he works very hard in Canada. He studied English by himself. When China was very poor, he became a success.

He helps me a lot in English. I have so many new words that I don't understand. So I bring them home and use the dictionary. When my father comes back home and looks at me, he says, "Don't use the dictionary. Many times the dictionary definition is not true. You can ask me. Don't waste your time on the dictionary." Therefore, I always get most answers from father.

Also he always tells me, "Studying is the best way for your future. You are not strong, but you can be learned. Your job is to study harder and harder for yourself." He never asks me to wash dishes or clothes, or do anything else around the house. He just says, "Go! Study hard."

I love my father.

Bobby Wang
China

Caring

Some Canadians do not care about being polite to their parents and their brothers and sisters. In our country we can never argue with our parents or disagree with them. We also cannot call our brothers and sisters names if they are older than we are.

I hope my children will keep our Chinese customs in their minds and not be like some Canadians who, when they are older, leave their warm homes and forget what their parents have given them. Our Chinese system is that you take care of your children, and when they grow up and you have grown old, then they must take care of you.

Cecelia So
Hong Kong

Control

My parents control us very tightly. They decide when we go out, come back, and with whom we make friends. Although I am over 18 years old, my parents still ask questions about school life, teachers, people, and homework.

Every time I go outside my parents ask many questions. With whom? Where? What time will you be back? What kind of activity is it? Sometimes I hate to answer those questions, but I feel they take care of and pay more attention to us than Canadians do with their children. When Canadians are growing up, they seem to have many rights and freedoms. They can do whatever they want. The parents and children seem like friends rather than parent and child.

Our Chinese parents give us good food, clothes—everything—and work hard to earn more money for their heirs or grand-heirs. They devote their whole lives to their children who will be obedient heirs.

In China, if you have a big family with many children, you all live together. The father is a God in the family. His speech is an imperial order, and no one can disagree.

If I have children one day, I will wish them to keep the Chinese marriage customs and to be obedient to their parents. They should be diligent persons, overcome difficulties, make improvements, save each penny, and fall into good habits.

Tung Shiang Hsiung
China

My Parents Are Part of Me

One day I was working in my father's store, and a seventy-year-old man came in and bought some cookies We talked to each other, and I found out that his married sons and daughters were in Canada, but they did not want to support him and just sent him to an old folks' home. This seemed to be very sad.

I began to compare the Canadian family system and the Korean family system. In Canada parents treat children as individuals and give them rights and freedom and also expect them to take responsibility for what they do. There seems to be no strong relationship between them. They do not have the heart to sacrifice themselves for their children. They think of themselves first and then their children, and so they never expect their children to support them after they get old. Also, their sons do not feel it is their duty to support their parents when they get old.

I was very depressed to realize that the seventy-year-old Chinese man had taken the North American way of thinking about parents and children. I felt very glad and lucky that I had been taught the Korean way, and I really regretted that I had once demanded payment for working in the store from my parents.

There is a strong relationship between parents and children in a Korean family. My parents think of me as part of their body; therefore, they have the heart to sacrifice themselves for me and always expect me to obey them. I always try to obey them since I understand them. I am supposed to support them when they get old, and I really want it as if they were part of my body as long as I live.

Joseph Park
Korea

A Stinking Fish

I was brought up in a rather mixed-up fashion. My parents still cling to some of the centuries-old Chinese traditions, but are Westernized in some ways. Thus, I became aware of the good of both Eastern and Western cultures.

My childhood was nothing out of the ordinary. Like many, or most, children of Chinese ancestry, I was sent to a private Chinese school so that I would not lose track of my culture and become too Filipinized. Also, it was one way of learning to speak my mother tongue.

The school I attended was very strict. Closed circuit TVs were attached to every nook of each room, in the corridors, and in the hallways. One little error, and you got reprimanded. Two errors, and you had a detention. Three errors earned you a suspension. Four or more, and you got expelled. In spite of all the disciplinary measures, the school offered quality education. But I did not think of that then.

School for me was a drag. Classes started at 7:30 a.m. and lasted until 12:30 p.m. This was the English session, which meant that all subjects (history, math, economics) were taught in English. A one-hour lunch break followed. For the Chinese session, classes recommenced at 2:00 p.m. and lasted until 4:00 p.m. Work didn't end there—we were burdened with approximately two hours of homework each night.

I passed through elementary school without whispering a voice of objection. It wasn't until I was in Grade 9 that I started to voice my opinions and my disgust over the school policy. I started to hate school, especially my Chinese classes. Intentionally, I failed all my Chinese subjects so that I'd be expelled from the Chinese department.

By the end of the term, I had failed five out of five subjects in Chinese. My father couldn't believe his eyes when he saw my Chinese report card. It looked more like a birthday card than a report card, because all my marks were in red ink. My name was the only thing not written in red. (In the Philippines, failing marks are written in red, while passing marks are written in either blue or black.)

When we got home, all hell broke loose. I saw steam coming out of my Dad's ears. I prepared myself for whatever punishment he might give me. One, two, three minutes went by, and still he didn't say a word. After five more minutes, he stared at me with those cold, melancholy eyes and one word came out of his mouth.

"Why?"

I was speechless. No matter how hard I tried, no word came out of my mouth. I only gazed awkwardly at the bedroom floor. After a while, I managed to muster enough courage to answer him.

"I don't know, Dad."

"Why, son?" Silence filled the room.

"I guess I'm just not cut out for it."

"You can be anything you want, if you try. Tell me honestly. Did you exert effort?"

"Yes, Dad, I did, honest!" I lied.

"No, you did not try hard enough. Go to your room and think for five minutes. If you believe you tried hard enough, or at least exerted a little effort, then come back."

It only took me three minutes. "Yes, Dad, I tried very hard."

"No, you did not. If you tried hard enough, you'd get satisfactory marks. I do not have stupid sons, only lazy ones. Go to your room and do a little soul-searching, then come back here."

At that point, I was fed up. I was set to explode at the slightest provocation.

"You want the truth, Dad? I hate Chinese. I don't want to have anything to do with Chinese."

It was my Dad's turn to be astounded. He couldn't believe his ears. I knew I shouldn't have said that. I knew he felt hurt, for I saw his face grimacing in pain.

"John, you are old enough to know what is good and bad, what is right and wrong. If you think that Chinese is too heavy a burden for you to carry, then do what you think will ease your load. But let me tell you this. The old Chinese proverb says that he who knows not his native language stinks more than a stinking fish."

Time healed the rift between my Dad and me. It wasn't until I went to Taiwan that I learned the wisdom of his words. I found, to my amazement, that I wasn't able to speak a word of Mandarin. My pidgin Mandarin was worse—I didn't do justice to such a beautiful language. Worse still, the American boy beside me spoke Mandarin as if it were his own tongue. Then I remembered what my father had said. And I felt ashamed. How I wished I had listened to him!

All is not lost yet. I may have lost the battle, but I still have the war to win. I have taken my Mandarin seriously from that time on. Isn't it ironic that now I'm studying Chinese, my hated nemesis, in an English-speaking country?

John Madarang
The Philippines

Thank You, Dad, for Everything

My father is an energetic man. He is generous, understanding, and, most of all, loving. Dad is like a philosopher to me, and to this day he continues to give me worthwhile lessons about life.

Many of my present attitudes about education and life in general come from Dad. He was the one who taught me the multiplication table, who taught me Chinese, and who gave me my first driving lessons. What I have learned from my father will always stay with me. Even now, when I multiply, I do it in Vietnamese because I was taught that way.

Dad's parents had a little drugstore, and they were very busy in running it. It was a routine for Dad when he was young, that every day after school, he would spend his evening helping out with the business. However, he didn't find the job oppressive and enjoyed helping out around the store. Often he stayed up until midnight to do his homework. This job had no effect on Dad's schoolwork since he always turned out to be an "A" student in his class. Besides working really hard on his grades, Dad got involved in many extracurricular activities. He did basketball, track and field, and soccer. He was known as a great athlete.

My father was 18 when he finished his high school education. He wanted to continue his studies in sciences at college, but unfortunately his parents couldn't afford this. The first job Dad had was working for the government as a translator. Very often he travelled with Chinese businessmen to Vietnam to do translation in their business negotiations. Dad became very fluent in both languages, Chinese and Vietnamese. After working five years as a translator, my father decided to move on to another career. Based on his good knowledge in sciences, he was able to obtain a job as an engineer in fixing measurement equipment. Again, Dad became skilfull in this job. He now has great ability to fix little things. Whenever the clock or the hair dryer breaks, he will take out his toolbox and start to dissemble the little screws. It ends up that we use the hair dryer over and over again.

The person who knows me best is Dad. When I first started to take the Chinese course, I was faced with difficulties in reading and writing. This was obvious because Chinese is not my first language. However, my father stood behind me and gave me his support. Even though it has taken me a lot of time to pick up the right pronunciation, he didn't give up hope for me. Every night he would spare a moment of his time, teaching me how to read. At the end Dad was proud of my accomplishment. I thank him for his time and patience and also for the confidence he has in me.

I was motivated by my father's persistence. I am typical of most immigrants. Since I am aiming at achieving a university education, I have to use the opportunities that Dad never had. When I study for a test, I make sure I put all my energy into it and give it my best try. As Dad always says, "Whatever you do, do your best." This has given me the little push that I need.

When I decided to get a part-time job, Dad didn't interfere, even though he thought I should concentrate on my schoolwork. He has always respected my ideas and decisions, and in return I have respected his.

It was my father's idea to immigrate to Canada, because he wanted the best for his children's future. He never shows his love through words, but rather through actions. When he bought our house, his intention was to leave it to his children in the future. Dad is not a person who only thinks of himself; he always thinks about what is best for his family. Constantly, he reminds me to do well in school so that one day I can be my own boss.

As Dad grows older, I learn to appreciate him more, and as I grow older, I become more and more like him. I have always looked up to him and always will. His guidance has led me through the darkness that I thought I could not overcome. He is always there when I need him. This is often. Thank you, Dad, for everything.

Tim Hoang
Vietnam

Smile!

"Smile!" said the genial voice of Uncle Ching, who had his camera glued to his left eye. Hang Chan's jaw felt very sore. He had been taking photographs with his relatives for the past half hour. Despite that, he still had to squeeze out another reluctant smile.

Indeed, it should have been a happy day for Hang Chan. It was the day he had longed for all these years. His university graduation ceremony had just been completed a minute ago. Now he was standing on the big lawn in front of Convocation Hall with his academic gown on and his graduation diploma gripped firmly in his hand. Even the weather fit the happy mood of the day. It was the first sunny day after many days of drizzle.

"Now it is Aunt Jade's turn," said Uncle Ching, the geniality and zeal in his tone still unchanged.

"Cut out this picture taking nonsense! I'm fed up with it!" Hang Chan wanted to yell out loud. But he did not. Instead he walked quietly to stand beside the slight figure of Aunt Jade, put his exhausted arm limply around her shoulder, and manoeuvred his stiffened lips to form a smile, or something close to one. He knew well enough that it was his obligation to pose for pictures. It is the way of the Chinese.

Never in his life did Hang Chan know he had so many relatives. His parents had been busy making phone calls all that week, inviting relatives, even the most remotely related, to his graduation. All this was understandable. After all, what would be a more worthy reason for a pair of Chinese parents to be proud than to have a son who was a university graduate? It has been the Chinese way for a very, very long time.

So it turned out he had to usher about forty people into the hall like a parade before the ceremony had begun. He knew they were really impressed by what they were seeing, for they kept making loud comments in the hall from the minute they entered. All the people were staring at this noisy procession as his relatives seated themselves; however, they were unaware of their conspicuousness, and were still talking loudly. All the solemnity in the hall was swept away. Hang Chan could do nothing but blush. Chinese are not supposed to criticize elder relatives and certainly not to tell them to shut up.

Hang Chan was so lost in his memory of the ceremony that it took him five seconds to realize there was a hand on his shoulder. He turned his head quickly and saw the familiar face of Professor Hoffman, his professor in Chemical Engineering.

"Congratulations, Hang!" said Professor Hoffman heartily. "I can see you have brought your whole family along."

Heavens, who would not see it, Hang thought to himself.

"I never knew you had such a nice family. I even thought you did not have one because you never talked to me about it at all. Why are you keeping them a secret?" asked Professor Hoffman half-jokingly.

Hang Chan's reply was an embarrassed smile. Suddenly, he remembered he had to introduce his parents to Professor Hoffman, according to the unwritten Chinese doctrine or custom.

"This is my father." Hang pointed to a man in his early fifties, fat, with a double chin, wearing a tie so obsolete that it could only be found in movies of Charlie Chaplin's time.

"It is easy to tell with all these resemblances," commented Professor Hoffman good-humouredly.

"And this is my mother."

Professor Hoffman saw a woman quite a few inches shorter than he was, grinning shyly at him like a frightened kid.

"Would you and your parents care to dine with my family tonight? My wife would be most delighted to have you as our guests. Why? You will know if you come tonight." Professor Hoffman winked at Hang Chan after he finished the last sentence and smiled mischievously.

Uncle Ching had been following the conversation all along. He uttered a rapid-fire translation to Hang Chan's parents. They nodded without a moment of hesitation. It is an honour, according to the unwritten doctrine, to dine with a well-educated man, even though Professor Hoffman's manner was quite different from their image of a well-educated man. Impressed by Uncle Ching's ability to translate English, Professor Hoffman also invited him to dinner.

What Hang Chan dreaded most before the graduation had come true. Professor Hoffman had become more than just a teacher to Hang Chan through these years in university. In fact, he and Hang Chan were more than intimate friends. Hang Chan had done exceptionally well among his classmates, and Professor Hoffman always said he would like to see the family from which such a brilliant, well-bred student sprang. Now all Professor Hoffman's images of him and his family were going to be shattered because he would see what kind of parents Hang Chan had. Hang Chan's father was a cook who owned a small restaurant in Chinatown. His education had ended in Grade 6 when he had to go to work in order to support his family. After being in Canada for 15 years, he managed to learn to speak English, in the typical Chinese way—very awkwardly and without all the end sounds. His mother was even worse, for she knew no English at all. She had never gone to school and at a very young age had married Hang's father. Because she was always shy in front of strangers, she worked only in the kitchen of their restaurant.

"What am I going to do?" he asked himself as he drove his parents and Uncle Ching to Professor Hoffman's house. A memory of the past flashed back into Hang Chan's mind. It was of the time when he first came to Canada. He had gone to a high school in which he was the only Oriental. He remembered the jeering laughter and whispers of people when he passed by in the hallway. He was so lonely that he studied all the time and got very good marks. People started to accept him and make friends with him. Then Uncle Ching and his family immigrated to Canada. Naturally, his cousin clung to him all the time because he knew the school better. His cousin could speak very little English, and so he was always lost in classes. Hang Chan had to speak Chinese in order to explain things to him. Hang Chan could never forget the staring eyes that turned to him when people heard him speaking Chinese, eyes that seemed as if they were seeing creatures belonging to another species. Hang was eager to make friends, but the segregation between him and other students widened more and more. The same questions went round and round in his head. "Why am I Chinese? Why can't I be a totally Canadian Canadian? And what can I do? Change the colour of my skin?"

From then on, Hang Chan always tried his best to cast away all the Chinese ways so that he could be more Canadian. However, every time he saw the grey hair of his father grow whiter or the wrinkles at the corner of him mother's eyes become deeper, he knew he could not do that. He did not want his relatives to look down on him as a traitor to Chinese customs and thus a disgrace to his family. He was caught in a struggle to find balance between his identity as a Canadian and a Chinese.

Hang Chan was forced back from his thoughts when he realized they had arrived at Professor Hoffman's home. He quickly stepped on the brake and parked the car outside.

As they entered, Mrs. Hoffman was busy setting the table. Hang Chan's heart started to beat vigorously and his palms were full of sweat. He had given his parents a one-hour lecture on Western table manners, but they had seemed uninterested.

The main course of the meal turned out to be rice and chicken wings. Obviously Mrs. Hoffman intended to suit the tastes of her guests, and her Chinese cooking was not bad. "My wife always said her Chinese food is as good as in a Chinatown restaurant. That is why I invited you all to verify the truth," Professor Hoffman said, smiling.

"I have always liked Chinese cuisine but I could never do it well. So maybe I could get some lessons from Mr. and Mrs. Chan," said Mrs. Hoffman. The spitfire translation of Uncle Ching followed.

Hang's parents said they would be most honoured to help Mrs. Hoffman with her Chinese cooking. Uncle Ching translated. Then the Hoffmans turned their attention to Uncle Ching. They were amazed to learn that Uncle Ching never went to learn English in school. Uncle Ching had come from China just eight years ago, and he knew no English then. His determination enabled him to speak and read English fluently now.

After dinner, Hang's mother tried to pick up the dishes to wash them in the kitchen. Hang stopped her immediately.

"This is not our restaurant, Mother!"

Hang's mother was so nervous that she dropped the dishes, which crashed into pieces on the floor.

Hang Chan was frozen with shame. He thought he was going to lose Professor Hoffman as a friend, as he had lost all his friends in high school. It was then that Professor Hoffman took him out to the terrace. "I notice you have not been very comfortable at the dinner table. I know the reason. You are ashamed of your own culture. I noticed it back at the university. You think people will look down on you because of your ties to your culture."

"But people *do* look down on me because I am Chinese."

"Only those people who do not understand the spirit of Canada do. They think Canadian culture has been invaded by outsiders. What they do not know is that Canadian culture is a mixture of many cultures. Canada has had a long history of accepting immigrants who brought into this vast country many different cultures. Every one of these contributes to the Canadian culture. Thus is formed the multiculturalism of Canada. Have you ever seen the stained glass in a church? Is it not much more beautiful than just plain glass?"

Hang Chan was thinking as he walked back into the kitchen. He found the broken pieces of the dishes were gone already. He saw his father teaching Mrs. Hoffman how to carve a carrot into a rose. Hang's father, like a conjurer, skilfully cut pieces of the carrot, and all of a sudden, there was a rose staring right at everybody. Hang Chan fully understood Hoffman's speech now. There is unique beauty in every culture, and so even though they are different, they can be put together like a mosaic of colourful pieces of glass. He had never seen beauty in his own culture because he was so busy trying to belong to the new culture.

Later on, Hang's mother went to do some knitting with Mrs. Hoffman. They showed each other in turn some special patterns they had created. Uncle Ching got no chance to exercise his spitfire translation skill because the two ladies got on well by themselves. So he went to join Hang Chan, his father, and Professor Hoffman to watch the hockey game on TV.

At nine-thirty the Chan family left. At the door, Hang Chan's mother said the only English word she knew to the Hoffmans: "Thank you."

And the Hoffmans understood all the underlying meanings hidden in the words. After all, people do not communicate only by words.

Kit Wong
Hong Kong

What I Believe

Dear Mrs. McDougall:

I received your letter last week, but I could not reply to you right away because I had to study for a big pharmacology exam. I hope you will forgive me. I was very sorry to hear of your husband's death. As you mentioned in your letter, you would like to know more about my culture. I am very pleased that you are interested.

Confucianism is actually the root of my family religion, which emphasizes much devotion to family and relatives, and ancestor worship. However, my Dad is the root of my religion. When I was a small child, he used to give me the task of lighting an incense stick every night to put on the family ancestor table, which had my father's grandmother's picture on it. Then another table was added after my brother's death. As I grew up, more pictures of my relatives were added. I was very scared the first few nights, but then my Dad told me stories about my grandmother and how beautiful she was when she was alive. After that, I never missed my task a single night because I believed that the burning incense warmed up their spirits, and also I had a chance to tell them my wishes (usually, to pass a test/exam or to cancel class the day after.)

Every year, on the day that my grandmother died, we had a special little meal prepared and placed it on the table, and we burned incense to invite her spirit and others to enjoy it. When the incense was finished, it was our turn to enjoy the meal. This way we never forget those who are no longer alive, and we don't feel empty because their spirits are still around.

On New Year's Day we used to go to the cemetery to clean up their tombs, have tea, and tell stories about them. In Vietnam my ancestors were buried in the country; therefore, we used to have to cross one rice field after another to finish cleaning up all the tombs that we could remember and locate.

In my family particularly, we have a tradition on New Year's Eve. We always have a fresh coconut and cut off the head to make a little spout so that we can drink from it. After being on my ancestors' table, we pass the coconut around from an older person to the younger ones to drink from it. It is said that the coconut juice, pure and made by nature, untouched by any living things until this moment, sweet as honey and fresher than anything, will connect us all together. After all, we all are from the same bloodstream. (I guess it's like drinking wine from the Holy cup in the Christian mass.)

When I asked my Dad who was our God, he said that Buddha is our God, Christ is our God, my ancestors are our God, anyone with good deeds, any humanitarian, is our God. The good thoughts and behaviour in ourselves are our God. God is the person who lives inside me, who guides me to do good things, and God does not live in temples nor in churches, but the true God lives inside each person. You don't have to bring fruit and money and incense to the temple to be loved by God. You don't have to go to churches to be with God. God is right inside you, and to be loved by him all you have to do is to be a good person.

Actually, I've found this philosophy of God good because then whenever I discuss religion with other people I never have any conflicts in terms of which God is the real God or which God is the better God. I believe in all of them, and all of them to me is only one God who lives inside me.

Also death to me does not mean losing someone. Death does not terrify me at all. From the day we are born, we all know that there will be a day when we will die. It's the law of nature. Rich or poor, high or low, no one can escape death, no one can control death, but there is one thing that one can take control of—how to live life. Life can be good or it can be bad; it can remembered with honour and respect or it can be remembered with hatred and disgust. It can be cheerful, happy, full of colour, or it can be sad and grey. It all depends on the person who chooses how to live life.

I wish you good health and peace of mind.

Sincerely yours,

Tuan Nguyen

Tuan Nguyen
Vietnam

Student Activities

Talking and Writing*

"You Can Ask Me," "Caring," "Control," and "My Parents Are Part of Me"

1. What do you learn of the traditions in the Asian family from these stories?
2. What contrasts do these students believe exist in Asian and Canadian families?
3. Prepare to interview your partner about the traditions in her/his family. Write questions on each of the following topics:
   - Education
   - Relationships with brothers, sisters, and parents
   - The boss in the house
   - Choosing a girlfriend or a boyfriend

Talking and Writing**

"A Stinking Fish"

Explain why John considers it ironic that he is studying Mandarin in Canada.

"Thank You, Dad, for Everything"

Give evidence from the essay to show that the writer admires the character and values of his father.

"Smile!"

1. "It is the way of the Chinese." With what Chinese traditions is Hang Chan impatient? What evidence is there of his impatience and his embarrassment?
2. How does Hang Chan feel during his graduation and during the meal in Professor Hoffman's house? Explain his feelings by referring to details in the story.
3. How does Hang Chan's memory of the past help explain his feelings and his personality?
4. Do you think Hang Chan is self-centred and immature? Explain your answer.
5. What does Hang Chan learn from his conversation with Professor Hoffman and his observations of his parents during the visit with the Hoffmans?

"What I Believe"

What thoughts in this letter best express Tuan's philosophy of life?

Group Discussion

1. Do you agree or disagree with the following statements? Give reasons to support your opinion.

   - Children should look after their parents when they are old.
   - Teenagers should always tell their parents where they are going, with whom they are going, and what time they expect to return.
   - Men and women should be equal in a marriage.
   - Children should show respect to their older sisters and brothers.
   - Schools should teach heritage languages and cultures.

2. What qualities in parents do these writers in this section most admire? In your opinion, what is the most important quality of a parent? Illustrate how this quality might be evident in family situations.

Writing Folder

1. Write a paragraph in which you describe some of the traditions in your family.

2. In a short persuasive essay develop one of the themes that you discussed in your group.

3. Describe your future family. (How will you bring up your children? Which customs of your own parents will you wish to keep?)

4. Using the story "Smile!" as a model, write a story which focuses on the theme of family traditions.

Parents

The stories by the students in this section are accounts of incidents and times from the lives of their parents. In order to write these biographies, the students relied on stories told to them by their parents, their own observations of and reflections on their parents' lives, and, in some cases, personal interviews with their parents.

Most of the stories express the students' admiration for the love and devotion between their parents, and for their determination and perseverance as they struggled to survive in harsh circumstances.

As you read these accounts, you will learn not only about the lives and characters of the parents, but also about the student writers themselves.

Glasses

"Do not sit too close to the TV!" my mother said to me while I was watching cartoons.

"Why not? I am into the story. It's better to sit close," I cried, with my eyes still fixed on the cartoon characters.

"Because you will get nearsighted eyes. And you will have to wear a pair of heavy, ugly glasses on your nose."

In order to keep my mother silenced, I sat back half an inch. Mother sighed and went on with her business.

During that summer, almost everyday I went to my little friend's house to play. There I could sit as close to the TV as I wanted. When the summer was over, I went back to the school, but something strange was happening. The words on the blackboard seemed blurred. I told my mother, and she took me to the optometrist.

From that time on, I had to wear a pair of heavy, ugly glasses on my nose.

Peggy Lok
Hong Kong

Love at First Sight

When my mother was young, she was beautiful. She met my father when she was 17. My father is seven years older than she. He was her teacher. He fell in love with her at first sight. She fell in love with him at third sight. They married a year after they met. My grandmother disapproved of their marriage, but my mother said, "It is not *you* marrying him, and if something happens, I won't bother anyone." Then my grandma let her do what she wanted to do.

Li Minh Tseng
China

Suffering and Sacrifice

Life is just like a wheel. There are rich and there are poor. If there is laughter, there are also tears that each of us may encounter. For example, our family suffered sadness as well as happiness. I was only five years old, but I can still remember that in that year my father died. He left his nine children, and a month after his death our youngest brother was born.

Suffering and sacrifices were what our mother endured, but in spite of those difficulties, she never became impatient with her children. Instead, she tried her best to manage the position of mother and father at the same time. She never let anybody take away any of her children. She also did her best in sending her children to school. She used her strength and willpower in continuing the plan of our dead father. She continued tilling our lands and sent her eldest child to college—not only the eldest but also the second, third, fourth, and the rest.

And as the world changes, life also turns. Year after year passed until our eldest brother reached his goal. He graduated from the Philippines Maritime Institute as a marine engineer. Then he helped our mother in sending us to school until the next brother graduated and could help.

Alma Morales
The Philippines

Living Inside a Smile

My parents grew up together because my father's mother knew my mother's mother very well. Together my mother and father developed their love from playing hide-and-seek, going to the seashore, and finally, building their home together.

Since my father knew what love meant, his love towards my mother increased every day. He found that he could not leave my mother for a moment because my mother was so attractive and was once called a "beautiful little woman." My father was afraid to lose her so he kept in touch with her. However, my mother's family was quite traditional. She was not allowed to go out alone unless she had her parents' permission, and she was forbidden to go out with my father because her parents said she would have to marry him in the long run, if she was to date him. They did not want people criticizing their daughter as a fickle person; therefore, my Dad suffered because of this for a while.

My father never called on my mother because whenever he did my mother's parents and sisters would be there and would talk with them together. My father felt very uncomfortable in these circumstances, and the romance was almost ruined. Therefore my parents' love was demonstrated in a strange way. They mailed letters to each other almost every day. Sometimes their letters contained only three words: "I miss you," or "I love you." Yet they never tired of reading them. Furthermore, my father used to go and try to see my mother. He would stand under a light opposite my mother's window every night, no matter whether it rained or a tiger fell from the sky. All night, they just looked and smiled at each other.

My mother could not be free until she was 18 years old. At that time she told her mother that she was going to marry my father. Also, my father's prudence and honesty had impressed my grandparents. From then on she could go out with my father without further investigation.

They enjoyed themselves a great deal during those carefree and delightful times. Together they counted the countless stars, watched the sunset, swore upon a wishing-well that their love would last forever, went to the beach, and wrote down "happy land" on the sand with a stick. Saigon was covered with their footprints. There was no reason, no rhyme, and no need for them to keep track of time. They were living inside a smile.

My parents married each other within a few years. My father had his mother ask for my grandparents' approval to marry my mother. After thinking deeply, they approved of the marriage. According to the custom for a Chinese marriage, the groom's family had to ask the bride's family how many cakes they would need to assign to their relatives and how many seats for a meal in a restaurant. On the other hand, the bride's family had to carry over some jewellery, clothing, and furniture to show that her family was rich.

Being together, they were as free as in solitude. Their trust and confidence in each other was total. My mother always said, "I hold myself supremely blest—blest beyond what language can express because I am my husband's life as fully as he is mine. We will be forever together."

Donna Phung
Vietnam

Arranged Marriage

I didn't know how my mother and father got married before now. I always wanted to ask, but I was not brave enough to do that. It is because I'm their daughter that I could not ask such a question of them. I felt it was impolite. One day, I made up my mind. I went to ask them. At first my parents felt angry, but later they smiled at me and told me how they got married.

It was about 31 years ago. My mother was just 18 years old. She lived in a rich, old-fashioned, traditional family. My father was 19 years old. He lived in a rich family too. One day, someone came to my father's home and wanted to introduce a girl to his parents. When my grandparents saw the picture of my mother, they found that my mother was beautiful. They didn't ask the agreement of my father or my mother. My grandparents decided to let them be a couple. At that time my mother did not say a word. She just obeyed what her parents said. My mother felt shy because she was going to get married. She felt frightened because she did not know what the boy looked like, and she felt happy because she was going to have a husband. My father also had the same feeling as my mother, but he was not shy. He just could not sleep until the day he got married.

The day came. That morning my mother woke up early before the sun rose. She sat on the bed and wondered how my father looked. Was he smart? Would he be a good husband? Oh! There were so many question marks in her mind. She knew that she would solve some of the problems soon. But she found that a minute passed like an hour. On the other hand, my father woke up early that morning too. He just walked around the house without stopping. He found that it was hard for him to stop walking and thinking.

The time came. My parents dressed in their own houses, My mother was taken to my father's house. At that time my father still could not see my mother because there was a red cloth covering my mother's face. When the ceremony began, my mother held one end of the red silk cloth and my father held the other end. My mother had to pour tea for my grandparents. Then my grandparents gave her Red Pocket Money to show good luck. My mother and father went into their own room after the ceremony. At that time, after my father took away the red cloth which covered my mother's face, he found that she was beautiful, but he did not know how to talk to my mother because he had never met such a sweet lady before. My father just looked at my mother, and my mother kept her face down because she was shy.

Ming Szeto
Hong Kong

Traditional Korean Marriage

A lot of time I wondered how my parents got married. I never asked them, for I thought it was impolite.

My mother's family was well educated and very respected. When she was a teenager, her father never let her wear a pin in her hair or put on makeup or read magazines or listen to music. Her father stressed that a good girl should not get involved in these things but should study hard, obey her parents, and stay home to help with the mother's work. My mother was told not to do so many things that her ears were sick and tired of hearing them, and many times she hated her father. However, her father did this because he cared about her a lot and loved her very much.

My father's family was Christian and well-educated. His parents were not as hard on him as my mother's parents. From boyhood my father was taught to help other people, respect parents, and study hard. Above all, his father thought helping other people was the most important thing. He told my father that if he helped people when they were in trouble, they would never ever forget the incident. The people would always remember the help even though my father died, his father said. As my father grew up, he never gave any trouble or problem to his parents.

The day of the wedding, my mother was dressed in a long Korean dress. She had two little red dots on her cheeks and a small ornament on her head. The little dots and the ornament symbolized that she had become a woman. She had to tie her braided hair up high and clean her face. She did not put on any makeup.

My father wore a "hun-oak" (Korean men's suit) with a tall black hat. Early in the morning my father rode on a horse and came to my mother's house in order to take her to his house. My mother and my father had never met before. She could not lift her head or touch or even talk to my father.

The wedding took place on a patio. My father and my mother had to sit on the floor facing each other between a small table full of rice cakes and some special wine which is for weddings. There would be traditional Korean music, and one person had to stand between my parents and give the same bowl of wine to both my mother and father. Each of my parents had to drink three times, and every time they drank, they had to bow to each other in a very formal way. Drinking the wine three times with the same bowl meant that my parents had shared food.

After the wedding they had to bow to my mother's parents in appreciation of them as parents. Then there would be a party celebrating the wedding. My mother was always surrounded by ten people, who protected her. They followed every-where my mother went and helped her with her clothes and food.

After a few hours my father and mother headed to my father's house. My father rode on a horse as usual, but my mother rode a "game" (Korean wagon with no wheels, which was carried by people on their shoulders). Again, they had to bow, thanking these people for what they had done. Then my father's parents called the neighbourhood friends and relatives and invited them to the wedding party to share the joy. They drank and ate until all the food was gone. Their wedding party was the biggest in town.

It was not that simple after my mother had married. For three months she had to get up very early in the morning before the rooster crowed to make breakfast for everyone. When my father's parents got up every day, she had to greet them by saying, "Good morning, mother and father. I hope you had a good night's sleep."

My mother had to wash everyone's clothes, clean the house, make everyone's bed, iron and starch the clothes. It was very hard work, and she was exhausted in the beginning because she had never worked so hard; however, later she got used to it. Still that was not all. She also had to stay up very late besides getting up early. She had to be the last one to go to bed, and before she slept, all the work in the house had to be completed. Every day my mother only slept four or five hours and if she slept more, she would be kicked out of the house.

The work we do now is nothing compared to work in the old times. I feel sorry for my mother, who has worked very hard, and I would certainly never want to be married the way my parents were.

Monica Kim
Korea

Mother's Influence

My mother, who is a wise, kind, hard-working high school teacher, has greatly influenced me and helps me to find my own way in life.

Mother is such a wise and understanding woman that she rarely hit and scolded me even if I sometimes really provoked her when I was a naughty boy. Whenever I did something wrong, she had a heart-to-heart talk with me instead of scolding me angrily. Once I skipped school and went to a movie. After the teacher had complained to her, she surprised me by not blaming me. Instead, she talked to me, gently explaining why I should not have played truant. From then on, I never was absent again and tried to do my best in school.

Mother not only taught me how I could make good in my life, but also gave me strength and advice when I was confused and faced with difficulties. In China, the school system was destroyed thoroughly after the Cultural Revolution, and politics and ideology began to be emphasized in school. The one who knew the most slogans of Chairman Mao was considered the best student in school. Since the universities were closed, no one was interested in studying anymore. During that time, I was so disappointed and confused, wondering what great change had taken place in China and how we were going to cope. Since studying was useless, we played all day long, ignoring our homework or going to school just for fun. Everyone was facing such a terribly dark future, for the only choice seemed to be to go to the country to do hard labour. Mother was so anxious and worried about me that she often could not sleep well. She encouraged me, insisting on my studying even in such bad times. She often reminded me: "Knowledge is Power." From her, I received strength and continued my studies.

Mother is also such a hard-working, self-confident person that she never gives up whenever she faces difficulties. She is always an example to me. After we came to Canada, our family, like so many other newcomers, had a difficult time adjusting. We had neither money nor experience. Even worse, we could not speak any English, and we had to do such hard work in Chinatown. I continually recalled the good times in my country and even hoped to go back to China. I was disappointed that Canada was not the heaven which I had dreamed of before, but rather a real hell. But at that time, mother was so optimistic that she never complained about her two jobs. It gave me enough strength and confidence so that I gradually was able to adapt to the way of life in Canada.

After a few months, we bought a house and I had a chance to get further education. I feared that I might be too old to study and that I might have forgotten most of the mathematics and science that I had studied before. Mother again encouraged me to go back to school to learn more. She said to me, "It does not matter whether you can get into university or not. The more education you have, the better off you are."

In my heart, mother is great although she is not a well-known person and has not done anything significant. But she has greatly influenced me, and I will remember her all of my life.

Kenny Chou
China

Admirable Parents

My father has been the cleverest, kindest, and wisest man in my life ever since I was a little girl.

As a boy in Hong Kong, Father was a "pearl" in his family because no one in his family had received as high an education as he had. Father was so bright that his parents treated him like a businessman when he was only 15 years old. During the day Father went to school, but at night he helped his parents in the store and counted the money.

After Father graduated from high school, like many idealistic young people, he was influenced by leftist philosophy. He chose to sacrifice a rich and comfortable existence in Hong Kong and went to Communist China to study and to start a new life. Since my father's math was very good, he was accepted into one of the best universities, Peking University, to study aerodynamics. After he graduated, he got a job as a university professor.

But the Cultural Revolution smashed Father's dream. He was classified as a capitalist because his parents had a business in Hong Kong and also because he was an intellectual, according to Chairman Mao's thought. Father was sent to a farm in the countryside to do manual work—cultivating the fields, mining, and cutting down trees in the forests. This was a terrible experience for Father, yet it was a good thing too. The sunshine and hard work made him physically strong, and he learned to be industrious and resourceful.

It was a great pleasure when Father was near because he always saved us from Mother's harsh punishment. It is hard to remember whether Father has ever beaten me; instead he always used his knowledge and reason to teach us. I still remember the time when some neighbours looked at me with contempt because I had done a very bad thing to them. Father learned of it afterwards, but he still did not punish me; instead he gave me some very good advice. "Your life is in your hands. Nobody can change it except yourself. Although you may have been a very lovely child around the neighbourhood, they will be disgusted with you because of your bad behaviour." I found that Father's teaching methods were much better than Mother's, because every time I got severe punishment from mother, I knew only that I had done wrong and didn't know what my behaviour might lead to in the future.

Living in a foreign country is very hard, especially for people of my father's age. He has applied for many jobs for which his background should fit him, but he has always been rejected because he does not have Canadian experience and Canadian degrees. Because of this, the only kind of job Father can get is working in a factory. Sometimes I feel unhappy because his excellent knowledge is useless in this country, but Father does not give up. He works by day and studies by night. Although it is very hard for him, he says that he enjoys studying in the university and being a student again.

Never in my life have I known a more powerful, strong, independent, straightforward, yet rigid woman than my mother, who acquired these qualities through hardship and misfortune.

Her mother died when she was only ten years old, and as her stepmother was indifferent to her, she developed an independent spirit. Lacking a mother's love, she turned instead to studying and joined a leftist group—a Communist organization for young people in Hong Kong. Every time her father signed her student report, he always smiled with pride, but he could never believe that his proud daughter had joined the Communist party.

As soon as Mother graduated from high school in Hong Kong, Grandfather busied himself finding a husband for her. He chose an old and wealthy Chinese immigrant from America, but before this man could come to get her, she told Grandfather that she wanted to go to Red China to continue her studies. At hearing this, Grandfather became furious, for he was not only mad at Mother's rebellion, but also mad at her communist beliefs. A few months later, Mother left with her classmates. She did not ask Grandfather for permission.

My parents were schoolmates and good friends at Peking University. Mother loved and admired my father not only because he was very intelligent, but also because he was an optimistic man. They were both concerned about each other because their relatives were far away. Both of them studied very hard because they loved studying. Years passed. They fell in love and married after graduation. After finishing university, Father taught aerodynamics in the university, and mother taught in a college.

Mother was so energetic and strong that you would hardly ever see her ask someone for help. During the Chinese Cultural Revolution, according to Chairman Mao's ideals, the intellectuals had to do manual work—this was called "washing the old brains of the bourgeoisie." Father put away his teaching and went to a farm far away to work as a farmer. Although Mother was not sent to the farm, she had to tend pigs for half a year. Even though it was very hard for her because she had never before done any manual work, she did not complain a bit. Every time I saw her carry a heavy burden on her shoulder or pull a heavy wagon full of pig's food, I felt terrible. Whenever my brother and I tried to help her, she always commanded, "Go home to finish your homework!" Actually, we did not have any homework during the Cultural Revolution. Any homework we did have was all given by Mother, and it was always more than the school teachers gave. If we did not finish it that night, we received a beating. We always wondered how Mother had such strength to beat us after her hard work!

After immigrating to Canada, Mother still has great energy! Although living in a foreign country is so hard that many women my mother's age give up and just work in a factory for the rest of their lives, my mother is so marvellous that she takes both a part-time English course on the weekend and a part-time electronics course at night on the week days.

Li Yuin Tam
China

Do Better!

Today I told my father I was going to write about him. He smiled. And said nothing. He does not want my admiration. He wants me to make him admire me.

He is the kind of father who gets angry with marks below A. When my brother got home this week with five B's and said he did very well for a student with English as a second language, we almost had a private war. My father does not like B's, and never tell him you did a good job, given your limitations. Better still, erase this word from your dictionary. It is a four-letter word for him. My brother is still fighting him because he thinks he deserves some credit for getting a B, and not a C. But my father would have to be sick to say "Good!" for a B in school.

My father has a PhD in engineering and a bachelor's degree in Physics. He did two degrees at the same time. And he is a teacher. He knows every single excuse we could present about mediocre achievement, and he never accepts any. He has proved he can succeed; he wants us to do better.

On the day of his marriage, he woke up at five o'clock in the morning and wrote a test in Physics. Then he ate lunch and wrote the final test of the engineering program. Finally he took a bus and travelled two hours to meet his parents in the city where he was supposed to get married. He got home half an hour before the wedding which half-killed my grandmother. She says her son was almost the first groom who arrived in the church after the bride. When he came back from his honeymoon, he spent his first weekend writing the final test of the Physics program. He half-killed my mother, alone in the new apartment on the first weekend of her new marriage. He is always half-killing somebody, mainly if "somebody" is the kind of person that expects normal behaviour from him. He is not an average person.

If I had to describe my father in a single word, I would say "beyond." This is his favourite word. He always wants to go "beyond" everything. Mainly, he does not accept limits. Not ours, not his. And it makes us develop ourselves. My brother now is so angry that he will get more than A's in his next report card.

Moreover, my father's desire to succeed is not only in intellectual but also in physical areas as well. He used to play soccer on the beach when he was 17 years old. Sand is the hardest surface possible for soccer. Shoes are not allowed, and the sand makes it extremely difficult to kick the ball. As a result, his feet, even now, are covered with hard callouses. He can walk on extremely hot surfaces and feel nothing. He calls it adaptation. The last game was played in a heavy rainfall. If you have ever felt wet sand, you know you cannot walk without making holes, and you cannot run. The sand is too heavy. I can imagine him pushing the whole team, screaming and doing more than just the possible. He was the captain of the team, and the team won the championship that year. This persistence is his most admirable quality.

My father never gives up. He spent two years trying to come to Canada. He was a fighter in his country too. He did not agree with much of the Brazilian way of thinking. This is what I admire the most in him. He is not afraid of fighting for what he believes in, and he does not stop until he gets what he wants. He makes us understand the need of being strong and of making up our minds. He is always pushing himself or somebody else. He is never afraid of criticism or change.

Whenever I have the strength to do what I want, or say exactly what I think, it is because he has shown me it is right. Moreover, if I have the self-assurance to pursue my goals, it is because I know he admires me and will always be by my side.

Caroline Moraes
Brazil

Did Father Care?

The tick-tick sound of the rain hitting the window wakes me up. It sounds just exactly as it did 15 years ago. I began to remember.

It was my second day of school and it was raining heavily. I could not resist the habit I had at home, so I fell asleep right at my seat. I woke up to find that my father was carrying me on his back. We were halfway home. It was the last time I felt close to him.

After that he practically never carried me or hugged me as other fathers in town hugged their children. I was not bothered much by this though; in fact, I was proud of it, for I felt independent and "grown up." There were occasions when I felt depressed but could seek not comfort from him; that was when it bothered me. I stopped telling him stories and asking him strange questions that came off the top of my head. I did not know why I reacted to him in such a way. Did he notice it or not? I never knew.

I thought he did not like me for some reason, but I did not see any. So I dropped the subject. One day, I was printing Chinese characters as homework. I hated doing this more than any other homework. My father came and stood behind me for a moment, watching me scratching the paper. Then, right off the bat, he said, "This kind of writing needs patience. And to have a proper character, it must be balanced." Then he picked up another piece of paper and commented, "Your writing is not strong enough, press harder." I followed his advice for the next two words, but as I could see little improvement, I followed my own method—the fast way. His advice did not improve my writing, but it improved our relationship. I could see that he still cared for me.

That was about all he taught me because as I found out later he did not know anything else appropriate to teach me. He had finished his education in Grade 6 without writing the final exam, and spent his teenage life hiding from the bombing of French airplanes. All he learned in school was Chinese literature, the four basic mathematical operations (addition, subtraction, multiplication and division), art, and music.

At that time Grade 6 was the highest grade in town, and so he was considered to be one of the scholars. People used to ask him to write them verses from famous poems or worthwhile proverbs in big characters so that they could put them on walls or on poles in their houses. He even had his writing on the flag at the entrance of the one temple in town. I thought that he was the best calligrapher and was very proud of him. Later I saw that he was not the best, but it no longer mattered by that time. Another of his accomplishments was winning the chess tournament. I was there, watching each day for three whole days.

Enough of his virtues. I saw more of his weaknesses as I grew older. He swore a lot, especially when he talked to his buddies. You should have heard him. He swore more than I do. The funny thing is he used the stick on me if he heard me swearing. He also gambled, but he beat me when he caught me doing it. I was really angry about that, but nothing could be done. I had no voice. He prohibited me from playing billiards, learning the guitar, or reading novels. He explained, "Billiards is for street people. Guitars and novels only make you a dreamer." The only approved sports left were table tennis and basketball. I eliminated basketball for I was only one-metre-fifty something tall. Thus, every time I came home from the sports centre, the answer I used to give, if I had to, was "I've been playing ping pong."

His ambition for me was well defined. He confessed, "As you can see, this family is going to count on you. You've got to try. I'm no good as a man, I know. You can't be like me. Get an education."

As a result of his ambition for me, I have made it through high school and perhaps will make it through college.

Mit Ly
Vietnam

Student Activities

Talking and Writing*

"Glasses," "Love at First Sight," and "Suffering and Sacrifice"

Read these three stories. Give examples from each story to show that the daughter admires her mother.

Talking and Writing**

"Living Inside a Smile," "Arranged Marriage," and "Korean Traditional Marriage"

What do you learn about dating and marriage customs in Asia a generation ago?

Group Discussion

Read the stories in "Parents."

In your discussion of the following topics refer to your reading of the stories in this section and your own experiences to support your opinion. You might be interested after your discussion to have a more formal debate on the topic.

- Marriages should be arranged by parents.
- Parents should sometimes use physical punishment on their children.

The Writing Folder

1. Interview your father, mother, or any older relative or friend. In preparation for this interview make up questions which demand more than a yes/no answer. Questions might focus on the following topics:

   - How parents met;
   - Attitude of grandparents towards romance;
   - Courtship, marriage customs;
   - Education and family values;
   - Memories of early childhood experiencess;
   - Interests, significant experiences.

   Write an account of the interview. Concentrate on a few topics only and develop each in as much detail as possible.

2. Ask the person you are interviewing to talk about the most interesting event that ever happened to him/her. Write about this event in the first person as if the person interviewed were telling the story.

3. In the first person tell about an incident from your childhood. Focus on your father or mother as you narrate the incident. (For an example, see "Glasses.")

4. Do you believe in arranged marriages? Write a persuasive essay defending your point of view with strong arguments. (Try to anticipate arguments on the other side and refute these.)

Grandparents

Often there is a very special bond between grandparents and grandchildren. For grandparents, their grandchildren represent renewed life and the chance to love a young child again. For grandchildren, grandparents offer wisdom, understanding, and affection.

Here, the students write nostalgically about the delightful moments they shared with their grandparents as they were growing up. They remember so clearly songs, stories, conversations, and words of advice and warning. They express admiration for the quiet perseverance of their grandparents, who survived hard times, and appreciation of the patient understanding offered by them.

One of the most painful repercussions of coming to Canada for many young people is the separation from grandparents. Too frequently they are left behind as parents and children pull up roots and leave for a new country and a new life. The profound sense of loss in being separated and the deep love of these young people for their grandparents are vividly expressed in the following stories.

Footprints

If my grandfather were still alive, he would be almost 100 years old. He died when I was three years old. I cannot remember clearly what he was like, but my grandma told me that he was a diligent man who worked from morning to night when he was in Canada. He never smoked, drank, or gambled.

Before the Second World War, my grandfather and my grandmother left my parents and went to Canada with my granduncle and grandaunt. They ran a laundry. Since it was not near the downtown area, they needed to walk from door to door to collect the dirty clothes, and send back the clean clothes house-by-house. Their footprints were over all Toronto.

After many years of hard work, they saved a little money, but my grandfather got high blood pressure, and my granduncle's feet didn't move very well. Therefore, they decided to close the laundry. My grandpa brought the money and my grandma back to Hong Kong and built three houses in the countryside because the land was much cheaper. My granduncle used some money to buy some houses in Toronto.

Three years after my grandparents were back home, I was born. When I was three years old, my grandfather's health became worse, and he died in that year. I didn't know what death was, because I was so young. I just felt he had suddenly disappeared.

When I was four years old, my grandmother brought me to kindergarten. She said, "Early to school, early to graduate, and early to get money." My grandmother was a supplementary teacher to me when I was in kindergarten. She taught me to sing some short Chinese country songs. She said, "Try to remember all the songs in the brain, then your brain will become bigger, and your memory will improve."

Every day Grandma brought me to school and also brought me back home. One day when we were walking to school, she told me, "Today I may not have time to bring you back home. You may go home by yourself."

Since she was not sure whether she would be back or not, I thought of a signal. If she didn't have time to bring me home, she would pick up a stone which we had noticed. If the stone was not picked up, I would wait for her. After school, the stone was still there so I thought she would be back. After a long wait, I decided to go home by myself. At night when I saw her, I asked her angrily, "Why didn't you pick up the stone? You know so many songs that your memory must be very good! Why did you forget that?"

"Gold is never changed by time, but man declines in old age!" she answered regretfully.

Esmond Szeto
Hong Kong

I Love My Grandfather

My parents divorced when I was three years old. I lived with my mother and her parents. I did not really notice any change in my life, or at least I did not feel any change, as I was only three years old. I loved my grandmother and my grandfather a lot—I loved them more than my life. They really treated me very well, much better than my mother and father.

I remember when I was a child, I went to an Italian school and spent one year there with the nuns. They treated me so strictly that my mother moved me from that school. In those days I had to wait for the bus at 6 o'clock in the morning in front of my house. My grandfather used to wait with me in the cold until the bus came. In the last days of his life he refused to eat from anyone except from my hands.

When he died I was really shocked, and I could not believe that he was really dead. They tried to convince me that he would be happier with God, but I stayed in bed for a week. I did not eat. I cried a lot. But because I was a child, I began to forget quickly.

Hussam Abou Dan
Egypt

To the Rescue

My father lived in a small village in China in his early childhood. When he was a little boy, he was very naughty. He played truant and did not do his homework. Once his teacher asked him to recite a very difficult chapter from the book. Because he had not studied it, he could not recite it. The teacher used a very thick cane to hit him right on his head whenever he made a mistake in reciting.

This seems cruel and is unlawful nowadays, but at that time it was acceptable. Teachers were extremely respected by plain peasants who were not educated. For that reason they wanted their children to be educated in order to lead a bright, comfortable life. They believed that only harsh punishment could make children good and useful for the rest of their lives. Thus they supported the teacher's punishment, even if the teacher had misjudged the children.

My father was ordered to stay after school to learn that difficult chapter. He could not go home until he could recite it perfectly and had the teacher's permission to leave. All the other students had gone home for their supper. My father sat on a stool, feeling lonely, tears in his eyes, pain in his head, haunted by hunger.

His grandmother was waiting for him, anxiously looking for him over the fields. My father's classmates ran to tell her what had happened. Without a second thought, she hurried to the rescue. When she saw her grandson, she hugged him tightly in her arms while he cried. At first, she begged the teacher to let him go, but she was disregarded. Seeing her grandson in pain, she began to threaten that if her grandson died of his wounds, the teacher would have to give her back another grandson. At last, the teacher gave up.

Unlike the other timid, old Chinese women, Grandma felt she knew best how to deal with her grandson, who was deeply impressed and decided to be a good student in order to please her.

Fung Yue Wong
Hong Kong

His Favourite

I was born in Peking, China. Because my father was in Canada, my grandparents looked after me. My grandma was very warm and soft, but my grandpa was exactly the opposite.

My grandparents' apartment was at the edge of the city. Sometimes Grandpa took me with him to his office when he was in a good mood. I had not seen so much traffic and so many huge streets before so that when we came to cross the street, I got frightened even though I knew the cars were going to stop. I was shaking and sweating because my grandpa did not like to hold hands, and he walked so fast that I had to run after him as if there was a ghost after me.

Maybe you think my grandpa did not like me, but you are wrong. I was his favourite, because at that time I was his only granddaughter, and he liked girls more than boys. This was the opposite of other old Chinese people.

There was something wrong with Grandpa's stomach. It always hurt. One day Grandpa took me with him to work. On the way back we stopped at a noodle factory. After eating, I was tired and sleepy. It was nearly the time for my afternoon nap. I was too lazy to walk. I wanted Grandpa to hold me and I knew Grandpa had a bad stomach, but I asked, "Is your stomach hurting now?"

"No," said Grandpa.

Without thinking what I was going to say next, I said, "Grandpa, if your stomach is not hurting, can you hold me for a little while?"

My grandpa looked at me and laughed and he carried me for a long time.

Emma Yu
China

Left Foot, Right Foot

When I was about five years old, I often went to play with an old man who lived across the path from our house. He was about 75 years old and lived with his wife. Since my real grandparents were living at a great distance from me, I didn't get a chance to see them very often. So I called this old couple my grandparents. I loved them as much as my own.

I remember every other day the old man taught me how to play checkers. We played for hours, and while we played he asked me about my interests, and he often talked about his only son who had been dead for ten years. He told me that I resembled his son. We played checkers and laughed, ate cookies, and cheated sometimes.

Every other day he taught me how to dance. He had been a professional dancer when he was young. He usually said, "Now your left foot, now your right foot," and he expected me to imitate him. When I did, his wife applauded loudly, smiled, and hugged me. After we finished the games or dancing, he would tell me some folk tales and teach me how to read and write the Cambodian alphabet. I loved being with him.

About twice a week, we went swimming in a swift-moving stream located about a half-mile from our house. We picked wild spinach in the forest when we came back. Every weekend, my mom would cook delicious food and invite them to join us for dinner.

One day he caught a cold and had a headache. He took some aspirins and thought that he would be cured soon. The next thing I knew was that he was in the hospital. His wife came over and slept at our house. She was frightened sleeping alone. She said that he would be okay in a couple of days.

A week after he had entered the hospital, my mom arranged for us to pay him a visit. He was delighted to see me when we got there. I found out that his flu was cured, but his legs were so weak that he couldn't walk by himself. I encouraged him to try to walk and he did, with the support of my mom and his wife. At that moment, I remembered the dancing lessons he had taught me. I told him to place his hands on my shoulder to support himself and to follow my steps. I said to him, "Now your left foot, now your right foot," just as he had taught me. He laughed.

In the next couple of days he was able to walk again, and his health was even better than before. Then back at home we did the usual things. We danced, ate, played checkers, and cheated.

About two months later my dad died, and my family was forced by the Khmer Rouge to live in a new district which was about ten miles from our old place. I felt very depressed. I didn't know what would happen to that old couple later on, and I didn't know how they would feel without me around to cheer them up.

Sangva Sok
Cambodia

Don't Waste Your Youth: Go Dancing

My grandmother is a seventy-four-year-old woman with grey hair who always shows happiness in her kind face. She gives the impression of kindness and honesty.

She was born in China and moved to Macao during World War II in order to escape the Japanese invasion. She never had been gone to school because in old China, girls without any culture or knowledge were considered good to marry. Usually, a girl was supposed to learn some cooking and sewing techniques and to wait for a woman who represented a boy to ask her parents for her hand in marriage. If her parents were willing to give their daughter, then the boy would send thousands of cakes and choose a lucky day to marry.

According to this traditional custom, my grandmother married at the age of 18. She never saw nor knew anything about her husband before her marriage, and even after a week of marriage, she still couldn't see his face clearly because a woman was not supposed to hold her head up before her husband.

My grandfather was a rich businessman, and also handsome and sensual. During the following five years, he married twice after marrying grandmother. He kept three wives at home and gave them no money.

Unfortunately my grandfather was paralysed after a car accident and also became senile in his late life. His two younger wives left him and married other men. My poor grandmother stayed with him 20 years and took care of him without any grumbling. In these 20 years, not one of their five children stayed home. They left for China, America, and Canada, I cannot imagine how my grandmother could stand those 20 years. I think she was the most good-tempered woman.

In those years, her only source of pride was her older son, my uncle. He graduated from the University of Hong Kong and went to Australia, where he got his master's degree. Then he went to England and finally got his doctorate in Chemistry. All the education fees came from scholarships. Not only did he not get any money from home, but also he sent money home every month to support two old people. Now he is working in Canada in an inland water centre.

In 1974, my grandfather died; for this reason our family was permitted to go to Macao. At the end of 20 years of a miserable, lonely life and on seeing her son and grandchildren, she felt a hopeful life starting again. I have loved Grandma very much from the first time I saw her. Although she grew up in the old society, she does not have a conservative mind. Sometimes my mother criticizes me for knowing no cooking or sewing, but Grandmother says: "Don't worry about this and don't waste your youth in the kitchen. Go dancing. Go to a picnic and do whatever young people do." Then I understand Grandma. She knows how unfortunate her life has been, and she does not want us to have the same fate as she had.

Two years ago we immigrated to Canada. Grandma seems to like this new country very much. She is not like other old people because she never complains about the cold weather, the Canadian food, and the transportation. She spends most time helping in my father's noodle plant. This is the only thing we worry about. We cannot stop her working. She cannot rest. She always says: "My hands will feel itchy if I have nothing to do every moment." This is how I see my grandmother!

Nora Chao
China

Inside My Heart

My grandpa was born in the early 1900s, and he died in July 1977 when he was only 69 years old. He was a very honest, well-educated man, a man who was always full of energy, a man who had a lot of experience and patience with children.

After his death, I found out from my grandma's letter that the cause of my grandpa's death was cancer, the most prevalent death-causing disease in China. I did not attend his funeral because my family and I had left China and immigrated to Canada. The last time I saw my grandpa was at the train station, saying "Good-bye" to me. At that time he was still healthy and very active, and I still couldn't believe that he died so quickly. He loved me very much since I was his only grandson.

I can still remember the scene when I said farewell to him. It was three minutes before the train departed. All my relatives and the good friends of my parents were there wishing us good luck in the future. I was crying because I did not want to go with my family, but my grandpa confided that he would immigrate to Canada shortly and live with us for the rest of his life and I believed him. When the train began to move, I saw my grandpa was in tears and waving at me.

I loved my grandpa too, because whenever I was in difficulties he was always there helping me, explaining the facts to me, and making me happy again. Sometimes I wondered what I was going to do without him.

I lived with my grandparents when I was very young. My parents, who were teachers, lived at the university. They visited me every weekend because the university was very far from my grandparents' home. My grandma cooked my favourite food and my grandpa played with me and taught me lessons. Every morning my grandpa accompanied me to school, told me to behave well, and told me why I should go to school when I did not like to. He seemed to understand me better than I did myself.

My grandpa was an understanding person, who did not get angry very often. One time I accidentally smashed a window at the school with a ball. I ran home and cried because I thought my grandpa was going to punish me severely, but he did not get angry and told me not to cry. He paid the damage for me. The only thing he told me was that he wanted me to play more carefully next time.

My grandpa had a lot of patience and experience with children. He taught me English, word by word, sentence by sentence, until I understood. He did not force me to study, but he told me the importance of knowledge. He told me that I needed English because I had to speak English in Canada. He did his best to satisfy me.

Now, my grandpa is dead. His dreams of seeing me again and living with us for the rest of his life cannot be achieved, but his love and image stay deep inside my heart.

Ted Liu
China

Visit to Our Ancestral Tomb

Ching Ming Festival is on the fifth day of the fourth month. It is a festival for descendants to pay respects to their ancestors at their graves. Because our ancestral tombs were far away from Saigon, I had never been there before. Every year my grandparents, my parents, and my uncle went there to sweep the tombs. My sisters, my brothers, and I stayed at home because the Communists often appeared in the forests or the villages outside Saigon.

Before the Ching Ming Festival, my grandmother and my mother were busy making cakes and cooking the food which our ancestors liked best when they were still alive. At night, my grandmother put incense candles and some paper money into a basket. Then she put some fruit into the other basket. Why don't I ask Grandmother to let me go tomorrow, I thought. My grandmother was a kind and gentle person who had the most authority in the family. I asked, "Grandmother, can I go with you tomorrow?"

My grandmother smiled and replied, "My girl, certainly you can go, but don't tell the others now."

The next day, after driving for three hours, we had to walk for about one hour in order to get to the tomb. When we got there, my grandparents burned some incense and some paper money. We lit two candles on each side of the tomb. My family made three bows to the grave and then it was my turn. As I was looking at the tombstone, my grandfather seemed to be plunged in thought. I moved towards him and asked curiously, "What's wrong with you Grandpa?" He did not answer, but forced a smile.

Without answering my question, he sat beside the stone with his head down. Then he turned to me suddenly and said, "Thirty years from now, you will visit the tomb of your grandmother and me with your husband and children." I felt sad at these words as I hoped they would live for a long time.

That was the first time I went to sweep our ancestral tombs, and also the last time, because we were forced to leave Vietnam. If we go back there one day, I do not know whether our ancestral tombs will be there or not, since the war has destroyed and ruined the countryside and villages.

Juliana Ly
Vietnam

An Ordinary Hero

Last summer my grandfather died. When I heard it, I felt a sudden stab at my heart. The thought that I could have seen him, and did not, and would never see him again—this bitter thought buried itself in me with all the force of an unanswerable reproach. "He is dead," I repeated, staring dully at the telephone and then making my way noiselessly into the street, wandering off without knowing where I was going. The past suddenly rose and stood before me.

"You will come back some day, won't you?" he asked hoarsely, holding my hands tightly. It was a winter day and we were at the airport. I was about to leave for Canada.

"Certainly I will. Don't worry about anything, Grandpa. I will study hard and be healthy. I will come back soon and tell you about my experiences in Canada."

Tears fell down his wrinkled face. After a long pause he suddenly said to me, "I have some money to give you. As soon as you arrive in Canada, please buy whatever you want with this money." He took a bill folded at least ten times out of his shabby pocket and tried to smooth it out with his trembling hands before giving it to me. I could not help weeping.

"Grandpa, Canadians use different money than we use in Korea. I can't buy anything with the bill that you are giving me. So just keep it." I wanted to say this, but did not. The bill folded carefully ten times was the only way that this old man could express his immeasurable love towards me at this time. Without a word, I carefully put the bill in my pocket. After hugging me tightly, he disappeared into the crowd. As I saw the back of his grey head and his slim figure, I felt an unfathomable affection towards him. It was the last time that I saw my grandfather.

My grandfather was not a hero nor a distinguished person. He was just an ordinary person who was born in an epoch of social unrest, torment, and war. He had poor parents, was poorly educated, and lived most of his life in a foreign country in frustration and agony. Maybe he might have tasted a little happiness when his son entered the best university, although he did not even know what "university" meant. I think he just naively assumed that his son would have a much better life than he himself after spending four years in something called "university."

Although he was not a great man whom many people admired, I find greatness in his ordinary life. During the Korean war, an American war correspondent, Margaret Bourke-White once wrote, "What is the invisible power which keeps this small nation from being broken? Is it military power? Is it political power? No, I don't think so. It is the farmer whom I am looking at right now, who is ploughing his field quietly regardless of the frightening sound of bombs overhead."

Whenever I think of my grandfather, I am reminded of the farmer. If our society were filled with ordinary and good people like my grandfather, we would not need a hero.

Oh, I miss my grandpa.

Anonymous

My Amazing Grandmother

At 78, Grandma is still as strong as ever. She would do battle with Iron Mike Tyson and knock him down cold. Yes, energetic she is. Every morning, Grandma wakes up at five (ever determined to put the rooster out of commission), goes for her morning stroll in the garden, and comes back for her morning tea. At her age, she is as nimble as a lamb and robust as a twelve-year-old. Though the years have crept up on her, her wit is still as sharp as ever and her eyes still sparkle as if in a kaleidoscope.

Grandma was born to the gentry in China. As she was the youngest, her father kowtowed to her whims. She could have anything she possibly wanted. During her tantrums, the maidservants would cower in fear, but they provoked her even more. She was indeed the epitome of a spirited brat. Her anger would ricochet around the house.

All her worldly pleasures came to a grinding halt when the Nationalists fled and the Communists ascended to power and took everything. Fearing an inquisition by the Communists, who wanted to rid China of all the bourgeoisie, my grandmother fled the country. She went to the Philippines to eke out a new life and to escape Communist persecution.

Unable to speak a word of Tagalog, she was scoffed at and ridiculed by the Filipinos, but she took everything in stride. Slowly, she learned the language and was able to communicate with the people. Having led a luxurious, if not decadent, life, Grandma was unaccustomed to hard work, but she did not bewail her fate. Instead of cursing the heavens for this strange twist of fate, she decided to work hard and overcome the obstacles in her way.

Grandma was determined. She did all sorts of odd jobs. She sold noodles at the street corner during All Saints' Day. She did the laundry of the wealthy Chinese. She worked night and day, from dawn to dusk. Slowly but surely, she managed to save enough money to form her own business. She assured herself that her children would not undergo the ordeal that she had been through.

Dad attested to this when he told me of an incident that happened while he was in high school. Determined to help his mother, Dad skipped class and worked part-time to augment Grandma's meagre income. When his folly came to light, Grandma gave him a tongue-lashing that he has remembered to this day. Grandma told him that it was enough that she had suffered, and she would not let her son suffer as well. She told my father to study hard, and eventually he would succeed.

Dad also told me of the hardships that Grandma went through during the Second World War. When the Japanese conquered and devastated Manila, Grandma fled to the hills. She carried her son, my six-month-old father, 130 kilometres north of Manila. The journey took her four and a half days.

Grandma is indulgent, sometimes too indulgent. When we were small, Dad did not hesitate to use physical punishment, and so every time we saw the stick, we ran to hide behind Grandma's skirts. We knew she would pacify Dad. She told him that she had never hit him when he was small. Dad grumbled that she was spoiling us rotten. I think she did.

Despite her indulgence, Grandma can also be an authoritarian. Once when she caught me smoking, she handed me straight to Pilate—Dad. I thought my crucifixion was imminent, and it was. I was grounded for two months and that stopped me smoking.

She is an enigma which will take me a lifetime to comprehend. And I may not be able to fulfill that Herculean task in my lifetime. She never ceases to amaze me. I haven't seen her since coming to Canada. How I wish to tell her, "Look Grandma. Look at my report card!" How I wish I could see her again. Next year, maybe. Next year.

                                        Anonymous

How to Be Clever

It was ten years ago on the day when I first enroled at Yu-Hwa primary school. Early that morning my grandmother woke me up as usual and got me ready for school.

On the breakfast tray I saw no milk, bread, or my favourite peanut butter jam, but there were two boiled eggs, some tiny spring onions, and a cup of Chinese tea instead. I looked up at my grandmother with my eyes full of questions.

"Sing-sing, it's your first day of school. I have made you a special, good breakfast. Hurry up and finish it. The school bus will be here in five minutes," said my grandmother. My family called me Sing-sing—"Little sweetheart." I was the youngest daughter.

"I hate boiled eggs and those stupid spring onions. I want my peanut butter jam," I yelled.

"Sing-sing," my grandmother shook her head. "Chong" (spring onion) and "swam tan" (two eggs) provide you with a flexible brain so that you will become very "chong-ming" (clever).

I was always an obedient girl. I did not say anything more; in fact, I started eating my "clever" breakfast. Those spring onions tasted like medicine, and they made me lose my appetite. As a result, I left one egg and those spring onions unfinished on the tray.

"Sing-sing, you must finish the eggs and Chong. If you eat only one egg, you will get a zero mark. If you eat two eggs, you get two zeros. So, you have to eat one Chong and two eggs in order to get 100 marks," my grandmother called, running after me as I got on the school bus.

The bus left, leaving my grandmother crying in her trembling, angry voice. "Sing-sing, I taste salt more than you have eaten rice. Chong always makes intelligence. You do not finish your Chong, you cannot be a 'Chong Ming Girl' and you will get a zero mark." For the next two weeks, I was forced to eat Chong every morning for I missed the first meal which was so important.

Huey Seen Yeoh
Malaysia

No Kowtow

My grandmother was from a large family of 13 children. As a young man, her father, with many other Cantonese, went to America to find gold. He didn't find gold, but he worked as a labourer building the Pacific-Atlantic railway. It was in those days that he learned the skills of building houses and laying railway tracks so that when he returned to China, he was able to start his own business.

Grandma received much more education than most Chinese women did at that time. She went to excellent universities and was quite remarkable academically. In Beijing, she met my grandfather, who is from an old family in Suzhou.

After graduation they decided to marry. On the train back to Suzhou, Grandpa asked her for a big favour—to kowtow before his parents on the wedding day. Grandma refused immediately. "I never did this before, even in front of my own parents. No kowtow or no marriage. You decide!"

Shortly after the wedding, the war between China and Japan broke out. The Japanese invaders captured many cities, and there was much bloodshed. The government moved the capital to Chongqing, a major city in the western part of China. Hundreds and thousands of frightened refugees rushed westward to seek protection from the government. My grandparents were among them. When they approached Wuhan, about halfway to Chongqing, they could get only one ticket to move farther west. So they promised to meet in Guiyang, and then my grandmother had to make her way alone. At that time she was already pregnant with my father. After a terrible trip, she arrived at the wharf just as the last ship was ready to leave. It moved slowly away from the shore attached only by a strong cable. With great effort and courage, Grandma hung on to the cable, swung across the water, and climbed onto the deck. The people on the ship were dumbfounded at such a scene. At last, she marched to Guiyang, where my father was born. That's why my father's name is Qian Li—a thousand kilometers.

Jonathon Song
China

Student Activities

Talking and Writing*

"Footprints"

What lessons did Esmond learn from his grandparents? (Sometimes lessons can be learned from a person's actions as well as words.)

"I Love My Grandfather"

Explain why Hussam developed such a close relationship with his grandfather.

"To the Rescue"

The writer has been told this story about her grandmother by her father. Why do you think she remembers this story and is able to describe it in such detail?

"His Favourite"

1. What incident does Emma describe?
2. How old do you think Emma was at the time of this incident? Why?
3. Why does Emma remember this incident so clearly?
4. What characteristics of Emma's grandfather are suggested by this description?

"Left Foot, Right Foot"

1. What activities does Sangva enjoy with his grandfather?
2. Why is the title appropriate?

Group Discussion

You might use the "jig-saw method" as follows. Form several groups. Each group reads and discusses one or two stories. Then one member from each "expert group" becomes part of a new group to "teach" the stories.

Stories:

- Don't Waste Your Youth: Go Dancing
- Inside My Heart
- Visit to Our Ancestral Tomb
- An Ordinary Hero
- My Amazing Grandmother
- How to Be Clever
- No Kowtow

The following questions might be used to guide you.

- What incidents involving the grandparent does the writer focus on?
- Why does the writer remember these particular incidents?
- What impression of the grandparent's character is communicated?

• How does the writer communicate a clear sense of the grandparent's character and the relationship between them?

Writing Folder

1. Choose one experience that you shared with your grandparent. Describe this so as to reveal the character of your grandparent and your relationship with him/her. Try to include dialogue.

2. Write a biography in which you describe events which reveal your grandparent's character and your feelings towards her/him.

MEMORIES

Childhood

Memories of childhood experiences become very precious as we grow older. When people and places have been left behind in the move to a new country, these memories are often all that remains of a past life.

Childhood experiences, whether beautiful or painful, have helped to make us what we are today. Among the bitter memories are loss of parents, quarrels and rivalries with sisters and brothers, punishments, and the images of war. Even memories of love in the past become tinged with sadness in the realization that people are gone forever.

Despite the pain, the memory of love and happiness makes the heart sing. Hwan Lee expresses the bitter-sweet feelings of remembering love experienced long ago:

> Ten years passed
> He does not know where she lives now.
> He does not know what she is doing now.
> He cannot remember what her name was.
> But
> He can never forget
> The purest feeling ever
> On that winter day.

Among the joyful memories described in this section are family holidays, close friendships, childhood games, the sights and sounds of home, and conversations with parents.

Writing about the past sometimes helps us remember our roots and understand ourselves better. As you read these selections, you will find you have many experiences in common with these students even though you may come from a very different background.

First Love

At the beginning of a new school year I noticed a girl who was good-looking and graceful. For the first few days in the class, I tried to concentrate on the lessons, but her long, black, smooth hair was like a small brook flowing in my soul. Sometimes I caught myself looking shyly at her, not daring to look straight into her eyes so that I had to pretend to scratch my head or watch the teacher to hide from her glance.

How many times did I intend to speak to her! Always I would lose the courage. One evening when school was over and many long, white dresses overflowed from the classes, I waited impatiently, looking for "my girl," until her pretty silhouette appeared in front of the gate. Under the setting sun I followed her leisurely pace. As I was passing her, I knocked her arm deliberately and scattered all her notebooks on the street. I said, "Sorry, I didn't mean that." Gathering her books together, I gave them to her and hesitantly apologized. She smiled a smile brighter than the sunshine, prettier than any flower in blossom. I became more courageous and carried on the conversation with her. We talked easily.

After that I was happy in love. Studying together and going out together made our friendship grow more tender. But the pleasant times never last as long as one wishes. I had to say goodbye to her forever. I will never see her again.

> Dear Nga, do not doubt my love,
> Please understand my leaving.
> Now, apart from you
> Far away from our motherland
> Whenever I recall your face
> I feel so lonely.
> Oh! How I miss you, Ngoc Nga.

Viet Kiem Ngo
Vietnam

Games

When I was young, I used to play "holen" (marbles), "sipa" (kicking a bundle of rubber bands or a small paper balloon), and most especially "bahay-bahayan" (doll house).

I remember every time I played marbles, I always lost the game, because all my playmates were boys and they were good at shooting the marbles in the holes. I remember when I was playing marbles with my playmates, I cried because my marble was broken into pieces, and I knew that the boy who hit my marble had a steel ball. That's why I said to myself that I was not going to play with them any more.

Instead I played doll house. I found it so interesting because I could dress my dolls in different styles and colours. I could fix their hair. One was so pretty with long black hair and big dark eyes. Also, with my doll house, I had a few small cooking pots and pans made of clay. They were dear to me because they were my first set of cooking toys, given to me by my mother. My playmates and I cooked rice with real fire in a vacant lot where nobody could see us. When I look back now, I'm afraid we could have burned down houses, but thank God nothing happened.

Another favourite game was "tumpang preso." This game was a favourite of all kids, boys or girls. In it there was no limit to the players as long as you had a wide playground to run in. The players could be from five to ten, the more the merrier. There was a player called "it." He or she had to chase the players from a line if nobody was able to make the tin can fall on its side. The players had to run from the "it" without being touched by the "it" who was guarding the tin can and whose duty it was to keep the can in its upright position. Very seldom did I become an "it," because I could run faster than other children.

Loida Rivera
The Philippines

The Boss

My sister was very wild like a boy. She had many gangs which followed her. She was like a boss. I had a lot of fun when I was young. My sister and I played father and mother games and train games. When we played train games, my sister was always the conductor and I was the passenger. So I complained about that a great deal because I wanted to be a conductor. But she was the boss!

Mi Suk Pong
Korea

New Year

In two weeks, the Chinese New Year will come. This year I don't think I can have a happy Chinese New Year, because in Canada few Chinese know when the Chinese New Year comes. I like the Chinese New Year better than any other festival. I cannot forget how I passed the Chinese New Year when I was young.

I remember I knew that I would be happy at the Chinese New Year because I would have a new dress and new shoes. Everything would be new. About three days before the Chinese New Year, my parents, brothers, sisters, and I would go out and buy new dresses and shoes. At that time, we could choose whatever we liked. We bought new things because the Chinese thought that when the new year was coming, every old or bad thing should be forgotten. Therefore, they bought new clothes to represent the new life beginning again in the new year.

The night before New Year's, we had to go out and buy flowers. There were two meanings for that. We thought that if we went out and had a walk, all our laziness would go away and we would become hardworking the next year. Second, if we could buy some beautiful flowers at the flower market, we believed we would have good luck the next year. And on that day, even though the weather was cold, we had to wash our hair and have a bath. It meant all our bad luck would wash away.

We had to wake up early in the morning of the Chinese New Year, because we had to pour tea for our grandparents and parents and say greetings to them, such as "Kung Hei Fat Choi." After that, my grandparents and parents would give us Red Pocket Money to show good luck. On that day, we would not go out to visit our relatives. Our family members would group together and have a meal.

The next day, we would go to visit relatives. At that time, all the children would receive Red Pocket Money from the couples so that we could buy as many candies as we liked.

On the third day of the Chinese New Year, no one would go to visit other people. This was because the Chinese thought that if you visited others on that day, you would have a quarrel with them.

The Chinese New Year ended the seventh day after the New Year. That day was the birthday of all the Chinese. We would burn firecrackers and cover the house with red paper. The colour red represents good luck to the Chinese. After that day, we would wait for the next Chinese New Year to come.

Ming Szeto
Hong Kong

Bamboo Stick

I remember my mother as being a very unpredictable woman. When she was angry, I always expected a severe punishment. Yet sometimes, she just talked to me and told me not to do the same mistake again.

My father never gave me any punishment. It was always my mother. She used to have a stick made of bamboo hanging innocently on the wall. That stick was my most hated enemy. I have no idea if my mother made it for me, or if she made it for my three brothers when they were still small and, I guess, hardheaded. Maybe it was so feared by my brothers that it stayed around long enough to make itself useful on me again. The stick measured 15 inches long and was about an inch wide.

Once I tried to hide the stick so that my mother could not use it. Just as I was hoping for the better, it got worse. She made an even larger stick which made the punishment deadlier. I then thought that it would be a wise idea to give the first stick back, and so I did.

I remember asking my friends what their parents used for punishing them. They all replied that their parents used the handle of a feather duster. So I thought that I had a unique mother, who had a custom-made punishment stick. Maybe the reason is that she loved me.

Johnny Lim
The Philippines

The Man on the Mountain

When I was 13, I went to Beijing in the summer holidays. One day I went to visit Xiang Shan Mountain. Xiang Shan is the most famous place for sight-seeing. It is especially famous for its red and gold autumn leaves.

It was a very beautiful day, and so there were many visitors. As soon as I arrived at the foot of the mountain, I began to climb. At the beginning, I was full of zest, but I got tired gradually. I walked slower and slower.

Suddenly, I saw a young man who was climbing step by step, carrying two baskets with carrying poles. His clothes were soaked with sweat. I asked him, "What are you doing?"

He stopped, and smiled, "I'm carrying food for people on the mountain."

I was surprised and asked, "Are you tired?"

"Yes, but when I think the visitors will have a good rest and when I see their smiling faces, I'm satisfied. And I forget tiredness." He lifted the baskets again and climbed ahead.

I stayed there, gazing at this receding figure.

Jennifer Yu
China

Best Friend

> We have joy. We have fun.
> We have seasons in the sun.
> But the hills and the trees
> Like the seasons all have gone.

You always said that this was your favourite English song. I still remember once you attempted to learn it, but you did not get it by heart. Since then, I have never had a chance to hear you hesitate over the song again, but your voice still haunts me, and the song still touches me whenever I think of you, my best friend.

You were the first friend in my life. We were born in the same year, but I preferred to be an older brother just because I was born a few months earlier. My mother and yours used to be good neighbours. They liked chatting on their porches every evening; their chats always concerned their children. My mother had great expectations for her son just as your mother had a sweet dream of the future for her daughter.

When we were five, you and I were in the same kindergarten class and through-out the years in elementary school you were always my classmate. School was three blocks from our houses. At times, your parents were too busy with their hardware store, and my mother would come across to pick you up. Then we went to school and came home together. I somehow rejoiced in those occasions as you and I chased each other all the way to school. I liked playing marbles and sliding, but you only stood apart and watched. I liked to show off jumping over the puddles. You only smiled when I could not make it and fell into the stagnant water.

Grade 5 was our last year in elementary school. My parents hired a tutor to help me with my homework in order to give me a good preparation for middle high school. Since you were in the same grade and the same class as I, my mother had an idea to have you join me every evening with the tutor. We studied and did home-work together. The tutor, Miss Lam, seemed to be fond of you, for she said that you were an industrious and quiet girl. You were upset by my jealousy when you did well in school. I seldom talked with you or even glanced at you then. I had a medium-sized bicycle which I loved to ride up to the school backyard where I enjoyed watching the cricket-fighting games, playing soccer, or sometimes racing my bicycle.

The next year we both left for a middle high school. I was transferred to Bac Ai School, a school chosen by my father. His ambition was that I become a doctor or a pharmacist. At that time, the major modern language in universities was French, and so I had to learn French in Grade 6. Your parents had different ambitions. They wanted you to go to Taiwan after finishing high school. You were in another school called Minh Vien.

My schoolwork was not so good after I went to Bac Ai School, partly because of the great grief I experienced when my father left. I quickly learned some bad behaviour, such as skipping school and going to the swimming pool. But the worst thing was that I attempted to smoke. Knowing that I had changed and that the school discipline was not tight enough, my mother decided to send me to your school. Perhaps I was ashamed of what I had done and so I felt dislike and kept away from you. Time passed. I found that I had a lot of trouble with my Grade 7 work. Schoolwork seemed to be too hard for me to catch up with until I was inspired when you were willing to study and discuss homework with me. You were enthusiastic when you saw I was anxious to learn. I had the feeling that you were my most thoughtful friend.

You and I were still going to school in 1978 when great changes happened to your family and mine after the Communists annihilated the bourgeoisie. Your house was confiscated and your family sent to the "New Economic Zone." My family fled to Kien Giang to prepare to leave the country. At first, I expected you would come along with my family, but later I was told you felt you should go with your family. You would embark at Vung Tau on the boat VT-1502. I tried to reach Vung Tau by noon so that I could see you off. You had changed after a few months in the "New Economic Zone"—you were still quiet, but you did not smile as you usually did, and your eyes were thoughtful. "When shall I see you again?" you asked. I did not answer. I will never have an answer.

The next morning I was still in Vung Tau. News came from the ocean that two fishing boats had rescued nine people on the sea from a boat that had sunk the previous night, just about 50 miles away from shore. I tried to ignore the news. People gathered at the harbour to wait for the two fishing boats to come back. I was there as well. The boats approached and the fishermen screamed, "VT-1502." The crowd understood.

"It can't be true. It's too cruel," I said in a trembling voice, paralyzed with fear because you were not one of the nine survivors.

I will miss you forever.

Dan So Giang
Vietnam

One Winter Day

When the white beard of Santa Claus
Occupied their minds
Instead of a multiplication table,
When thick turtleneck sweaters
Did not feel stifling any more,
When they saw their moms
Knitting their mufflers out of wool,
When there was fog near the river
So thick that they could cut it with a knife,
When they heard their friends
Boasting of their new sleighs,
And thus
When they felt like
Teasing their dads to make sleighs for them,
Children in the town
Knew that winter was coming.

"Two times three? Five times four?"
The old teacher kept on asking arithmetical questions.
There was a rather strange punishment
For a child who gave a wrong answer.
The child had to
Stand at the back of the classroom
Holding one hand of the previous child
Who gave a wrong answer.

A girl with sparkling eyes and a neat ponytail
Was standing at the back silently.
She was the brightest of all.
Unfortunately
She was watching the white snow castle
When the teacher fired a question at her.

A boy sitting in the front row
Had a hidden ambition.
"In order to hold the pretty girl's hand,
All I have to do is
To answer incorrectly
When the teacher asks me."

The boy's dream came true.
Right after his confident answer
"Two times five is eleven!"
He was sent to the back
Had to hold her hand.
The romantic boy
Traded his honour
For ten minutes' happiness of
Holding the hand of
The girl he loved.

Without a word,
He expressed to her
All
His love
With strong beats of his heart,
With warm sweat in his palm.

Ten years passed
He does not know where she lives now.
He does not know what she is doing now.
He cannot remember what her name was.
He cannot even remember what she looked like.
But
He can never forget
The purest feeling ever
On that winter day.

Hwan Lee
Korea

The Red Scarf

When I was young, I liked sports. I had learned every sport that I possibly could, such as swimming, soccer, basketball, roller-skating—but not riding a bicycle. The happiest day in my life was the day I learned how to ride a bicycle.

My parents were afraid that it was dangerous for me to ride on the street. Because I lived in the biggest city in China, Shanghai, where several serious accidents happened every day, I was strictly forbidden to ride a bicycle. However, the longer I was kept from riding, the more eager I felt. One day, I took my mother's bicycle without her permission. I thought I would enjoy the speed of riding.

Nevertheless, this was not as easy as I wished. The main problem was that I could not balance very well. The bicycle always fell on one side as soon as my feet left the ground. My bicycle went nowhere, staying in the original place as if I were glued there. My funny actions made people laugh; moreover, even the policeman came and interfered with my "business" and said that I was blocking the traffic. Therefore, I was forced to leave the street.

On the way home, I felt as if I had been defeated. As I was approaching home, suddenly I heard a clear and sharp voice, "Hai Bo, nice riding!" I turned my head back. "My God!" I shouted inside my heart, and I blushed because I saw a girl, a classmate, riding her bicycle in a carefree manner. She smiled and asked, "Were you that powerful guy who made such a traffic jam on the street just a little while ago?"

Her words really upset me. I knew she was teasing me. I had always looked down on girls in sports. Today it was her turn. She said, "Okay, I'm joking. Riding a bicycle is easy as long as you learn some main points. Come on! Don't stay there staring. I'll show you." Normally, I would not have accepted her "pity," but this time was entirely different. My recent experience had embarrassed me. Desperately I yearned to learn to ride a bicycle. Besides, this girl was to be my companion. Why not? When would I get another chance to be with her?

She began to teach me, one step after another, in a small alley. "Good, you're improving." Her words encouraged me a lot. Even on a wobbling bicycle, I started to taste the joy of riding. She was always smiling. I said nothing. I replied to her instructions only by actions. But I could hardly stop staring at her from beginning to end. I don't know what kept me balanced on the bicycle. I don't know how I learned it. It all seemed a dream. My mind was totally blank. But I knew that I could ride now! I did not fall down even once. But on the way home, I fell. I fell down deliberately and pushed her down on the ground too. "You stupid!" she said, half-jokingly.

Suddenly, an idea crossed my mind. I shouted out, "How about a competition on the street?"

"What? You're kidding, aren't you?"

"No, I'm serious," I laughed aloud. She seemed to be surprised and accepted my challenge.

I knew my skill was poor, but I was confident. We raced down the street. I almost forgot about the terrible things which had happened a couple of hours ago, about the embarrassment I had felt, and about the punishment I would get because I had taken my mother's bicycle. I did not care.

These feelings were all replaced by a feeling of joy. I went after her as if she were a star. Her red scarf was like a light that kindled the flames of hope. Through the crowd of people, through the traffic, I followed the red scarf. Although I was a loser in the game, I felt I was a winner.

Hai Bo Li
China

My Native Land

Burma

Sparrows chirping at sunrise and sunset
Frogs welcoming rain during monsoon
Thunder splitting the clouds
Raindrops beating against metal roofs
Pagoda bells laughing through the silent night
Chanting of monks from nearby monastery
Music joyously sung at the Water Festival.

Palm trees against distant blue mountains
Sun burning mercilessly
Lightning flaming against dark sky
Wind chase of whirling dark clouds
Dew gleaming on green leaves in sunny winter morning
Fragrance sweet of Padout flower
Glimmerings of candles and lanterns at The-Din-Kyut.

Sweet and bitter drinks from palm fruit
Natural honey in the forest
Wild mushrooms
Khallpoke with green tea.

Tze Kan Yeo
Burma

China

I remember:

Running of the Yangtze River
Cracking of yellow leaves
Screaming of roosters in the morning
Plums beautiful white in the schoolyard.

Burning smoke of coal and wood
Bikes in Peking: ding-a-ling, ding-a-ling,
Reciting of Chairman Mao's poems
   "If someone insults me, I will take revenge
   If someone loves me, I must be grateful."
Singing of the national song, "Get up my people!"
Shouting, "Go faster, Go faster!" at sports competitions.

Large, white pork burgers at New Year's
Moon cakes at Midautumn Festival
Green rice burgers at Dragon May Festival.

Snow Hsiung
China

The Philippines

Pearl of the Orient, strewn over the blue sea like a rosary
Shorelines with white beaches under golden sun
Pure white shells on sand kissed by rolling waves.

Friendly smiles on sunburned faces
Sweet smell of fruit: golden mangoes
Watery melons.

Ringing bell of Mr. Ice-cream Man
Shouting and laughing of children
Whistling horn of a passenger train
Moaning hoot of owls in the evening.

Ringing of bells sounding in the New Year
Echoes of laughter during parades
Murmur of a child cuddled by a sweet mother
Crackling of bamboo clapping into the air.

Clarita Cawagas
The Philippines

Hong Kong

Streets crowded with people
Heavy traffic, choking people
Screaming car brakes and screeching horns
Fog of black carbon dioxide trapping me
Skyscrapers, factories like cemented forest.

Markets trading busily, screaming hawkers
Muddy roads like swamps after rain
Stench of chickens in cages
Arguments about prices.

Swaying green bamboo after spring rain
Blowing winter winds howling on streets
Pounding on windows of typhoons and heavy rain
Leaves changing from green to red, and falling.

The New Year:
Cleaning the house in welcome
Smell of frying twisted flour ropes
Half-moon "Kok-chai"
Visiting relatives
Piles of red pocket lucky money
Deafening drum at Lion Dance.

Fung Yue Wong
Hong Kong

Korea

Forsythia blooming in beautiful spring
Butterflies fluttering in the sun
Little boys striking marbles, tick tack
Fresh scent after a heavy rain
Savory vegetable soup filling streets.

Sunflower staring at hot sun in sweaty summer
Laughing of students crowding through school door
Children playing with five stones, click clack
Merchants jingling bells to sell ice-cream
Choking dust and smoke from traffic and factories.

Cosmos waving back and forth in autumn breeze
Mothers beating laundry with sticks
Girls counting as they bounce their balls, to-dak to-dak
Delicious burnt sweet potatoes, roasted chestnut and hot cakes
Sourish smell of Kim-chi.

Snow covering the city in cold, stormy winter
Brightly coloured dresses on New Year's
Throwing yoot, tararak and cracking nuts
Cuckoo birds singing early in the morning
Hot ou-dong on the skating rinks.

Monica Chung
Korea

Music Box

In my early childhood, what I remember about my parents was that Father, a successful businessman, was always busy with his work, and Mother disappeared for months on trips. I was always left alone with my sister and a servant. My sister was eleven years older than I; therefore, most of her time she did not share with me but with her friends. I was always put in front of a TV set, holding my teddy bear, waiting for a postcard from Mother or a phone call from my father. This is the scene which is the most vivid in my memories. It was not a difficult life before I was five years old. My youngest sister used to play with me for a while before bedtime. My parents used to give my sister money to buy me a lot of toys. No one ever punished me, no matter what I broke or what kind of wrong thing I had done.

However, life changed for me at the age of five when my sister was sent to Canada to study and the servant was too old to stay and take care of me. Mother was forced to spend more time with me. Because of the numerous quarrels between her and Father, I was forced to admit the facts. Father was not busy with his business, but busy with a woman—a woman who had borne him three children. And mother went on trips in order to forget everything. Although I had reason to hate my father, instead, I wanted to be close to him and gain his love. This desire for his love became stronger and stronger.

At the age of six, I was put in a famous Catholic school, and in the same winter I started practising piano. There were two reasons for this. First, once I had heard my father talking to his friends, saying that he liked seeing girls playing the piano. Girls who practised piano were cultured, and in order to please him, at that moment I decided that if I had the chance I would practise the piano. Second, I still remember a terrible quarrel between my parents one winter night. My mother found a receipt in my father's pocket and discovered that he had bought a piano for "that woman's" youngest daughter who was one year older than I. At that time I was too small to understand the quarrel. What I knew was that a week later a new piano was delivered to my home to replace the old one. And that was the first time my mother had a serious talk with me. "If you are my good daughter, do well with that piano." This statement started my nine years of piano practice, three hours a day. Throughout that period, I never once asked myself if I really liked the piano.

Also, at the age of nine I started my ballet class for similar reasons. I tried my best to be the perfect daughter in order to please my father. However nothing changed because of my hard work. My father never appreciated what I did. For birthdays and Christmas I received an envelope with money inside from him— never a letter. Stupidly I never lost hope, never stopped dreaming that one day I would have my father's love.

At the age of 15 my dream was shattered. It was five days before Christmas. I went out shopping to buy a present for myself with the money my father had given me. When I walked into a small gift shop, I saw my father with a girl of my age. They were both laughing happily and were choosing a music box. I saw so clearly the happiness shining in their eyes. At the same time I understood that girl was my "sister" who had taken away what belonged to me. When my father looked at me, I ran as fast as possible out of that store.

That night I wandered around the park again and again, feeling stupid for wasting nine years of my life chasing things that never belonged to me. At midnight when I got home, I saw a little music box on my desk. But at that moment my heart was full of hatred towards my father. I suddenly took out all my piano books and ballet dresses, together with that music box, and burned them. In front of that fire I swore to myself that I would never touch the piano or dance again. Those things I had burned symbolized the end of the search for my father's love.

From that time on, I started to live entirely differently. I changed to a public school and started playing tennis. The reaction of my mother was anger, because I refused to explain. In my father's eyes all I saw was guilt. Throughout that year my father tried very hard to communicate with me; however I started to build a wall between us. My only conversation with him became:

"Do you have enough money?"

"Yes."

"If not enough, ask me."

"I will."

This conversation was repeated until I came to Canada.

I think deep inside me I still love my father; however, I cannot reach out to him. Maybe some day I will hold my father tight and tell him how much I love him, but now at this moment I just cannot do it.

Anonymous

Images of War

My childhood was broken
Broken by war.

Every day there were
Trucks carrying machine guns
Tanks gliding heavily.
Carts carrying corpses
Down the dusty road.
Men with broken legs
Leaning on crutches.
Blood flowing from wounds
Like lava out of volcanoes.
Mothers calling for their children
Children calling for their mothers.
Shattered buildings
Broken glass.

Since then
I have realized that
War is just another way of saying
I hate you.

I am willing to trade
My childhood
For anything else.

Chris Truong
Vietnam

A Brothers' Quarrel

I was going to school in Namur, a small town near Brussels, Belgium, where my brother and I were studying. Tired of a hard school year and exhausted from those late nights before exams, I was feeling worried. Here I was studying in an English-speaking school in a French-speaking country. I did not have any ideas about the future. I did not know how I could attend a French university because my French was poor. My brother was studying computers and was depressed because he had not been successful in his exams. He had tried so hard.

For three days we had been expecting our parents to arrive in Belgium from Iran via Germany, but they had not shown up. We used to go to the train station every five hours to check if they had arrived or not. There was no sign of them. As we walked back quietly, there was only silence between us. I was sort of mad, because of everything, mad enough to start blaming my brother. "What do you think has happened to them?" I asked quietly. "Maybe you didn't get their message right."

"I don't know," he replied impatiently. "Stop bothering me, will you?"

I felt worse. I started to think of him as an indifferent person who did not care about anything. I got furious. Then I heard a car behind us. I thought maybe it was a cab with my parents in it, although they had not been on the last train from Mainz, Germany. "Hey, there is a cab. They may be in it," I said excitedly. At this moment, as we were walking side by side, I leaned to take a look at the car. I stepped in front of him and blocked his way. He pushed me away furiously.

"What the hell is your problem? Do you think you're the only one who's upset and tired?" I said, ignoring his feelings and just being a real pain in the neck. He came up to me and punched me in the face. My glasses fell off. He kicked them off somewhere.

I was so weary. I went to a park close to our room and lay down on a bench. I must have spent about two or three hours there. It had started to rain about an hour before, and by that time I was wet from head to toe. Why had I been so impatient with him? I should not have started all that. I felt so sorry about bothering him and making him feel worse. I got up, and went home to find a way to talk to him. But I did not know what to say. If I told him "I'm sorry," maybe it would be even worse. I found an open window to a bathroom on the second floor. I climbed up the wall stepping on the window sill and finally got in. I started to panic about facing my brother. I hated those dark and quiet corridors. It felt just like a monastery. I could see the light coming out of the bottom of the door. I stood there for a while.

Suddenly I opened the door, and there he was. He stood up, stared at me, standing there. I was silent and speechless. He began to cry. God, it was the saddest moment of my life. I just wanted to throw myself out the window, but he came to me and said; "I'm sorry...I...I was just...I didn't know what I was doing."

"Hey, it's me who's got to be sorry. It's my fault. I was just being a real pain in the neck." My voice was shaking like hell.

We didn't say much more to each other, but each of us knew how the other felt. We didn't have to talk anymore.

Peyman Teymouri
Iran

A Golden Childhood

I would say that my childhood was a golden, happy, innocent time. There was much sweetness and beauty to remember. I wish I could be back in my childhood once again.

Life was beautiful when my family was on the way towards prosperity. In 1972, after my father had bought a car, we started travelling for every New Year's vacation. It was a really wonderful time, for it was the only family time we had together. I was excited because there were many places I wanted to see, especially Saigon, a beautiful city, about which I had dreamed since I was a little boy.

Even though these things have long passed, I still remember the first time I arrived in Saigon. The city was totally strange to me, not only because of its modernity, animation, and beauty, but also because the language was completely unfamiliar. Cantonese was spoken in the Chinese section, and I did not understand a word that was said. I was so excited about the city that I spent my days walking all over the city in order to discover it and to satisfy my yearning about it.

My family was large: I had seven brothers and one sister. My father used to say that we might form a band or a basketball team because we had enough people and we all liked music and basketball. My father first bought us a guitar. After we had played for about two years, he bought us drums and electric guitars. We were so excited that we played day after day, and we would not have stopped if our neighbour had not come over and complained about the noise.

There were many things I liked about the city in which I spent my childhood. That city was Ban My Thuoc, a small, not very modern city, famous for producing good coffee. For this reason there were many people who owned farms and managed their businesses at the same time, such as my father, who owned land and hired people to take care of it. He only visited the farm once a week. I liked visiting the farm when it was the season for collecting the ripe coffee seeds from the drooping branches. The farm not only grew coffee, but also grew corn and sugarcane, which I would never miss tasting on every visit.

Life would have been perfect had there been no war, no killing, and people could have lived peacefully together. Unfortunately, no such Utopia exists anywhere in this world. I remember when I was a child, I used to stand on the sidewalk clapping and yelling at the tanks, the soldiers, and the big guns. I did not understand the meaning of what I saw. These things all seemed natural to me because they had existed always in my memory.

Now I know very well what soldiers and guns mean. They mean killing, destruction, and savagery, so that I hate myself for clapping and giving a welcoming smile. On the other hand, I forgive myself, because, at that time, I was still an innocent, naive, little boy.

Chau Lien
Vietnam

My Mother's Favourite

If it were possible, I would like to be a child again. Childhood is the most peaceful, the happiest, and the most innocent period of life. Children do not know what to worry about because they have nothing to worry about; the only thing they know is to eat, sleep, play, and be curious about the surroundings they grow up in. It is a pleasure for me to recall my childhood.

I was born and brought up in Myingyan, Burma, a beautiful country, especially in the mountainous region where the beauty of nature is undisturbed and the climate is fair. My family is a big family. I have four brothers and five sisters, all older than I. My father originally came from Amoy, China, to Burma, by boat, via Hong Kong, Singapore, and Malaysia. My mother was born in Rangoon, the capital of Burma, but her parents also came from China. They lived in Chinatown, earning a living by opening an egg pudding shop.

I do not know how my parents met each other and got married. Once I asked Mother. She said, "Your father always came to my father's pudding shop and I fell in love with him." That was all she said, smiling. I thought it was a joke. After their marriage, they moved to Myingyan where Father bought the biggest supermarket, including a cafe and a restaurant, in town. Because Myingyan is located in the countryside, there were not many Chinese, and both Father and Mother started to learn to speak Burmese.

In 1942 the Japanese invaded the country to take it over from the British. My parents, with their firstborn daughter and all their relatives, including those from Rangoon, fled into the forest region, which is not far from the Sino-Burmese border, so that they would not be killed in the war between the Japanese and the British. After the Japanese won the war, they went back into Myingyan. In 1945 the British kicked out the Japanese again. This time my parents did not go away.

Many years later, Burma became independent. When Father heard the rumour that the government was going to socialize foreigners' properties, such as lands and companies, he sold all his stores and worked in a trade corporation. My mother made clothes and earned money.

Father was the only son of my grandfather, who was a rich man in China. He was lucky because a son is more important than daughters according to Chinese custom. My grandfather loved him very much. Father was very interested in bicycling, badminton, and tennis. He was a badminton champion and even went to the People's Republic of China with the badminton team of friendship.

Father loved all his children. He bought me ice sticks, chocolates, cookies, sweets, and sunflower seeds. He often took me to the movies with him. It was he who was the first to worry whenever any of his children were ill. As he had some knowledge of Chinese medicines, he made medicines himself and cured his children. He chose food for them and took their temperatures twice a day. He was very concerned about his family. Since he was eager to help with medicine, he was a friend of many people in town. He was always ready to give effective Chinese medicine to anyone who needed it.

Because I was the youngest in the family, I was my mother's favourite. When I was able to walk at the age of two, I accompanied her wherever she went. I still remember the day when my mother asked me, "My little son, I love you very much. I do everything for you. When you grow up, will you get married and go away with your wife? What will you do?"

"Don't worry, Mama. Never will I leave you. I will study hard at school to be educated and to earn money to support you," I replied to her from the bottom of my heart. At that moment, I so wished that I was grown up and could convince her.

There was a Chinese school in Myingyen until 1959 when the school was socialized and turned into a Burmese school. When my fifth older sister and I started school, since there was no Chinese school any more, we had to attend the Burmese school. The rest of my brothers and sisters had finished Chinese high school at that time. In the year my second older brother passed the last examination from a Chinese high school, there was violence between the Chinese and the Burmese. Chairman Mao was then popular among the Chinese students, and the Burmese did not like it. Unfortunately, my second older brother was not allowed to continue to university because he was accused of fighting against the Burmese although he had not. My eldest brother passed the university entrance examination with higher marks than the requirement to attend the medical faculty. While he was attending classes in the first year, the government discovered that he was not a Burmese citizen, and he was forced to attend another faculty, not a professional faculty. He had to change to a chemistry major. My parents were angry about it.

All my family loved me. My sisters did everything for me. I took it for granted. When I was three years old, my second older sister immigrated to the People's Republic of China. I still remember when my family saw her off at the airport. I was shouting to her not to go, but to come back. As the plane took off, I was still shouting, "Sister get off the plane! Come back!" From then on, I shouted those words to the sky whenever I heard and saw a plane, believing that she was still on the plane. Next year, again, my third older sister immigrated to the People's Republic of China. The situation was exactly the same as the first. I missed them very much. Sometimes even now, the sound of a plane arouses my memory of those moments.

Tze Kan Yeo
Burma

Student Activities

Autobiography

This term you will write an autobiography (the story of your life). The stories in this unit will help you with your autobiography. First of all, you will discover that you have a great deal to write about. You will recognize themes in these stories that relate to your past experiences and that you can write about easily. The stories will also help you with the organization of your ideas, and give you the vocabulary and structures you need to write about yourself.

Journal

In your writing folder keep a journal of personal responses to these stories. You may be able to develop some of these more fully for your autobiography.

Talking and Writing*

"First Love"

1. Where did Viet Kiem first see his first love and how did he meet her?
2. What details does Viet Kiem use to describe her appearance?
3. In your journal list the people that you most enjoyed being with when you were in elementary school.

"Games"

1. You may recognize the games that Loida played when she was a child. Which game does the writer describe most vividly? What details does she use to describe this game?
2. In your journal list the games you remember playing when you were growing up.

"The Boss"

1. What does Mi Suk remember most clearly about her relationship with her sister when she was growing up?
2. In your journal list incidents involving you and your brother or sister when you were growing up that you remember most clearly.

"New Year"

1. Ming remembers Chinese New Year as the happiest day of the year for her. What events made this a happy day for her?
2. How does Ming organize her essay? (What is the main idea of each paragraph?)
3. What was an important holiday for your family when you were growing up? In your journal list the events which made this day happy for you.

"Bamboo Stick"

1. How does Johnny feel about the punishments he received from his mother?
2. Do you think parents should use physical punishment in disciplining their children? Give reasons to support your opinion.
3. Do you remember any punishment you received when you were young? Do you remember why you received the punishment? (Make notes in your journal.)

"The Man on the Mountain"

1. Compare the attitudes of the writer and the man with the carrying poles towards climbing the mountain.
2. What lesson does Jennifer learn from the man on the mountain?
3. Do you remember an important lesson that you learned in the past? From whom did you learn it? What was the lesson? What conversation or event helped you learn this lesson? (Make notes in your journal.)

Talking and Writing**

"Best Friend"

1. In describing his friend, the writer almost seems to be reliving the happy times of his youth. Why does the writer consider his friend to be a *best* friend?
2. Examine the style of this story.
   - How has the writer organized his thoughts?
   - Why is the verse from the song effective?
   - Short sentences can be very powerful. How has the writer used these effectively?
3. In your journal list the events that you associate with the memory of a best friend.

"One Winter Day" and "The Red Scarf"

1. What similarities in theme and feeling are there between the poem and the narrative?
2. Which of these gives the most vivid picture of the writer's feelings?
3. In your journal list occasions in your childhood when you felt intense feelings of love or loneliness.

Poetry on "My Native Land"

1. How have the images in these poems been organized? Examine "Burma" and "Korea." For each verse what is the controlling idea which links the images?
2. Choose two of the poems and write the images from them which are most vivid.
3. What images might you use to describe the place where you grew up? Create images which appeal to each of the senses.

"Images of War" and "A Brothers' Quarrel"

The poem and story are both about painful experiences. Describe these briefly. *(Note*: The authors use language and structures in their writing that they have learned while reading literature. The structure of "Images of War" is similar to "Provincial" by Miriam Waddington, and some expressions in "A Brothers' Quarrel" are reminiscent of "Catcher in the Rye.") You might keep a section in your journal for beautiful or powerful phrases from the literature you read in class.

"A Golden Childhood" and "My Mother's Favourite"

Both these narratives focus on happy memories of the past. How have the authors organized their thoughts? Choose one of these stories and list the main ideas of each paragraph. (Remember that the topic sentence usually gives a clear sense of the main idea of the paragraph.)

Writing Folder: Autobiography

1. In your autobiography write about a childhood memory. Use your journal notes to get you started.

   Possible Topics:
   - Friends
   - Games
   - Sisters and brothers
   - An important holiday or festival
   - Stories I remember from my parents
   - Fears and superstitions
   - Family traditions and customs
   - A frightening experience
   - A punishment I remember
   - An important lesson I learned
   - Someone who influenced me
   - Growing up
   - My family history
   - My native land
   - Parents
   - Searching

2. In your first draft you should take time before you write to organize your thoughts. You might read the following stories again and examine their organization and style.
   - Narrating a single, important incident
        "First Love"
        "Climbing Up"

- Using dialogue in personal narrative
    "Climbing Up"
    "The Red Scarf"
    "A Brothers' Quarrel"

- Using images
    "Images of War"
    "My Native Land"

- Organizing the essay
    "New Year"
    "Best Friend"
    "My Mother's Favourite"
    "Music Box"
    "A Golden Childhood"

3. After writing the first draft, have your teacher and writing partner read it. Use their corrections and suggestions in your rewriting. Choose an interesting title for your chapter.

School Days

In describing the first days of school, students remember both the excitement of new experiences and the shock of separation from parents. Suddenly the world widens and life becomes more complicated. Children must learn to handle new experiences on their own as they begin formal studies, try to win the approval of teachers and parents, and gain the acceptance and friendship of other children.

Students here discuss the difficult adjustment to be made when the language of instruction at school is different from the native language, the pressure of having to memorize much information in order to pass exams, and the fierce competition to gain admission to colleges and universities.

Students in China who went to school during and immediately after the Cultural Revolution describe being uprooted and forced to live in villages in the countryside. There, rather than academic subjects, schools emphasized politics and ideology: the glories of Chairman Mao's reforms, the importance of physical labour, and the necessity of thrift.

As you read these stories, you may remember your school in your native country: the teachers who most influenced you, the fun of learning, the pressure of exams. If you remember your early schooling, compare it with the Canadian educational system—the course content, the teaching methods, the relationship between teachers and students, and the evaluation methods. Perhaps, as Yuichi does in "Sham Freedom," you will see the educational system as a reflection of the culture in your native country, and gain deeper understanding of the values which shape different cultures.

Special Day

According to Chinese custom, on the first day of school parents must bring a cooked chicken, vegetables, and fruit, along with their child, in order to have a formal ceremony. The first day of school is regarded as a special day when the child becomes a student and gains his "mental" teacher, Confucius. Of course, I was no exception.

That sunny morning my parents took me to school with that special food, a new small school bag, some books, a pencil, and some brushes. When we arrived at school, I saw a number of parents taking their sons and daughters to school as well.

Soon the ceremony began. A middle-aged teacher held my hand to write the first word "Van," which is my last name, and then my first name, "Sam." That process was called "opening brush." Many Chinese believed that if the teacher who held your son's hand to write for the first time had beautiful writing then your son would be as good a writer as his teacher in the future.

The next morning my mother took me to school again and stayed there until school was over. For a week, my mother kept staying with me at school. As a result, many other children laughed at me. These little monkeys said, "Don't you know how shameful it is for you to have your mother stay with you?" When I heard this, I almost cried, and my mind was full of various emotions: embarrassment, shyness, anger, and panic.

Hurriedly, I rushed to tell my mother to go home and come back at the end of the day. My mother wondered why I was so brave. Then she walked happily out of the school.

Sam Van
Vietnam

First Day

I still remember my first day of elementary school. My mother took me to the school, and I was wearing a small hanky on my chest which was to wipe my runny nose. At first I was very happy and proud of myself. It was my first experience meeting such a large number of children of the same age. I was a bit confused and depressed on seeing that all parents treated their child as preciously as my family had been treating me, and I realized that I was just the same as other children.

After the first day of school, my life seemed to be changing quite a bit. I discovered many new, sad facts. First, my father, who had always been on my side and who had never restricted my behaviour, was changing. He was not always on my side. Sometimes he scolded me for being rude to my elders. I really felt sorry for myself, and I wondered why my father was treating me so differently, but I did not know how to ask about my father's different treatment.

Second, my school life was not as I had thought it would be. I had to go to school alone, while the other children went to school with their parents. Also, I did not receive good marks in school. Some of my classmates were better than I was in schoolwork. Sometimes I felt lonely, inferior, and helpless, but I could not express myself.

Joseph Park
Korea

Cleaning Washrooms

We cleaned the classroom ourselves every day after school. If you were late for school, you had to clean washrooms because most of the students disliked cleaning washrooms. Because of that, most students came to school early. So did I.

Mi Suk Pong
Korea

A Little Red Guard

Throughout elementary school I always had been elected as one of the five leaders in the class who would discuss with the teacher where the class should go for a field trip, who would help students experiencing difficulty in their work, and who would decorate the class by putting up the excellent work students did.

If you were a good student, you were a "Little Red Guard" and wore a red handkerchief around your neck. That told people you were a good student and helped others. Children in China always wanted to be a Red Guard.

We had a lot of homework every day. It usually took me one hour to do it. In addition, after school we had to clean up the classroom, clean the tables, sweep the floor, and dump the trash because there were no caretakers.

Emma Yu
China

Force-fed Like Ducks

I liked my Grade 6 home-form teacher. He taught me English, and when pupils failed dictations, or tests, he used two long rulers to punish them. But I really liked him because he taught us many things, and I knew that he wanted to help us.

We had to write an important examination before we went to secondary school. If we succeeded in the examination, we could choose a good school and the government would help the students pay the fees for three to five years. This teacher always said that this was the most important chance in our lives so that we had to catch it. The examination was regional. All the Grade 6 students in Hong Kong, Kowloon, or New Territories took the same examination on the same day; however, some schools sent only the best class to take the examination. It included Chinese, English, and Mathematics. If students got a very high mark, such as one or two, they would have their first or second choice of schools.

Grade 6 students did a great deal of work before that examination. Every day I brought two packages of books and exercises to school. The pressure was very great. In Hong Kong, people called the educational system "duck-like" because hawkers who sold chickens or ducks wanted them to grow fat and large. If the duck was thin, they used things like strainers to put crops into the duck's throats so that the duck had to eat the food. Similarly, we had facts forced down our throats in school.

Pui Yu Tam
Hong Kong

Mathematics Test

When I was in Grade 4, my grades began to drop. I got 50 percent on the test, and I needed ten more marks in order to pass. It was the first time I had failed a math test since I could remember. I was disappointed and fearful too. I had to bring it home and let my parents sign it. So that night I was very afraid that mother would whip me. When I handed the paper to her, at first she was very angry, but finally she signed it. I didn't know why I failed the test. Maybe I didn't study enough, or I didn't pay much attention in class. Then I decided to work harder than before, and my grades improved rapidly.

James Ma
Hong Kong

What I Learned in School

When I lived in China, school educational policy emphasized politics and ideology, and the knowledge of academic subjects was put in second place.

From kindergarten to primary school, we children were taught to love our nation, to love Chairman Mao, and to work and serve our great country after growing up. All the lessons, books, stories, and songs were full of intense political content.

In high school we had three periods of politics lessons in which we studied Marxism, Lenin, Stalin, and Chairman Mao's philosophy, and we often had parties called "Contrast Between New and Old." Some old people who had spent half of their lives in the old society of China (before 1949, the year of the liberation of China) were invited to the parties to tell us the stories of how poor they were. They told us of having not enough food, no warm clothes, working 16 hours for an employer, and earning only a little money. By contrast, after Chairman Mao came, everything had changed. The purpose of the "Contrast" was to let us realize how fortunate we were and how we should love Chairman Mao because he was our benefactor, for he had liberated our generation from darkness, poverty, feudalism, bureaucracy, and the semi-colonial old society.

We were also taught to be honest and thrifty; therefore, nobody liked wearing new clothes. The popular colours were dark blue and white. Girls never wore makeup. I seldom had old clothes or hand-me-down things because I am the oldest, and my family was above the middle class. Besides, my grandmothers always sent me clothes from Macao and Hong Kong, although I never dared wear them to school, because if I did so, I was afraid the teacher would criticize me in class and force me to "wash out the dirty bourgeois thought from my brain." Sometimes I cut a small hole in the clothes and let my mother mend it because I did not want to appear special. I wanted to wear mended clothes as other people did. There was a slogan popularized in China: "New for three years, old for three years, and mended for three years." According to this slogan, clothing should be worn for nine years.

This changed when the former president of the USA, Richard Nixon, visited China. The foreign journalists always took many pictures of people with old, dirty clothes, and Americans said that the clothes of the Chinese represented their poverty. After that, the government began to encourage people to be more concerned about their clothes.

Nora Chao
China

The Cultural Revolution

When the Chinese Cultural Revolution started, I was in Grade 2 and Mother said that I was a "victim" of this revolution. According to Chairman Mao's ideals, the school had to educate us, the new generation, not only to be good students in academic studies, but also to be "Red" students as well; therefore politics became the first priority in schools.

From the time I entered primary school, I was always caught in the "middle way" between my parents' teaching and the school's teaching. For me life was a puzzle. From the very first day of my school life, I was always taught to love my nation, love and obey our benefactor, Chairman Mao, and work and serve our great country after growing up. The behaviour towards working was very important because it could decide whether you were a "Red" student or "White" student. Because we had no cleaners at all in our school, classrooms were all cleaned by volunteer pupils.

I still remember once our Grade 3 had a "Volunteer Working" competition. In three months the number of activities for which you volunteered would be counted in your politics mark. Before the competition, I warned myself, "This time I'm going to get a higher politics mark because I don't want other kids to keep looking down on me." But despite my efforts, my politics mark was still the lowest mark in the class.

When the competition started, I had tried to go to school a half hour earlier than usual to clean the schoolyard and classroom, but afterwards, I found out some had arrived even earlier than I. Of course, there was nothing left for me to do. So I tried to go even earlier, but my mother stopped me, saying, "Listen! You're not allowed to do that kind of useless activity any more. If you have the time, then use it to study!"

But I delivered my declaration of right: "Chairman Mao taught us that a good child should have a 'Red' brain first and then be a good student."

Mother stopped for a few minutes. Then she commanded, "You have to study now! I think you will understand me later."

After hearing this, I was deeply troubled and puzzled because Mother explained nothing to me, and I dared not ask the teachers why my mother behaved like that because she might get in trouble.

At the end of the competition I received drastic criticism from one of the teachers who said, "You should train your 'working' interest, especially since you come from an intellectual family."

I was upset and disappointed because my reputation among the students had been ruined again, but I simply said that I could not get up earlier. I knew it was not a good excuse, but what could I say?

My parents never criticized the government in public, but they always complained that my brothers and I were creatures of the Chinese Cultural Revolution and the only thing we learned in school was working in the fields. The Chinese educational system did change, however, before I left China. The government of China now encourages young people to study hard and even has scholarships to reward the best students. Mother proudly says to me, "You understand now why I forced you to study."

Yes, I understand and my puzzle is solved. I have started to realize that sometimes the government and the laws are not as good as they should be, and you have to use your brain to think so that you are not influenced too much by evil.

Li Yuin Tam
China

From City to Country

We were forced to move from Peking to a village. Then my father left us for Labour School, about a four-hour drive away. There he was working as a farmer with his company, while my mother, brother, and I stayed in the village. We met my father once a month.

In my new school I did well, and I got the highest mark in most subjects, but not in physical education and outdoor activities. There was a great difference between the city school and the village school. In the city, "outdoor activities" included garbage collecting. In the country, we worked as farmers, doing work according to the season. In the winter we collected manure. Spring was the sowing season, and summer was the harvest season. We would spend one or two whole weeks helping to harvest rice.

I will never forget the first day's work on the farm. When we came to the sunbaked field, the teacher gave each of us a scythe—a tool with a slightly curved blade on a long wooden pole. A girl next in line to me told me how to use the scythe and showed me how to cut the wheat. I did as she showed me, bowing the body and grabbing the wheat with my left hand as I used all the strength in my right hand to cut the straw. After the straw broke, the scythe cut into my shoe and left a crack. I knew I was using so much energy that the scythe could not stop and cut into my shoe, but I did not care about this. I was anxious to catch up with the others because I was behind them, but the scythe did not listen to me. After the second cut, my finger was hurt and it was bleeding, but I did not cry. Meanwhile, only one thought occupied my mind—to catch up to the others, not to let them think I was just good in class, but that I could be a good farmer too. I didn't care about the heat, the thirst, and the pain of the fingers, but I was scared of snakes. The first time I saw a snake, I screamed with panic. Then numerous eyes looked at me, and I felt embarrassed.

I do not know how I got through that day. When I went back home with the split shoe, dirty pants, sweaty shirt, hurt fingers, and haggard appearance, I saw my mother's eyes fill with tears, but she still smiled and asked, "How do you feel? How do you like the work?"

"OK," I said with a weary sigh. As I stretched on the bed I told my mother that I wanted to sleep for a while and have supper later. Then she left. Now I could feel pain from the finger, an ache of hunger, and the cool of the sweaty shirt stuck on my back, but I neither moved nor slept. A lump of frustration and dissatisfaction came to me. I felt tears running down my face. I began to be tired of living in the village and remembered the school in Peking and my tranquil life there.

I really did not understand why we had to leave Peking. I asked my mother later, and she said that Chairman Mao wanted me to be a good girl and not only have knowledge from books but also learn more than what could be learned from books. She said Chairman Mao wanted her and my father to do the same work as the farmer; therefore, we had come here, and I would understand after I grew up.

Indeed, three years of farm life trained me to be stronger physically and mentally.

Nora Chao
China

Cheating for a Friend

It happened during the last year in elementary school, a little before the midterm. We were having an important math test, and I felt very confident. Olga, my best friend, was very bad in mathematics, and you could tell that she was afraid. It turned out that she was placed right in front of me in the great room where we always had major tests. We used to call it "Alcatraz." The teachers did too.

We were divided into two groups so that every other person got a different set of questions from the person in front. My questions were easy. I finished them quickly and checked over my results. But I still had a lot of time left. I looked around to see if anyone else was finished, but I seemed to be the only one.

Then I looked over Olga's shoulder and saw her paper. It was blank. She was obviously lost and didn't know what she was supposed to do. I felt sorry for her and did not want her to fail this test, and since we were not allowed to leave the exam room before the time was over, I decided to do the questions for her.

It was a stupid thing to do and not really helpful to her. I know that now, but back then, it seemed like a good idea. I wrote solutions for five of the questions for her because I didn't have time to do all ten, and I wanted her to put at least something on that paper.

Then I waited for the teacher to look the other way to hand her back the paper, but somehow he saw me and started walking toward my desk. He made a sarcastic remark: "It seems we have a smart bird here who thinks I was born yesterday." He picked up the note with five neatly done solutions, and said, "Why did you have to do this?"

Someone else said, "Nice try, kid!" Everyone laughed but Olga and me.

Of course, we both got zeroes, but I felt so bad for Olga, and I was so angry at myself because I was pretty sure I had a perfect paper. Since then I take my time on tests and I don't look over other people's shoulders.

Marta Skalamara
Yugoslavia

Learning Languages

I began to go to school at the age of five. I was quite young, but my parents thought that it was time that I should at least begin to know about school and the life outside the house.

It was my older brother's responsibility to take care of me and guide me into this completely new world. I was really excited about the idea of going to school. It was amazing to think of all the kids my own age gathering together to play and learn.

The school was not so marvellous as I had thought it would be. There was, of course, lots of fun and joy, but there was also discipline. For the first time, I had to study words in books, read them correctly, and practise writing them properly and neatly as I was taught. My parents made great efforts to persuade us to study. Every night after dinner, my older brothers had to do their homework and apparently there was no reason not to have me study. My father then asked me to take out those colourful books, and he taught me word by word how to say and write each character. This teaching did not last long, for my parents worked really hard, and they were so busy that my father had no time to sit beside me and patiently teach me word after word every night. The duty then was given to my oldest brother, who was four grades higher than I. It was no problem for him to teach me; however, he had to do his own work, and thus I could spend only a short time period every night on my studying.

The primary school I went to was a private Chinese school. It was the only Chinese school in my small city and was built by the contribution of the Chinese people who invested as much labour and money as they could in the school. Their profit, in return, was the next generation. In my case, my parents were proud that I would learn to write and speak Chinese. For the first three years I studied all my subjects in Chinese. In the fourth year I began to learn Vietnamese as there was a law that all students in the school had to have some subjects in Vietnamese as well as Chinese. For the first time in my life I realized the importance of languages.

I was raised in a typical Chinese family. It was very important to my parents that all their children have a thorough understanding of our own cultural background. Our most important task was to master the dialect that my parents had inherited from their ancestors in China. It was called "Trieu Chaw." Once I asked my mother whether all people in China spoke "Trieu Chaw," and I was quite amazed to find out that there were many different kinds of "dialects" spoken there.

I learned Mandarin in school because it was a "united language" that could be written and read by all Chinese. At home I spoke "Trieu Chaw" to my parents, brothers, and relatives. Most times, I spoke Vietnamese to my friends except for those who could understand "Trieu Chaw." Later on, when my family moved to Saigon in the neighbourhood of a large community of people who spoke "Cantonese," I had to start learning to speak Cantonese.

Since there were two major languages to be taught in the school, I had to study both Vietnamese and Chinese geography, history, language, and even math and science in both languages; however, I did quite well during my school years despite the fact that there was a great amount of work.

Going to school, as far as I can still remember, was a great pleasure and a worthwhile experience. It gave me a basis for my whole life. Still, there are many more things that I need to learn about from school and people. I know that I have to learn throughout my life. I think school is a great place to learn. As long as I can concentrate on it, I will try my best. My schools in Vietnam have already given me a good beginning.

Thuan Lien
Vietnam

Sham Freedom

Dear Munetaka,

Hello, I know you're fine. I am quite fine too, as usual. I think that I am happy in Canada and going to stay here for another year. Actually I want to stay here much longer. I feel much more comfortable here and, to tell you the truth, I do not want to go back to the same school again, nor to Japan.

I know what you are thinking now. "Yuichi does not want to leave the coed school!" Exactly, isn't it? Of course it's a part of the reason. But there is one thing I cannot stand any more. I don't think you notice it. I didn't either, when I was in Japan. It's the "sham freedom" existing in Japanese society.

You know the motto of our school—"Freedom." Teachers keep saying that they are giving us freedom. It is not freedom. Absolutely not. Our school is no better than others, or might be even worse. No students know it though. They are deceived by the "sham freedom." They can never know.

Our school regulations are quite loose by comparison with other Japanese schools, as you know. But it does not mean anything, I tell you. Do you remember what teachers said whenever we did something wrong? They always said, "We do not have strict rules, for we believe in students. But if you cannot behave yourselves, we can make strict rules. Is that what you want?" This is not freedom. This is just hypocrisy. The teachers had absolute control.

I guess you have never noticed the lack of freedom in your school. The teachers control us more than they need to, using the regulations to deceive us. But you cannot change it, to my regret. For it's a part of Japanese culture.

Japan is a democratic country and all people should have freedom. It seems to be working well on the surface. But is there really freedom? Can you really do what you want to do? I am sure you can't, even if it's not violating the law. It is not only in the school but everywhere. You know how Japanese communities work. All the housewives gather around and talk. They "assess" what folks are doing and figure out if they approve or not. No one can say, "It is not your business." And if your behaviour is considered undesirable, you are an outcast. You will always hear people whispering behind your back. Other people are always interfering with you. Always you have to think about the reaction of others before you do something. There is no freedom. This is not just a matter of politics. It is the culture. It terrifies me.

It is the worst aspect of our Japanese culture, I guess. And it is not only in Japan. It is common throughout oriental cultures, as far as I know. I cannot stand it, and it is unchangeable. That is why I want to stay here in Canada.

I am sure that freedom in Japan is impossible, and we should at least recognize this fact. If I have made you feel uncomfortable to live in Japan, I am sorry for that. But I want you to know how I feel, although this is still an immature and undeveloped opinion.

I am going to see you again someday I hope. I will call you soon. Write before if you want.

Yours sincerely,

Yuichi Kawamoto

> Yuichi Kawamoto
> *Japan*

Special Teacher

There was a time when I really did not pay attention to what was going on around me; I was just concerned about how to get out of the house and enjoy myself. I had never stood up to my parents about anything; I just did what I was told with no questions asked.

I was about 14 years old when I had a new teacher, Mr. Vasakos. He was not like other teachers I had. He never tried to keep the typical teacher-student relationship; he wanted to get closer to us because he knew that our small village did not give us much space to apply our creativity.

He was the first one ever to introduce me to books outside the school, and I can remember how excited I was. I was actually introduced to a new world I had never known before. For the first time I enjoyed poetry and reading books by writers other than Greek. At that time I had no confidence in myself because I felt nobody believed in me. I was curious about life, but the narrow-mindedness of the people around me made me stop believing that I could someday be free and be my own person. I just had to find a way to get out of my small jail. I had to get the misery out of me and be happy. I wanted to make myself stop caring about what people thought of me. I wanted to gain control of my life.

Mr. Vasakos helped me to start working on being myself and being the best I could possibly be. He helped the class organize the publication of our own class magazine. We included poems, drawings, and personal writing. Although some people gave up, a few of us continued and succeeded in completing the magazine. Throughout all the stages of publication Mr. Vasakos encouraged us.

He gave me the experience of success and a new confidence in myself.

> Joy Mikas
> *Greece*

Student Activities

Talking and Writing*

In your writing folder keep a journal of personal responses to these stories and ideas. You may be able to develop some more fully for your autobiography.

"Special Day" and "First Day"

1. Why was the first day of school in Vietnam so special for Sam?
2. How did Joseph's life change after he went to school?
3. In your journal list the most memorable incidents from your first years at school.

"Cleaning Washrooms" and "A Little Red Guard"

1. What rewards and punishments were given to students in China?
2. In your journal list the rewards and punishments given to students in the schools in your native country.

"Force-fed Like Ducks" and "Mathematics Test"

1. Both of these stories stress the importance of marks. In Hong Kong how is evaluation different from Canada?
2. In your native country how are students evaluated?
3. In your journal list your best subjects and your most difficult subjects when you were attending school in your native land.

Talking and Writing**

"What I Learned in School," "The Cultural Revolution," and "From City to Country"

1. According to these stories what values did the schools in China teach during the Cultural Revolution?
2. Schools teach much more than the academic subjects. In your journal outline some of the values the school in your native country taught you.

"Learning Languages" and "Sham Freedom"

1. Contrast the attitudes of Thuan and Yuichi towards their past school experiences.
2. In your journal list what you liked best about your school in your native country and what you liked least.

"Special Teacher"

1. Why does the writer consider Mr. Vasakos to be a special teacher?

2. Think of some teachers you have liked most. In your journal list the qualities they have which make them special.

Writing Folder: Autobiography

1. After reading some of the stories in this section, write another chapter in your autobiography about your school experiences in your native country. Use your journal notes to get you started. In your first draft do not be concerned with grammar and spelling. You might, however, take some time before you write to organize your thoughts.

Possible Topics:

- First day
- Rewards and punishments
- My school—a good place to learn
- Learning languages
- An embarrassing experience at school
- Comparison between schools in your native country and Canada, including teaching techniques, evaluation methods, courses, timetables, relationships between teachers and students
- A special teacher

2. Before beginning to write, you might read the following stories again and examine their organization and style.

- Narrating a single, important incident
  "Special Day"
  "Mathematics Test"

- Using dialogue in personal narrative
  "The Cultural Revolution"

- Using descriptive details
  "Force-fed Like Ducks"
  "From City to Country"

- Organizing the essay
  "Learning Languages"
  "From City to Country"

3. After writing the first draft, have your teacher and writing partner read it. Use their corrections and suggestions in your rewriting. Choose an interesting title for your chapter.

War

Most of us are fortunate enough not to have lived in a country at war. In order to try to understand what it must be like we can read the firsthand accounts of people who have experienced the tragedy of war. The following selections, written by students from countries torn by conflict, present vivid and moving accounts of their lives during desperate times.

We see war through the eyes of an eight-year-old child playing "war games copied directly from the real game of war" undertaken more seriously by adults. Vietnamese, Tamil, and Iranian children growing up in countries at war describe scenes as "wounds" in their memories. Seventeen-year-olds drafted into the army begin to question the government which tells them it is "glorious" and "honourable" to fight. They must choose between disobeying their government, deserting the army, and fleeing their country, or fighting and dying in a war they consider absurd. Education is disrupted, homes are smashed, families are broken, innocence and idealism are destroyed.

In times of war there are also moments of heroism. Farshid Missaghi describes the last time he saw his father in prison in Iran before his execution. Farshid draws great strength and hope from the fact that his father died believing in his religion: "They could only destroy my father's body; they could not destroy his faith."

Parents, who see no future for their children, make the greatest sacrifice and send their children away, out of their native country to an uncertain future in a foreign country. Tuan Nguyen describes vividly the moment when he said goodbye to his father: "He was standing on the shore waving at us and smiling an uncertain smile. He knew we were playing with death, that we were being taken from his hands and that he might never see us again. His figure became smaller and smaller and finally disappeared."

These stories attest to the resilience and courage of young people who are cut off from their parents and must shape their lives independently. These stories are also a testament to the love and determination of their parents who suffer the loss of their children to save them from hopelessness and perhaps death in their native lands.

Now that they are in Canada many of the students who escaped war feel a great responsibility to help those who are still suffering a nightmare existence in their native countries or in refugee camps. They feel a great responsibility to remember the sacrifices of others, sponsor other members of their families, fight prejudice and injustice, and promote peace.

Saying Good-bye to My Father

I will never be able to forget the day I left my country. It was in the afternoon when I, my sister, and my brother finally boarded a little boat to escape Vietnam. My father had come to see us off. He kept telling us to remember this and to remember that. He was very calm on the outside and kept smiling at us. I was too nervous to show my emotion and too sad even to say good-bye!

When the engine started and the boat began to move slowly away from the shore, a sharp pain stabbed me, for suddenly I realized that from then on I would be far away from my beloved people and from the land where I had spent my most wonderful years.

I looked at my father for the last time. He was standing on the shore waving at us and smiling an uncertain smile. Because I did not want to hurt him any more, I smiled back at him, but I could not help crying. His eyes were also wet. I wished I could have comforted him at that moment. He knew we were playing with death, that we were being taken from his hands and that he might never see us again. His figure became smaller and smaller and finally disappeared.

I had never felt so much love for my father before. I kept asking myself again and again, "Why? Why? Why can't I live with my family?" Years have passed, but the question is still unanswerable. Every day I wish, I pray that some day I will see my father's smile again, hear his warm, deep voice, hug him tightly, and shout out loudly, "Dad, I love you," the words that have been choked in my throat for so long!

Tuan Nguyen
Vietnam

I Was Sixteen

When I was 16, my village in Sri Lanka was attacked. At that time my mother's two brothers were shot. While our village was under military control, the guerrillas attacked the military, and in retaliation the military forces shot innocent people on the street. One day a group of Tamil liberation fighters visited our school. They encouraged us to join them and wrote down our names.

When my family heard that I had attended a few of their meetings, they were very angry. Instead of beating me, my father gave me some advice. He said that I should be a role model for my three younger brothers, and I owed it to them not to get involved in life-threatening situations. Also, since my mother was in mourning over her brothers' brutal deaths, I owed it to her to stay away from trouble.

However, I didn't listen to my father. Within one week, I left home and went to a forest with some of my school friends in order to get training from the liberation fighters. I think my curiosity and thirst for adventure took me there. When I heard that they were not going to train me to fight, but rather use me to distribute notices, I was disappointed. But in a way, it was more dangerous than fighting because we didn't have any protection. We could be shot and simply disappear.

When I returned home after three weeks, I was scared to death to confront my father. He told me, "Because of you, all of us are in danger." He forbade me to go again. He restricted me from going outside our house. But I refused to listen.

One day, after my parents had left for work, my friends came to my house with three bags of notices. They asked me to go and distribute them. I couldn't resist. After we gave out some of the notices, we were bicycling home. But the military forces caught some of the people who were reading our notices and beat them until they told our names. Within a few minutes they rounded us up, and we were trapped with nowhere to run.

They arrested us and forced us to tell who had supplied those notices to us. But we had already been trained to tell the same story over and over again. We told them we didn't know who had given them to us. But they didn't buy our lies. In a final effort to make us tell the truth, they commanded us to put our heads in front of each of the armed truck tires. They threatened to run over our heads if we did not tell the truth. I fell unconscious.

When I woke up, I was in the hospital and my father was next to my bed. Because my father was working at the hospital, he knew all the doctors. With their help I managed to escape from the hospital and then from my village to our capital city. I went to India and then to Europe and then to Canada. After arriving in Canada, I heard that two of my friends had died in battle and one was still in prison.

I was 16.

Rajakumar Thangarajah
Sri Lanka

Remembrance Day

Six students speak at a Remembrance Day service about how war has affected their families.

Cambodia 1972

I was born in Phnom Penh, Cambodia in 1972. Life in Cambodia at that time was good and peaceful, until the Khmer Rouge marched into the capital city on April 17, 1975. The Cambodia I had known from childhood became a nightmare. The wheel of the Khmer Rouge revolution sought to crush the country, its people, and its culture—individuals, families, knowledge, beliefs, and even love itself.

The Khmer Rouge disposed of roughly two million Cambodians, nearly a quarter of the country's population, in just three and a half years. I lost all my relatives and friends. The one thing I didn't lose was my family.

Such tragedies have happened before. It is said that history is a mirror of the future. I pray that this is not necessarily so.

Edwin Ang
Cambodia

Vietnam 1976

I was born in Cambodia. When I was two months old, my mother carried me on her back out of Cambodia. The road was full of tanks and helicopters. For one month we walked until we arrived in Vietnam.

In Vietnam we were sent to the wilderness where we cleared forests. My father had been a school principal in Cambodia. In Vietnam he raised pigs to make a living. War came again to Vietnam. Again our family was uprooted.

War is not a game. It destroys hopes. It destroys dreams. It destroys families. Let's work together for peace. Peace in Canada. Peace in the world.

Cach Truong
Cambodia/Vietnam

Beirut 1978

Our family was crouched in our apartment for five days with little water and no food. Bombs whistled overhead. We lived in constant fear.

On the fifth day a bomb hit our building. We clung to each other in silence and fear, as the plaster fell on us. The whole building shook. Although we escaped unharmed, others were not as fortunate. Of our fourteen-storey building, only four floors remained. The rest had been totally obliterated. Nothing remained of the forty apartments above us or the people who had lived there.

The following day we fled from Lebanon. It was on my fourth birthday. The explosion and destruction had lasted a few minutes, but for me the fear and terror will last a lifetime.

Nadine Kharabian
Lebanon

Iran 1983

On Remembrance Day, I remember my country, Iran, where hundreds and thousands of young people our age are killing each other because of the war—a war that has been going on for seven years, a senseless war between two neighbouring countries of the same religion and the same culture.

A close friend of mine who was in the war wrote me about a father and son who were both fighting in the same trench. He said they were surrounded by enemy soldiers. The 17-year-old son burst out of the trench. He was fatally shot. When his father saw him, he ran towards his son to help him. Just before he reached him, he was shot. He crawled towards his son. They hugged each other and cried. Three weeks later, my friend was killed too.

In my country, Iran, members of the Bahai Faith are persecuted, tortured, and killed. I was expelled from my last year at high school because of my religion. I was conscripted into the army. My father was arrested and tortured, like many other Bahais, for refusing to deny his religion. Then he was executed. His only crime was that he believed in his religion—a religion not accepted by the majority.

Twelve hours before my father was killed, I met him for the last time. He was as strong as ever emotionally. He comforted us. He faced his death courageously, strong in the belief that a person must die for what he believes to be the truth. They could only destroy my father's body; they could not destroy his faith.

Therefore, because my family and I were denied legal status and human rights, because I did not wish to fight in the army, and because freedom no longer existed in my country, I escaped from Iran.

On Remembrance Day we remember Canadians who fought in the two world wars to preserve freedom. We, who are immigrants to Canada, appreciate this country where we have freedom, equality, and peace. We have experienced first-hand a nightmare existence in countries where freedom and equal rights have been destroyed. We remember also the courage of those who died for us. They sacrificed their lives. We have a great responsibility to them.

What can we do in our school to promote peace? We can oppose prejudice and injustice. We can act with compassion and sensitivity to all. We can try to understand people who seem different from us. Each of us has a responsibility to promote peace.

Farshid Missaghi
Iran

Iran 1984

I am from Iran. I grew up in the midst of war. There were constant bombs. My city was like a ghost town. I had to stop school. My older brothers and their friends were drafted into the army. Some young men never returned.

My uncle and his son were killed as they escaped from Iran. But I had to take the risk and try to leave. My parents sent me out of Iran so that I would not be killed in the army. I have been separated from my parents now for six years.

The war in Iran broke up my family, and killed my relatives. Now war again threatens the Middle East.

Esmaeil Shabani
Iran

China 1989

On this Remembrance Day we remember the soldiers who fought and died for freedom and human rights in World War I and World War II. They are heroes. We also remember those Chinese students who gave their lives for freedom and democracy in Tiananmen Square. They are heroes.

Many were killed in June 1989 in Tiananmen Square. The Chinese government persecuted those who supported the students. As a result, my family and the families of many Chinese students were forced to remain outside China.

On this Remembrance Day our hope for the people in China is freedom, the end of repression, and peace.

Fong Yuan
China

War Games

When I was about eight, one of my favourite games was the "war" game. Our game was copied directly from the real game of war played by the adults.

In this game we would do everything we knew to win, whether or not it was harmful or dangerous. There were no rules. I still remember the many times I ran to the homes of the soldiers who were on the other side to tell their mothers that they were fighting. Of course, their mothers would hurry off to find their sons and then imprison them at home. In this way, I eliminated some of the enemy who were most dangerous for my side. While they were in their parents' prisons, we tried to capture the others. The other method that I used was to run to the teacher's house to visit him and stay there as long as possible if the enemy was just outside waiting.

We had various kinds of weapons. We spent quite a lot of money for plastic bands to make our slingshots. Furthermore, we hooked them on gun-shaped wooden sticks to make guns. This kind of gun was much more effective than the slingshot. The stone that we shot could fly further. We could load it with two or three stones and shoot them at the same time, while we could only shoot one with the slingshot. Also, we did not have to pull it constantly like a slingshot, and it was much more accurate. Our grenades were made of real gunpowder, which we collected from the cannons about one mile from our town. We wrapped the powder in aluminum foil which we found in cigarette packs. The wrapped gunpowder would fly wildly in all directions and leave little burning marks on whatever it hit.

At that time, the adults were playing the game of war as well, but they did it at night and more seriously, with real machine guns, real tanks, and real bombers. Also, I was sure that they did it for other purposes, not simply for fun like us. While they were playing their game, we had to hide in some pits in our houses. Sometimes, I had to sleep in the pit for the whole night because I was too sleepy to crawl back to my bed. The next morning we would open the doors and walls around to see if everyone was safe.

Perhaps I was still too young to understand the real meaning of death, but to me, it was just a long sleep. It did not seem to affect me much. All I had to concern myself with was that all my friends were still all right to play with me the next morning.

One more year flew by. I lived with joy. It was a time of innocence in my life. I thought it would last forever, but it did not. In geography class, the teacher taught me the word "erosion" and said that everything was changing. But I did not believe him.

Mit Ly
Vietnam

Threats

I am from Sri Lanka—a Tamil and a Hindu by birth. Because I had to travel far to attend college, my friends and I rented a house near the college and stayed there. My mother sometimes came to see me, but it was very difficult for her because she had to pass three military checkpoints to come to my school.

During that time there was night curfew and checking of everyone moving around, even in daytime. Many were detained without reason, and one day I too was detained along with others for nearly eight hours before being released. I was lucky because many people taken by the army were tortured, and some didn't come home.

I was elected as a member of the Students' Union, which published a student paper. This paper carried articles about youth and Tamil problems. We also were engaged in collecting money for the displaced people who were refugees.

The Indian army, which had come to help the Tamils, attacked the Tamil people. We were arrested by the Indian army at the press and taken to their camp and tortured. We were released after two days due to the intervention of our principal and teachers. This situation became worse. The press where our paper was printed was blown up by the Indian army, and our college was turned into a refugee camp.

I left college and went home and stayed with relations. When the Indian army came to our house and questioned me, the principal was able to keep me out of jail because my final examination was coming. After the exam, when I was travelling home, I was arrested by the army. They accused me of being a Tiger, a member of the Liberation Tigers, who are fighting for the freedom of Tamils in Sri Lanka. They took me to prison and tortured me.

When my mother heard of my arrest, she got letters from my school principal and teachers, and she was able to obtain my release from the camp seven days later.

The Indian army threatened to kill me if I stayed in my village. That's why I decided to leave my village and country. After making this decision, I left my homeland and with the help of relatives came to Canada.

Nimalan Manickam
Sri Lanka

Living in Terror

The war was all around me. I did not know how long it had been going on or how it had started, but when I was six, for the first time in my life, I realized what it was like and how tragedy was brought to people by war. It is a wound in my memory every time I think of the scenes that I have witnessed at the time of war.

When I was about five years old, I was quite used to the sounds which boomed like thunder from time to time. One day I could not resist my curiosity. I asked my mother what they were and she told me that they were sounds of gunfire and cannons that people used for fighting, and she told me about the weapons that I saw those soldiers carry when they walked on the streets, such as guns, grenades, and many other different types of weapons. I did not know what the war was about, but I did know one thing—that people got killed in the war.

It was in 1968 that I had my first experience with war. It started at the time of the "Tet" festival. It was New Year's Eve and people were celebrating the feast with rocket firing and fireworks everywhere. Because it was a happy holiday, it was quite obvious that nobody seemed to have any instinct about the terrible disaster that was going to replace the happy atmosphere.

I went to bed quite late that night because I was having such a great time. A loud sound like lightning woke me up in the middle of the night. Everyone in my family was also wakened up at that time. Suddenly, there was another loud sound. I knew that the explosion had to be very close to my house. Then, there came from all directions sounds of gunfire and I could hear soldiers coming from the army's headquarters, which were about a hundred feet from my house. The noise lasted about 15 minutes and then stopped. After a while, all was silent. My eldest brother said that they were probably the sounds of rockets with which people celebrated the New Year. I was so drowsy at that time that I went back to sleep with the hope that tomorrow would be a happy New Year's morning.

I did not know what happened after I went to bed, but the next morning when I woke up, I saw my mother packing our clothes, and she told us not to go out of the house because the soldiers were battling out there. She wanted us to have our breakfast eaten and then we all had to stay home, instead of going out visiting friends and relatives as we always did in the New Year.

Although I was staying in the house, I could still hear the sounds of fighting outside in the streets. Along with those terrifying sounds, there were also sounds of explosions, planes in the sky, and people running in a crowd. I went upstairs to look out of the window although my parents had told me to stay downstairs in case we had to get out of the house. Outside in the streets, I saw people running crazily from all directions. Mothers had their little kids tied on their backs and their hands filled with packages of clothes and food. Children were crying with fear. I saw a child about my age screaming because he had lost his parents. Adults were shouting trying to find their lost children.

I was so frightened that I got away from the window and ran downstairs. My father was talking to some neighbours next door. From them, I found out that those people on the streets were coming from the outside of the city where the Communists were attacking violently. It was lucky that we lived in the centre of the city where defence was much stronger. The Communists could not get any closer to the city, and so they kept on fighting and surrounding the city.

At home, I could hear sounds of bombs and guns, which lasted for three days and nights. During that time, we stayed inside the house. My father said that as long as our house was not on fire, we would stay there because there was nowhere else safer to go. It was fortunate that we had enough food at the time. Because it was New Year's day, my mother had prepared a lot of food at home for celebration of New Year's feast. That made it much easier for us, because at a time like that we could not possibly buy any food.

The sounds of gunfire and explosions diminished gradually. On the seventh day I was told that the Communists had retreated after many of them had been killed. Relief was shown on my parents' faces after seven solid days of fear that something might happen to us. Although I was a little frightened, I never imagined any real danger, such as a bomb dropping on our house or the Communists getting into the city and killing people. I was too innocent to be worried.

When I had the chance to go around the city, there was so much evidence of the destruction of war. Many houses had been destroyed, either by bombs or fire or other terrible weapons. On the streets I saw relief on people's faces, but also on those faces there were undeniable signs of sorrow.

After that, there was quite a peaceful period for about seven years until war broke out again. During that time, there were only minor skirmishes far away from the city. But every day, I saw tanks and army cars filled with soldiers moving in the streets on their way to the front. Sometimes I saw trucks coming back from the front with fewer soldiers and Red Cross cars with wounded and dead soldiers.

On March 10, 1975, soldiers made a sudden attack on the city we lived in. This time, it was much more violent and effective. They managed to get into the city within ten hours of attacking. By noon that day, from the window, I saw them running through the streets. I was really frightened this time. The street in front of my house was empty. I saw smoke coming from the city centre where many of the government's agencies and offices were located. Suddenly I heard a loud shout coming from the corner of the street. There I saw two soldiers with rifles in their hands. They were shouting to a man walking on the other side of the street. The man turned his head and saw them. Perhaps he was so frightened that he started running instead of standing still. They shot him. I saw him die. I felt my breath choking in my throat. My heart was beating rapidly as if it was going to explode out of my chest. Soon, someone stood beside me and dragged me downstairs.

Those two soldiers had probably seen us looking through the window. Only a few minutes after we got downstairs, there was a sound of an explosion upstairs.

The whole house vibrated as if it was going to collapse any minute. I was almost frightened to death. When evening came, we went up to see what had happened. There was a big hole through the wall and everything was broken to pieces.

The strained atmosphere continued for the next few days, until one morning, the air force came and dropped bombs on the city. One of the bombs hit a house a block away from my house. We were all so frightened that nobody knew what to do; so we all got in the car and left. Driving the car was a young man who worked for our family. He was extraordinarily calm and unmoved by the terrifying scene. We got away safely. If it had been my father who had driven the car, I doubt whether he would have succeeded because he was quite nervous and frightened at that time.

We drove all the way to the next city, a few hundred kilometres away. When we reached this city, called Ha-Trang, there was no battle because the city had surrendered. We stayed at the house of one of my father's friends. Two days later, we sailed secretly on a rented boat to Saigon, which had not yet been taken over by the Communists. We went by boat because all the highways leading to Saigon were blocked at that time. It took two days and nights to get there because it was a small sailing boat.

We had had 20 days of living in terror. War is vicious. It is disastrous for mankind, and worst of all, unlike natural disasters, it is man himself who causes war through his ruthless ambition and greed.

Thuan Lien
Vietnam

The War Changed Me

The most horrible experience of my life was during the war in 1975. I do not know how I can to describe it so that my feelings can be pictured clearly through my words. This experience has influenced me profoundly because I saw the savagery and destruction of war and experienced such helplessness when my life was not in my hands, when it could be taken away at any moment. But, if it had not been for the war, I would not have grown up. Neither would I have known the real face of life. I find that a person matures only in hard times. My life was completely changed because of the war.

In the year 1975, in Ban-My-Thuoc, the small city where I used to live, war was in the air. The sound of gunfire could be heard in the distance not far from the centre of the city. The war had been going on between the North and the South since 1954, so the sounds of gunfire were not strange to us. In fact, we had all been numbed to these sounds so that we could do our day's work and sleep soundly, in spite of the continuous noise of gunfire at night.

On March 3rd, a small village, which was about a hundred miles away from the city, was invaded and occupied by Northern troops. It seemed that a battle might take place at any moment. People realized the danger and hurried to buy food and rice to stock up in case of war. Almost everything doubled or tripled in price. Money became worthless; however some people were still optimistic that the South Vietnamese troops would take the village back in the next few days.

My school was also affected by the war. All students in my school were to participate in a demonstration against the invasion of the troops from the North. I remember I carried a banner on which was inscribed a slogan, "Overthrow the Vietcong." I walked around the city with my banner without knowing why I had to do it. The demonstration ended after we burned several paper statues of the Vietcong.

My parents were worried. They were thinking of sending us to Saigon, far away from the war because they had suffered from the war of 1968, so that they knew perfectly well what would result from war. They knew that they could not stop a battle if it took place. They could neither stop the killing nor protect their children or their house with their bare hands. Besides, we were too young to suffer so that they decided if the situation became worse to send us immediately to Saigon where my elder brother and sister lived.

In spite of the fact that they avoided letting me know much about what was happening, I could feel the danger and the threat of war. I observed my father build a small fortress in which we could shelter ourselves in case of war. I also noticed that my mother had bought more and more food. One day, I was told that my father had bought us plane tickets to Saigon and we would leave within a few days. I knew that things must have become serious or he would not let us go.

In my heart, I felt excited about being sent to Saigon. After all, I had dreamed often of it. Besides, how could you expect a naive, innocent twelve-year-old boy to understand what war was really like? Do you not think it would be cruel if a boy actually understood what war was by that age? Even though I had heard so much about war, I had never witnessed any killing or destruction from it. In fact, I thought it was a very exciting game. So when it seemed that a real battle would take place in the city, I just felt excited about it. But if I had known the price I would have to pay for it, I would have changed my mind.

On the last night before we left for Saigon, my father visited his friend, our neighbour, who had a store selling rice. They usually talked about whether a battle would take place in the city or about how good or how bad the government was. As for us, after we had finished packing our luggage, we played our guitar and drums for the last time. We did not notice the silence, the death-like atmosphere pervading our small, peaceful city.

About three o'clock in the morning, I was awakened by a great explosion. I could feel the house and the windows vibrating as the next bomb exploded. My mother dashed into our rooms and told us to get down into the basement to the bomb shelter. Half awake and puzzled, I wanted to ask her what was happening, but when I looked at her anxious face, I kept my mouth shut. Swiftly and silently we went into the basement. I observed that the gunfire was getting louder. The sounds first came from one side of my house, and then a sharp, shivering tone cut through the darkness, and I heard it explode on the other side of the house.

My father came back later with the news that bombing at the military airfield, about two miles away, had begun. Standing by the window, I could see the red, burning sky and smoke covering the airfield. About six o'clock, the bombing stopped. We thought that the threat was over, but we were proved wrong when a relative of ours, who had driven all the way from the airfield, told us that the Vietcong had occupied the airfield.

At about eleven o'clock, I heard the tanks rolling down the street. The Vietcong had broken the defensive line and had entered the heart of the city. We also heard the rushing and crying of the people whose houses were ruined and were on the way to a school for shelter. Among them was my aunt's family. Desperately my aunt beat at the door until my mother opened it. My aunt and her two sons rushed into my house along with the people who were eagerly searching for a shelter. We could not refuse them; we let them in. The worst thing was that two Vietcong also rushed in. My mother did not dare stop them. She kept saying that we were only innocent citizens so that they would leave. Her urging proved to be useless. The two Vietcong started searching all over my house, and when they came to the shelter in which we were hiding, they held their guns high over their heads and aimed mercilessly through the window. I could see the bayonets flashing in the air. We screamed. I felt so helpless that I covered my face with shaking hands. I do not know what would have happened if my mother, who was standing beside them, had not yelled at them that there were only children and women hiding there, or if they had fired before taking a look inside.

By three o'clock that afternoon, I could still hear the gunfire in the distance. We were shocked when my father dashed into the shelter with the news that the market where our store was located was on fire. My mother jumped to her feet immediately as if she were shocked by electricity. She kept yelling, "We must do something. We cannot stand here and see our years of labour ruined in a cruel fire." She urged my father to drive the car to save the store, but he refused. He said that we could not risk our lives. The store was only a store! We could build another one later, but we could not replace our lives. The hideous fire burned not only our store but the whole market as well. I found out later that only the iron door, which had been burned black, remained. It stood there helplessly as if it was about to fall down.

The battle was now over, but then the robberies started. The first victim was my neighbour, who owned a rice store. A group of people led several Vietcong to his store, and they ordered him to open the door or they would break it. He hesitated at first, but when he heard the gunfire, he opened the door. I could see the people rushing and pushing each other towards the rice bags, as if they were a herd of hungry animals just released from their cages. They were busy helping themselves, grasping, carrying the rice bags on their shoulders, but they were not yet satisfied. They returned later with other Vietcong and stole more and more until the whole large warehouse was empty.

My neighbour was not the only victim of this kind of robbery. In fact, almost every rice store or grocery store had the same fate. I felt sympathy for the owners. For example, my neighbour had been very kind to people, some of whom, ironically, were among the people who robbed his store. I also wondered whom I should blame for the destruction of my family's store, as well as for all the killing and robberies I had witnessed.

Chau Lien
Vietnam

Drafted at Seventeen

When I was in Grade 12, I was drafted into the army. Because the Vietnamese Communists were at war with the Cambodians, they needed more troops. All men who were 18 to 35 years old had to join the army. Actually I was really only 17 years old, and I was furious because I was still going to school. I was told that I would be on an important mission protecting my country. At school, the principal encouraged me. In town, the communist official encouraged me and said that I was "lucky and glorious" and had "the honour" to be a soldier of the People's Republic Army of Vietnam.

I knew this was foolish. I was angry because I knew the war was absurd. It was not "glorious" and I did not have the "honour" at all because I would not really protect my country but would help the Vietnamese Communists increase their power in Southeast Asia. I knew that I was just one of millions of "chessmen" and that the Vietnamese Communists were the "chess players."

I was furious because the Vietnamese Communists ignored the danger we were in. They demilitarized the border of Cambodia and Vietnam in order to lure the Cambodians into attacking us so that they could blame them for starting the war. They were not concerned when many of our people were killed; they wanted to make us feel angry with the Cambodians and to have a good reason to invade Cambodia.

Also, my family and relatives had worked with the former government. All my brothers had been soldiers in the Vietnamese army. One of them had been killed and two of them had been wounded. My uncles, who had been officers of the former government, were in a concentration camp, and I did not know whether they were alive or dead. For these reasons, my spirit still belonged to the former flag and the former regime. Should I forget everything to follow the Communists? If I joined them, it would mean that I had betrayed my family, my brothers, uncles, and millions of soldiers who had sacrificed their lives to protect my country. It would mean that I had betrayed my nation. I cannot tell you how miserable and guilty I felt.

One month before I joined the army, I went to see my school and my teachers for the last time. I stood still in the schoolyard while the students were studying. I could not smile when some girls teased me about how funereal my face looked. When school was over for the day, I met my teachers and friends to say good-bye. My mathematics teacher sighed as he shook my hand and wished me good luck.

My heart was broken. My mother was sick because of her sadness and worry about me. She felt sorry that I had not gone to France before 1975. She was so miserable that she could not eat, and neither could I. I tried to comfort her. She wanted me to hide, but this was impossible for the Communists would have immediately given my family trouble. So I had no choice but to go. My brother suggested that I join the army first, and then desert. In that way my parents could not be held responsible for my actions and would not be punished.

Then I began to taste the life of a soldier. On the first day I was given some equipment, such as one military uniform (the officers promised we would have two uniforms but I never saw the second one), a hat, a pair of boots, a blanket, and a pair of sandals. The government gave us a salary of five dollars a month, but when we used our salary to buy our clothing from the government, we only had about ten cents left.

After being given the equipment, we went for dinner. We were divided into groups of ten. The meal included vegetable broth, rice, and a little meat. At the meal, the other soldiers ate very fast, but because I had never been in the army before, I did not know that there would be so little food and that I should eat as fast as the others; therefore, I was hungry that night. My neighbour, Thai, gave me food. He suggested, "You've got to eat fast. In the army, if you're so slow, you'll die of hunger."

"But I can't eat without chewing," I said.

"Well, you don't need to chew. Just swallow everything. It doesn't matter what it is. You need to be full. Also the food is so terrible that you can't enjoy tasting it."

I really enjoyed talking to Thai. He was only 18 and had also been drafted against his will. He used to ask other soldiers for cigarettes. He said, "I smoke so that I can decrease my homesickness." When he was sad, he used to sit with me at the flagpole as we told each other stories about our former lives. He told me that he hoped he would be able to go back to school when the war ended. But when would the war end?

We stayed at the military school for about five weeks while we learned about weapons, strategy, and fighting techniques. Although we were called soldiers, some of us were still children; therefore, we used to fool around every time we were trained in tactics. We often threw wooden grenades at the officers' bedrooms, and we were often reprimanded and punished. They used to sound the alarm at night and force us to walk or run with equipment for several kilometres. During the days we practised crawling over stones under barbed wire. We were trained in tactics such as the "A" or "V." Three soldiers, formed in one of these shapes, could pretend to be a much larger force and scatter the enemy.

After being trained for one month, we were sent to the southwestern border of Vietnam. All the way to the war zone, we did not talk to each other very much. Everybody held his gun and had his own thoughts. We did not even brush off the dust and red soil that covered our faces and uniforms. We did not know what would happen to us. When we arrived at the war zone, we were not even worried about our fate any more. We thought that what was going to happen would happen.

Life in the war zone was worse than life in the military school. At night when I patrolled the barracks, I felt a deep sympathy for my country. For so long Vietnam had been involved in war. As I was holding the machine gun that was made in Russia or China, I usually remembered 1975, when my brothers had held weapons made in the USA. I felt an overwhelming hatred for the large, powerful countries that specialized in inventing weapons and caused wars between small nations to sell their products. I also thought a great deal about my family. I could imagine my old father praying to Buddha and my mother going to the temple to pray that I would be safe in battle.

Our officers had told us to save bullets. They said that each bullet was worth as much as three kilograms of rice. I wondered why the government bought weapons when the people did not have enough rice to eat. As we went into battle, we could feel the coldness of the barrels of our guns although the weather was hot. Our hands were wet with sweat. In one battle, one of my friends was shot as he was charging with me. I was stunned and thought he had just fallen down, but when I came close to him I realized that there was a hole through his forehead to the back of his skull. I jumped up and just fired and fired.

Since the soldier's life was terrible and the war was absurd, many of us wanted to desert. Once I saw a squad leader beating up a soldier for trying to desert. Although I felt angry, I could not help that soldier. When I was patrolling the barracks one night and saw a soldier attempting to desert, I told him to be careful and let him go.

Increasingly, I was depressed by the cowardice and laziness of the officers. When we went to battle, they always used their shirts to cover their revolvers, pretending that they were just privates. Most of them did not dare go ahead to lead their troops when we were fighting. They were stupid because they had not received any education, and got their commission only because they were members of the Communist party. Because we were in the jungle far away from our families, most of us liked to carve wooden bracelets, hairpins, and chopsticks from wood to send to our families. Our officers refused to let us do this in our spare time because they said we were wasting government property.

I became more and more miserable and introverted. I could not really smile any more for I had seen the misfortune of my nation, the death of my people, and the cruelty and inhumanity of the Vietnamese Communists. I decided to desert.

Van Tung Bui
Vietnam

In Prison

Before 1975 I lived in a wealthy family because my father was a high official. Wherever I went, there were many bodyguards to escort and protect me from kidnappers. Also, a lot of soldiers guarded my house. I never walked or took a bus to school or anywhere because I had my own chauffeurs. At that time, I was just a young boy enjoying life. I didn't even know what was happening in the outside world. I was very naive, and my whole life was going to school and having a good time on my holidays.

After 1975 the North Vietnamese Communists took over the South. My father was imprisoned and we did not know the day that he would be released. I was very confused at that time. Two years later, my parents decided to help me escape from my country to find freedom and a better future. I know that was a difficult decision, but they had to face the fact that my future would be a dead end if I stayed in Vietnam.

When I was 11 years old, I began my dangerous journey to escape by boat, but I did not succeed even though I tried 12 times. I was caught three times by the police. The first two times, I was put in jail for two or three days and then they released me because I was so young.

The last time the police caught our boat in the ocean. They put us in a large jail which was far from my house. The police treated the prisoners like animals and insulted us. They made us work without pay, and nobody could avoid the work because they kept checking every minute. We had to cut trees and dig wells. They gave us a bowl of rice without any other food and two bottles of fresh water every day. Also, at night, they tied all of our feet with two iron circles for each person and a long steel stick through all the holes of the circles. Nobody could escape. In the same prison were thieves and murderers.

I saw many events which astounded me. One time I saw a fight between two men over rice; one of them was a teacher who was well educated. Also, every time we got water there was always an argument because some got more water than the others. All my clothes were stolen, even my socks.

Fortunately, I had a friend who had been there for two years. He was very kind to me because he saw I was so helpless. On visitor's day, while most people had visitors, my family did not know I was in jail.

One bully made my life miserable. "Hey, little coward," he called me. "Hey, your 'father' is talking to you. I'm the king of this place. Whenever I tell you to do something, you have to obey it. Even if your father were here, he would still have to listen to me," he threatened. I kept trying to avoid him. When I showed I wasn't afraid of him, he came and tried to be friends with me.

I always kept a piece of broken glass in my pocket wherever I went, especially at night.

Quang Ly
Vietnam

A Cry for Freedom

I was born and grew up in Vietnam. Days passed and grew into memories. After living there more than 20 years, I would never have believed that one day I would leave my country. There I could speak my language; I understood my people and never felt lonely. Like other young people, I had a dream that one day I could contribute my effort to build up the country. Life seemed simple and smooth, and the future looked golden.

Then one day the war broke out seriously. Our northern brothers did not keep their promises. Thousands of them with tanks and explosives occupied the south. They reddened it and pushed it into hell. Many people were forced to leave their homeland to go to the new "economic zones" in the jungle. Many people who worked for the former South Vietnam government were forced to labour in concentration camps. Children had to leave school and go to work. Churches and temples became military camps.

Vietnam was then enclosed by an iron curtain; the whole country became a big prison with more than half a million people in jail. We all suffered from dictatorship, threats, and poverty; no human rights were respected, and we lost everything. We didn't even belong to ourselves! We had to struggle every minute to survive. Life seemed to be endless dark nights; and freedom, like the sun, was hiding itself behind the iron curtain. It was then I really understood that freedom is something very precious, but we don't realize it until we lose it.

Day was lengthened by hardship, and night never seemed to end. We couldn't live there any longer. We had to run away from the evil, whatever the costs we might have to pay. We all gave our last breath in an effort to escape. Day after day, thousands of people crossed the Cambodian and Thai borders, where a brutal war was raging, and many of them risked their lives there. Other people used all kinds of boats, ranging from small fishing boats to large cargo vessels, to ferry our people away from Vietnam. Thousands of them died at sea because of bad weather and a shortage of food and water. Many were robbed and killed by pirates, or they were confined in "closed refugee camps."

Refugee camps were very lonely and depressing places. There, new challenges awaited. Once again our lives were enclosed by barbed wire fences. We were isolated from other people and treated brutally by the local police. We lived there in a closed camp which looked like a zoo, and waited—waited for the door of mercy to open. I waited five years, and finally was accepted by Canada.

On the first day in Canada, it seemed to me that I was really born again. Oh Canada! I want to say "Many thanks." You are shelter and we were boats which were shattered. You relieve our anguish. The land seems cold, but the people's hearts are warm.

In Asia there are thousands of people still living in those refugee camps. They are still mistreated by local authorities. They patiently wait for the door of conscience to open. But nowadays people tend to think more about themselves and wish to remain ignorant about the suffering of others. As a result, the door is closed, and my people, whose eyes are tired of waiting, whose hair is getting grey with sorrow and time, are still waiting to be born again. They are all human beings, but they cannot contribute their efforts to improve the world. The world seems small to them. There is no place for them to go where there is love, understanding, and sharing. Nobody responds to their calls. They are gradually dying in those camps from physical and mental illnesses. Some of them feel so despondent when they hear that they will be returned to Vietnam that they kill themselves. It would be too painful for them to return to that hell. To them the nightmare seems endless.

Day by day I hear their cries from isolated islands or in closed refugee camps in Thailand, Malaysia, the Philippines, Indonesia, and Hong Kong, or right in Vietnam. They seem to be abandoned and are living in utmost despair. They feel they were mistakenly born on this planet.

I myself experienced this sorrow. For many years I was in prison, a concentration camp in Vietnam, and in closed refugee camps. I understand how they feel. Many times I wish I could do something for them, but regretfully my arms are short and weak. Every time I think of this, I feel heartbroken for all my people who were born into this world, but whose presence is rejected.

Phu Ha Phan
Vietnam

Student Activities

Talking and Writing*

"Saying Good-bye to My Father" and "I Was Sixteen"

1. In "Saying Good-bye to My Father" what do we learn about the relationship between Tuan and his father?

2. In "I Was Sixteen" why does Rajakumar get involved in such a dangerous situation?

3. When these young men left their countries they were sixteen years old. They came by themselves to Canada. Do you think that their fathers were right to send them away? Explain.

"Remembrance Day"

On Remembrance Day students remember the destruction and suffering caused by war in their native countries. They feel a strong responsibility to speak out for peace. The six stories under the heading "Remembrance Day" express these thoughts and feelings.

1. How has war affected the lives of the writers of these stories?

2. Why do you think it is important to read about the tragedies caused by war?

Talking and Writing**

Do you understand why so many Vietnamese have immigrated to Canada? These accounts by students will explain their backgrounds, their reasons for coming to Canada, and the influences of the war in Vietnam on their families.

"War Games"

1. The author speaks of his childhood in Vietnam during the war as a "time of innocence." Give evidence to show his innocence.

2. Why does Mit mention the geography lesson?

"Living in Terror" and "The War Changed Me"

1. Two Vietnamese brothers describe how the war affected their family. What do you learn about the effects of war from their descriptions?

2. "If it had not been for the war, I would not have grown up. Neither would I have known the real face of life. I find that a person will mature only in hard times." Do you agree with the writer? Explain.

"Drafted at Seventeen" and "In Prison"

1. These Vietnamese teenagers experienced personally the terror of war. What incidents do they describe to show its horror?

2. Do you feel it is ever an "honour" to fight for one's country and that war is "glorious"?

"A Cry for Freedom"

1. Why does the writer consider it important to talk about the thousands of people in refugee camps?
2. How does the writer make his essay persuasive?

Writing Folder: Autobiography

1. If you come from a country at war, write about your experiences. Include this chapter in your autobiography.

    Or

    After reading these stories, write an essay on the horror and absurdity of war. Refer to individual stories to give specific examples of the effects of war on young people.

2. Before writing you might read the following stories again and examine their organization and style.

    * Narrating a single, important incident
        "Saying Good-bye to My Father"

    * Using descriptive details
        "War Games"
        "The War Changed Me"

    * Organizing the narrative
        "Living in Terror"
        "The War Changed Me"

3. After writing the first draft, have your teacher and writing partner read it. Use their corrections and suggestions when you edit your work.

Why We Left

A Cambodian student writes: "Realizing that I would not be allowed to go back home, that any career I might want was doomed, that I had no future in Cambodia, I determined to gamble my life. Life is valuable for everyone, especially for young people, but when you lose all your basic freedoms, you feel you must risk everything to escape. If I succeeded, I could start again. It was the most difficult decision I have ever made."

Why would someone give up friends, family, and country to set out alone to shape a new life? Many of these young people did not know if they would ever reach safety or be reunited with their families or even be accepted as refugees in a free country.

For those of us raised in Canada, who take freedom for granted, it may help us to understand why many new immigrants deeply appreciate the freedom in Canada when we read about their lives in Iran, Vietnam, China, Sri Lanka, and Cambodia. An Armenian girl from Iran speaks of the constant threat of being jailed without trial and of the oppressive restrictions on women. A student in China describes the shock of university students after the killings in Tiananmen Square and his parents' pressure on him to leave China. Vietnamese youths describe their experiences in schools where politics became more important than academic studies, in the army fighting a war they could not believe in, and in prison.

The following stories help us understand why so many sacrificed so much and even risked their lives to leave behind the homes and countries they loved.

My Parents Sent Me Away

Who really wants to leave the native country? Who wants to leave parents, sisters, brothers, friends, and relatives?

First, my father's business was taken away. If you did business, you were said to be a thief who seized money from people. In a Communist country there are no rich people, only the poor, poorer and poorest people, because what people had done or made all belonged to the government, and what people got was just a little from it. People could not even support their families.

One day when I arrived home from school, I saw many Communist officials at my house. They told my father that the government had given an order that we had to go to a government farm and work while the government "took care of" our house. My father knew that the land we would be given there was bad, for he knew many other businessmen who had been forced to move there and who had died.

My father decided we could not go there, and so that night we left our home and hid in my aunt's house. It was a really difficult time for us. We were like beggars with no home, totally dependent on the generosity of my aunt. Every day I took my bicycle and went around and around the streets and did nothing.

Luckily, my father still had some money with him, and he decided that his children must escape to another country. My parents told us that they could not go with us because there was not enough money. Also, they said that they were too old and would be useless in another country. In contrast, they argued that my older brothers and I were young and healthy and could have a bright future in another country.

When we left Vietnam, we left our parents behind. My brother has just applied for my parents to come to Canada to join us. If I had one wish, it would be that I could see my parents again.

To Phan Luc
Vietnam

Rules and Penalties

We left Iran because we wanted more freedom. There were many rules and regulations that made our life difficult. I honestly don't know where to start, but I'll start with a rule that affected me every day. I had to wear a scarf and a long, dark-coloured uniform. I had to wear the same clothes everywhere—on the streets and at school. I guess this was so that we wouldn't attract the opposite sex by our clothes or our hair. Just imagine what it is like in summer! One side of the world is wearing bikinis; the other side is sweating under long, dark uniforms and scarves.

This rule was compulsory for all ethnic groups. I am an Armenian, but I and all other Armenians had to cover ourselves with the same uniform.

Not wearing the uniform brought a penalty. There were cars everywhere with government guards in them. They drove in the streets from dawn until dusk. If they found a woman with a little hair out of her scarf or a little makeup on, or with a shorter skirt, or with thin nylon stockings, they would stop the car. If they were pleasant, they would warn her not to repeat the offence. Most of the time they would take her to jail. Whenever we saw those cars, we were frightened. They could always find something wrong if they wanted to.

I remember when I was growing up, my uniform became a little short; it was just below my knees. I think I was 14 or 15. A guard stopped us and warned me about my short uniform. I was very afraid, and my sister promised him that we would buy a longer one that day.

Music was banned. If the neighbours who were on the government's side heard loud music, they would report us to the guards. Fortunately, we lived in an Armenian territory where most people were opposed to these restrictions.

I remember when we went to high school, they checked our nails to see if they were too long. They even checked to see if we were wearing a necklace under our uniform or any other piece of jewellery. They said that we had to dress simply in school. We weren't allowed to wear different colours. Our scarves and uniforms were mostly black and blue.

Food was very scarce because Iran was at war with Iraq. We got our food at the end of the month with ration coupons. They didn't give these coupons to the families in which the men refused to go to war. Such families had to buy their food on the black market, which was very expensive.

These are some of the reasons we decided we had to leave Iran.

Janet Nazarian
Iran

They Arrested My Brother

One day when I came home from school, the door was open, and I saw three military jeeps on the street with armed soldiers in them. When I went in, I saw more soldiers searching our house, looking for something. Later, I found that they had taken my brother away to a station for questioning. Usually, if someone was taken away for questioning, there was no coming back! My mother was very worried, and so she called my uncles and my father. One of my uncles had a connection with one of the men inside the station, and they let my brother out.

What had happened was that when my brother was talking to his friends, someone overheard his last words, which were, "See you there." He thought that my brother and his friends belonged to an illegal group and that they were going to have a meeting. But my brother and his friends were just going to the movies and wanted to meet each other somewhere first so they wouldn't lose each other and could go together. The man followed my brother, found our house, and called the soldiers to arrest my brother.

It was events like these that persuaded my mother to send us out of Iran.

Anonymous
Iran

My Last Days in China

I was a freshman at university in 1989 when the demonstrations for democracy took place in China.

My friends and I were deeply concerned about our country. Most of us felt despair when we talked about the future of China. When we heard that the students of Beijing University were demonstrating for freedom and democracy, we went into the streets day and night to support them. We demonstrated peacefully, as did the students in Beijing.

When we heard that the army was killing students in Tiananmen Square, we went into the streets carrying flags and chanting. We were shocked and angry.

But we were still young. We had families. Parents did not want their children to die. They came to the school and requested that we go home. One week later there were no students on the campus. My mother, who was in Toronto, phoned every week and begged me to go to Canada immediately.

Two months later I left my motherland. I was full of bitterness, but I had no other choice.

Xiao Miao
China

We Must Remember

It's already been a year. I remember that last year at this time I was in Beijing, exhilarated by the demonstrations of the students. A few days later I went back to Shanghai, filled with their revolutionary spirit. I walked with the students in the streets of the largest city in China, fired by the strength of their spirit, and wanting to be part of making China more prosperous and pure. But one month later, on June 4, 1989, as tragedy struck Beijing in Tiananmen Square, with a lost heart I flew to Canada, a peaceful and free land, to accomplish my dreams.

As time passes, a leaden feeling weighs me down. People seldom talk about June 4 now. Have they forgotten already? I know memory may be diluted by time, but it is important not to forget this day on which thousands of lives full of vigour and vitality were sacrificed for a democratic China.

These days my unhappiness has been getting stronger and stronger. How can that notorious regime stay in power for so long? How can a government kill so many innocent youths! But Premier Li Peng is to visit Russia as the leader of my country. People have to put their anger deep in their hearts, pretending to eulogize Deng Xiao Ping. Watching communist regimes falling one after another and people celebrating their freedom ecstatically, how can I not feel sad and indignant?

I remember faces of students, once eager for freedom, and then twisted by shock and outrage. These students, after learning more and being influenced by Western thought, had decided to push society beyond totalitarianism and poverty. What they sought is happening in Eastern Europe now. But those who sacrificed their lives can never know success.

I will never forget one day in a parade several students with handcuffs and chains put themselves in a prisoner's cage and sang the Chinese National Anthem. Their solemn and stirring voices stay with me day after day: "Stand up, people who do not want to be slaves any more." I just wonder how many years some people can exist before they are allowed to be free. I do not believe that the desire for freedom will "blow in the wind" forever.

Less and less information about Tiananmen Square is being reported now. This may be because the students' blood has been bleached by time, or because people are frightened by the possibility of another massacre, or because recent events in Eastern Europe eclipse China, or because people in the West are just too comfortable and complacent. Whatever the reason, we seem to have forgotten already that people in China are still suffering.

Even if we cannot be like the student leader Wuer Kaixi, who now is on a ship in the ocean sending anti-government broadcasts back to China, we still can send letters or photographs to break through the bamboo curtain which destroys the truth—the truth that thousands of people died in Tiananmen Square. We Chinese who have escaped must try to help change the present government.

I am too meek. I'd better begin to forget. But then I remember those young faces full of indignation and determination. Those young students inspire me. People can learn to forget. But the true warrior marches forward dauntlessly.

Qi Zhang
China

No More Lies

My father was a doctoral student in Canada, and my mother had joined him, hoping my sister and I could come to Canada at a later date. I was sixteen, living with my younger sister in a suburb of Beijing.

I had worked for eight months to get permission to visit my parents in Canada. My parents told me to go to the Canadian embassy in Beijing to try to get a visitor's permit for Canada. It was April 27, 1989. I heard there was a demonstration of students because of the death of Hu Yao Bang, who was the chairman. Students were warned that peaceful protests would be very dangerous and that they should keep off the streets. My relatives warned me to be careful whenever I went out. But I had to go to the Canadian embassy almost every day. People from all over the country were massed in front of the embassy. We had to line up and officers called our names in order. Because my relatives' home was so far away, I was always late and ended up with nothing. While I was waiting in front of the embassy, I got to know a lot of people. I was the youngest person there. Almost everybody that I met told me secretly: "It is hopeless to stay in China." Was there anything wrong with China? I could not tell!

When we first applied to leave China, the Canadians had rejected our forms. Now, however, as student protests increased, they seemed more willing to welcome us. It began to look as if our hopes would be realized. The atmosphere of Beijing was getting worse and worse. Students were leaving school and were going out on the streets every day. On the one hand, I resented the demonstrations. The crowds of people brought transportation to a standstill, and I could not go to the embassy. But I was sympathetic to the students. I saw them holding hands and singing national songs together on the streets. In those days the students refused to eat anything, and the government still refused to negotiate with them. Cold and hunger oppressed the students in Tiananmen Square. They were dying. They sacrificed their young lives to get democracy for everybody. When hospitals were full of students, the government still made no response to their concerns. Everybody in Beijing was angry with this. As a result, workers started to strike. By talking to students, hearing the facts, and reading the posters, I gradually learned what the students were protesting about.

History will never forget that day—June 4, 1989. Because I lived far from Tiananmen Square, I did not see the events myself. I heard that the army killed students my age, as well as old people and pregnant women. A woman who was in Tiananmen Square that night recorded the sound of machine guns. When I heard the tape, I was shocked. Several days later, I went to Tiananmen Square to see for myself. I could still see the blood on the ground, the bullet holes on the sides of buildings, and the treads of tanks on the streets. Although the government said on TV that they did not use violence, people believed nothing. From that day I no longer believed the Chinese government. The blood in Tiananmen Square had destroyed my innocence.

Although Chinese people have been silenced for now, the desire for freedom has taken root. I believe that one day the Chinese people will establish their own government—a real one, which will be in tune with the wishes of the people.

Fong Yuan
China

Outlaw Without a Future

The small boat on which I escaped held so many people and the ocean was so vast that even a small storm could destroy the boat and sink it. I had been forced to choose one of two alternatives: to live with certain suffering forever under the Communists; or to escape, risking many dangers in order perhaps to find freedom. I chose to risk my life on the sea.

Why did I leave my country which I loved? When South Vietnam fell to the Communists, I was a student. On that day my father stood sadly when he saw the flag of South Vietnam taken down and thrown on the road. This was the flag which my father, my brothers, and my relatives had fought under. Their blood had been spilled for it. Now it was finished.

My life as a student changed dramatically. Almost everything I had to study was related to communism. Even if you were the best student and studied hard, you were allowed to continue studying if someone in your family had worked for the former government. In my case, almost all my family had worked for the old government so that I was not allowed to go on.

One year after I had left school, another problem occurred. The Communists wanted to recruit troops. When I received my draft notice, I made up my mind not to join the army. I was not frightened of becoming a soldier. I was not frightened of fighting in a war if it were under a decent government and if I fought for a just cause. But the Communists wanted to invade other countries, Cambodia and Laos, and Russia was behind their aggression. So I refused join the Communist army.

From that time I lived as an outlaw, hiding out in places only my family knew about. If the Communists had arrested me, I would have been put in prison. I lived like that for one year. I was living without a future. Then I realized that my only choice was to escape from Vietnam by boat.

Long Bui
Vietnam

Imprisoned Without Cause

I was brought up in the city, and although I sometimes yearned to visit the countryside, every time I asked my parents for permission, they would never let me go since they were afraid that I would be captured by the Communists and forced to join the army or be caught up in the war.

The first time I was in the countryside was a few months after the Communists had taken over my country. Like many Vietnamese, I believed that from then on our country would be free and peaceful. Life would be better and happier. Everybody would be ready and willing to participate in rebuilding what had been destroyed by the war. Believing that it was now fairly safe, my parents agreed to let me take a trip to Ben Tre, a village about a hundred kilometres southwest of Saigon.

On the way to Ben Tre, I was fascinated by the beauty of the fields of rice stretching endlessly in front of me. Every breath of wind brought with it the fragrance of new, fresh rice, and it also seemed to bring the promise of a new, prosperous, and happy life.

The two weeks I spent at my friend's place were wonderful and unforgettable. Since my friend's parents were farmers, their house was in the middle of rice fields which descended to the river. We used to go fishing every morning after breakfast and swimming on hot afternoons. Along the riverside, there were many long, green rows of coconut trees from which we used to get milk after fishing and swimming.

In the evenings, we sometimes used to catch frogs or eels in the fields under the light of a petrol lamp, or we used to run after the fireflies all over the rice field. Sometimes we organized a camp fire by the river.

One evening, when we were looking for worms in the middle of a field under the full moon, we suddenly heard many gunshots not very far from us. Then we saw two dark shadows running and then disappearing into the darkness of a nearby garden.

Afraid that we might be hurt if we stayed, my friend and I started to run away, but suddenly many men armed with guns appeared and ordered us to stop. They ordered us to follow them to the police station.

At the police station, my friend and I were taken to two separate rooms. I was made to sit in front of four policemen who started to ask me questions. I showed them all my papers: my student card, my permission to go to the countryside issued from the chief of the district, my identity card, and other papers to prove that I was a good and loyal citizen.

They hammered me with a hundred questions about the reason for my visit, my reasons for being in a field in the middle of the night. They tried to turn the questions in many ways in order to make me confused so that I would not know what I was talking about. One of them, angry or wanting to terrorize me, suddenly seized my hair and pulled it as hard as he could. Pointing his finger at my eyes he threatened me if I did not tell the truth. He hit me in the face and at the same time kicked the chair so that I fell down on the floor.

From that moment, I realized that what was said about the Communists was true. We could be arrested and tortured without even having committed a crime. I also realized it was hopeless to protest my innocence.

I was thrown into prison after being beaten until I lost consciousness. When I awakened, I found myself in a small room with more than 50 other people. My whole body hurt from the previous night's torture. My eyes were all red and swollen and I felt an incredible pain every time I tried to keep them open. My two lips were horribly deformed and I couldn't feel anything except a numbness and inertia. For the whole day I could not eat anything.

The next morning I was awakened by the sound of a horn. Everybody stood up as the door swung open. At once, we could hear the shouting of the soldiers making people stand in single file to be ready to go to work in the field. I thought they might leave me there for a few days before sending me out to work like the others because I had been so badly beaten and was weak and exhausted.

As soon as the last person left the room, a soldier with a lantern stepped in. When he saw me lying on the floor, he stepped on my chest and ordered me to get up and go to work as the others. When I could not get up, he kicked me in the stomach.

That was my first day in a Communist prison. My friend's father learned of our fate and paid money to the assistant director of the prison to have us released.

As I left my friend's house to return home to Saigon, the countryside had a different meaning for me. I could not concentrate on the beauty; I saw only the corruption and brutality. I was so tired—tired of the lies I had learned at school, tired waiting for the promises to be realized. As a result of my experience in the prison, I was completely disillusioned with life under the Communists. I knew that I would never find security and freedom again in Vietnam and that I would have to leave my country.

Cuong Vu
Vietnam

Army Deserter

At the end of May 1978, 1 had planned to be busy studying for the entrance exams to university. I would have preferred to study rather than to become a soldier or a "volunteer" in the New Economic Zone. Unfortunately, in a general mobilization, all the youth between 18 and 25 had to leave school, work, and home in order to become reserve soldiers. If we refused to join the army, our families would be in serious trouble and probably would be sent to the New Economic Zone or have their rations cut off. I had no choice. In order to protect my family, I went to a military camp and was trained for three months to become a soldier.

From early morning to sunset we had physical training and practised close order drill and how to use machine guns. At the end of the day we were forced to help the farmers who were harvesting their rice. At night, in the middle of a deep sleep, we were sometimes awakened for combat practice. In addition, we were taught many tedious political lessons: the structure of the Communist party, the reasons for the conflict between the "free" world and the communist world.

During the training a few friends and I left to visit our families three times, although we were not allowed to leave without permission. As a result, I was punished in front of my platoon for violating military law.

After three months we were transferred to the border between Vietnam and Kampuchea. We were to open a military attack directly against Kampuchea. When my parents heard this, they sent my elder brother to tell me that if I was really being sent into battle I should desert. It was too late because I was already in Kampuchea. The images of that time stay in my mind to haunt me. I saw Kampuchean children lying with open eyes waiting for death.

While our troops were resting to gather strength for the next great attack, I made up my mind to escape. I had to walk nearly 30 kilometres to reach the border. Luckily I reached the border and bought some old clothes to disguise myself as a civilian. Then I went directly to Saigon where I had relatives who could conceal me for a while. There my mother met me, and we decided that I should risk leaving Vietnam for freedom and a brighter future in a foreign country.

Since I had been away from home, my mother treated me as an adult. At our last meeting I hugged her tightly and listened to her words: "From now on and forever you have to take good care of yourself. I won't be with you any more. Before you act, think carefully and try to remember what your father and I have taught you." I knew that she wanted to say that she loved me much more than her words could express.

Viet Kiem Ngo
Vietnam

Scapegoats

As my friend and I were walking on our way home from school, we dragged our feet along the sidewalk that was covered with a few inches of thick snow. The bitter cold and wind made the two of us tilt our heads while we were talking.

"Did you ever imagine that you would be walking in such a cold place when you were in Vietnam?" Ted asked curiously.

"No, I never did," I answered.

"Do you suffer from this cold weather?"

I smiled and shook my head. It was not his question which made me smile, but rather my good luck in arriving in this country where the people are my benefactors.

April 30, 1975, was a time when people in my country felt relief as the long civil war actually stopped. Everyone believed optimistically that there would be no more war and cruelty. The people longed for peace and approved of any change that would end the war. For years in countless battles they had seen many deaths. Husbands had been killed; thus it was particularly horrible for mothers to see sons grow up to fight in that senseless war. Yet the war did not end. Even though there was no gunfire, there were still starvation, "re-education," and the perils of escape by sea after the Communists took over South Vietnam.

A few months after their victory, the Communists accused the bourgeoisie of being the second most dangerous enemy of the country after the former government and the USA. That was how they started their "war" to stir up hatred against businessmen and factory owners. They used the middle class as scapegoats for the postwar economic crisis. Many successful businessmen were jailed.

My family was not a "first class" enemy, as far as they were concerned. They used another cunning but slower method to destroy my father's business. They established a labour organization in our factory. Every day workers had to study "workers' rights." They discussed and analyzed the relationship between bosses and workers. The guide, a Communist officer, would lead the workers to the conclusion that the owners had defrauded and taken advantage of the labourers.

As a result, a small revolution occurred in our factory. Slogans were hung all over the walls. My family was forced to sign a letter giving up the factory to the government. Later, they sent a note that they wanted to have our private house as headquarters for the local women's organization. Realizing that we would lose our house anyway, we gave it up. From then on, none of my family's activities was unknown to the government. Our life was uncertain until the second war against the bourgeoisie in 1978.

Schooling was absurd. Political activities were more important than studies. Besides, "labour" was an important subject on which I had to spend every Friday afternoon working in the schoolyard or somewhere nearby. We dug pools, planted vegetables, collected garbage. A teacher, who was usually a member of the Communist party in the school, came to mark our labour achievements. He was the individual with power. The marks we received in the study of politics and labour determined social rank and entrance to university. Normally the students whose families had belonged to the capitalist class stood no chance of going to university.

The Chinese in Vietnam were exiled; all the stores run by Chinese were closed. Schools were not allowed to teach Chinese anymore. In order to control people's finances, the Communists changed the currency several times. They collected all the old money and exchanged it for new money. The attack on capitalists, mainly the Chinese in Saigon, began.

Five young non-uniformed soldiers with arms stayed in my house for two weeks. No one in my family could go out of the house in the first week as they were investigating our properties. They made us sign a promise to move into the "New Economic Zone" just because we were unemployed. How could we be otherwise when none of the private businesses was allowed to operate and my father had had to give up his factory?

I stopped school. With my family, we fled to Kien Giang. At this time, there was a great movement of the Chinese to the maritime provinces, where the Communists collected gold in return for permission to board some small boats. "Floating back to China" was the slogan that they always used. In fact, people would rather risk their lives with some hope of a better future than give up all prospects in the "New Economic Zone."

On April 10, 1979, we sailed out on a small boat with 194 people aboard. The tiny boat struggled to reach Pulau Bidong, a refugee camp on a small Malaysian island. By the time we reached this camp, I had seen the second body drop into the sea. An old man was just too weak after the boat had drifted for seven days and died. The first victim was a woman who had been very ill on the third day of the trip and finally died two days later.

About 45,000 refugees were in the camp. Supplies of food and water were often held up by storms that delayed the supply ships coming from mainland Malaysia. Fresh water was the most precious commodity, and we could only obtain it from the suppliers because the water from the wells on the island was not fit to drink. Although life was harsh in the refugee camp, nobody complained. People were waiting for humanitarian offers from other countries and their turns to settle in a new land.

Delight came to my family when the Canadian delegation accepted our application forms to immigrate to Canada. One month later, I arrived in Toronto.

I realize why life is so precious.

> Dan So Giang
> *Vietnam*

Disillusionment

Although I was only 13 years old when the Communists took over Vietnam in 1975, I began to experience many changes in my life which were not easy to deal with. For some people, those changes might seem unimportant, but I found it difficult to adjust to different circumstances, tolerate disappointments, and face hardships.

A few days before the Communists took control, some of my relatives and my father's friends tried to convince my parents to leave the country. They kept saying that lives would not be secure under Communist domination. My father refused to take the risk; moreover, he doubted whether we could survive if we did leave the country where he had devoted his life to building a secure future for our family.

I still went to school when it reopened. But everything was different then. Many teachers were replaced by devoted communist teachers. Only those who taught mathematics and science and those who were considered "clear-minded" were allowed to keep their jobs. As a result, many good teachers had no chance to teach, and in turn students occasionally were taught by an idiot who knew nothing but a little communist ideology.

Life became more difficult as time went on. My father was accused of being a capitalist. He was forced to stop his business, which eventually was taken over by the government. My family lived on the money left over. My mother tried to hang on to a little store which the government had not yet discovered.

That was not all. The government then forced young people to work in some of the fields which had been abandoned because of war. Students had to take part in field labour in order to gain extra credits for higher grades. Travelling was restricted. People had to have permission to go from one town to another. Entertainment in theatres was discouraged because it was considered decadent. Most incredible of all, the government banned all types of music because they called it "music of capitalism," which was harmful to the spirit of communism. I bet they had absolutely no appreciation of music or literature. As a matter of fact, people had absolutely no freedom at all.

I saw nothing hopeful about my future. For me, going to school was an excuse, so that I would not have to join the "Labour Forces," organized by the government to keep people whom they called "parasites" of society working in the fields. Academically, we did not learn much at school. Most of the time, teachers were trying to brainwash us with political beliefs: how bad the former government was, how perfect the Communists were, and how to be a good Communist.

When there was war between the Vietnamese and the Cambodians, people from the ages of 18 to 35 were called to join the army. Two of my older brothers were called. My parents had four sons still at home. My parents then had to decide whether we should try to escape from the savage domination of the Communists.

My father decided to take his whole family out of Vietnam. We moved to a tiny village in the very south of Vietnam facing the ocean. We lived as farmers, but in secret planned our escape by boat. When seeds were planted, there was not much work on the farm. We then went out to the sea to fish so that we would be quite used to the ocean when we escaped.

It was almost two years later when we finally escaped from Vietnam. Life under communism had taught me perseverance. Most of all, I was completely disillusioned by communism because of what I had seen and experienced.

Thuan Lien
Vietnam

Genocide in Cambodia

A cruel war, a ruthless tyrant, and frightful starvation forced me to leave Cambodia, once called "The Land of Peace," where I was born and grew up. After the revolution of March 1970 and five years of civil war, most of the farmland had been destroyed. Farmers were compelled to abandon their ruined homes and lands and poured into the cities. The government was feeble and its officials were corrupt. The rate of inflation was incredible. It was impossible for the salaried class to catch up with the increasing living expenses. In order to survive, many of them became peddlers and petty tradesmen. The troops could not survive on their meagre salaries. They became outlaws and threatened civilians to get free goods and meals. Bombs were dropped frequently on the cities; thousands of people were killed. The whole nation was in chaos. Everybody was weary of the war and hopeful that the nation would once again become normal.

But calamity struck soon after the war ended. On April 17, 1975, the Khmer Rouge captured Phnom Penh, the capital city of the nation, and the rest of the country surrendered. The war ended and "peace" came upon Cambodia. Everybody was excited, celebrating and enjoying the "great day." None of us could foresee the imminent disaster. A week after the "liberation," the "peace bringers" suddenly turned out to be devils. They forced all people to leave the cities and towns by deceiving them that the USA, our number one enemy, would bomb the cities and towns, and we would have to retreat for several days. In Phnom Penh, the dispersal of residents was enforced right after the capture. Knowing nothing of what was going on, I followed the crowds leaving the town and began three unforgettable months of misery.

Then a savage despot and a group of ignorant followers made Cambodia a hell, full of misery and despair. They destroyed all civilization and took us back to a primitive stage. As we were dispersed further and further into the forest to uncultivated land, the food supplies diminished and eventually money was useless. By that time, we realized that going back home was only an hallucination, a dream that would never come true. The administrators started to "settle" us. New villages were formed and moving was forbidden, thus ending our wandering.

We were responsible for rebuilding the nation and had only our two hands to carry on this great commission! We had to cut the trees and build shelters ourselves. It was impossible to obtain even a nail. We used creepers to tie the pillars and reeds to cover the roof and walls. Whatever we had been accustomed to in our daily lives was considered a luxury. Education was thought to be nonsense. Everyone was encouraged to get involved in farming. Above all, rations were tightly controlled by the "organization." Everyone was given just enough for survival. Since our bellies were never filled, each morning the first thing that came into our minds was how to seek something to eat. We lost all our strength to rebel. We never thought of what our future would be like; we were only interested in eating.

Disease increased. There was no medical care or treatment. If you got ill, all you could do was ask someone who knew about herbal medicines and try to cure yourself. If it did not work, no one knew what your fate would be. Old people and infants were the first victims. The number of deaths increased every day. In addition, the "Highest Organization" started to "clear out" the former soldiers, government officials, and intelligentsia, whom they believed could organize rebellions against them. This was genocide. The number of deaths escalated incredibly.

The primitive life, the horrible diseases, and the terrifying starvation made me decide to risk escaping to Thailand. Realizing that I would not be allowed to go back home, that any career I might want was doomed, that I had no future in Cambodia, I determined to gamble my life. Life is valuable for everyone, especially for young people, but when you lose all your basic freedoms, you feel you must risk everything to escape. If I succeeded, I could start again. It was the most difficult decision I have ever made.

My escape took ten days. We walked through the forest during the days and used the sun as our guide. The little dry rice we had only kept us for three days. On the fourth day, we had to eat the leaves and stalks of plants and wild fruit. We did not even care whether they were poisonous because we needed strength to continue walking. Not only did hunger trouble us, but also wild animals, the patrols who moved through the forest to track people escaping, and the mines under the ground—all these were our enemies. However, these threats still could not destroy our will to seek freedom.

Finally, we arrived at our destination, Thailand. We were born again.

Chauncee Tang
Cambodia

Student Activities

Talking and Writing*

Each of the following stories provides insight into the conditions in countries which forced people to immigrate to Canada. Explain why students left their countries to find a new life in Canada.

- Vietnam
    "My Parents Sent Me Away"
    "Outlaw Without a Future"
- Iran
    "Rules and Penalties"
    "They Arrested My Brother"
- China
    "My Last Days in China"

Talking and Writing**

"We Must Remember" and "No More Lies"

1. Why is Qi filled with gloom when he remembers the events of June 4, 1989?
2. What is the attitude of the writers of these essays towards the students who protested in Tiananmen Square on June 4, 1989?
3. Are these writers hopeful or pessimistic about the future of their native land, China? Explain your answer with references to the two essays.

"Imprisoned Without Cause," "Army Deserter," "Scapegoats," and "Disillusionment"

1. Each of these stories gives a different perspective on why young people left Vietnam. In point form list the reasons why they left.
2. In these stories the writers describe their lives in Vietnam after the Communist takeover in 1976. How did harsh circumstances and painful experiences influence their characters and attitudes towards life? Support your opinions with references to the stories.

"Life in Cambodia"

In "Life in Cambodia" Chauncee Tang comments, "When you lose all your basic freedoms, you feel you must risk everything to escape."

1. What basic freedoms did Chauncee lose in Cambodia?
2. Do you agree with him that one must "risk everything" for freedom?

Writing Folder: Autobiography

In the next chapter of your autobiography, explain why you left your native country. Before beginning your first draft, reading the stories in this sections will give you some of the vocabulary and structures you need and some idea of how to develop and organize your thoughts.

1. With your partner or in a small group, compare your reasons for leaving your native country. Then write another chapter in your autobiography, outlining the reasons why you immigrated to Canada.

2. Before writing you might read the following stories again and examine their organization and style.

   - Narrating a single, important event
       "They Arrested My Brother"
       "My Last Days in China"

   - Organizing the narrative
       "Scapegoats"
       "Genocide in Cambodia"

3. Before editing your first draft get feedback from your writing partner and your teacher on what changes you should make to improve the clarity and persuasiveness of your composition.

Escape

Hungarians, Russian Jews, Vietnamese, Tamils, Iranians describe the difficulties and dangers in getting out of their countries and the long, torturous years in camps before being accepted as refugees into Canada.

The deep sadness felt by a child in leaving behind his native land is described by a Vietnamese boy who, at the age of ten, after the fall of Saigon, saw the Vietnamese flag pulled down on his ship, sang the Vietnamese national anthem for the last time, and watched while the captain threw the flag into the sea.

A Jewish girl describes the fear of being arrested as her family prepared in secret to escape from Russia, and the bewilderment and anger she felt as she left behind her friends, without being able to say good-bye.

One Chinese father created a careful step-by-step scenario over two years to take his family of eight out of Vietnam. He moved his family near the sea where they worked as fishermen, learning the schedule for fishing boats so that they could get out to sea without arousing suspicion.

The terrible conditions on little boats—cramped space, lack of food and water, sickness, storms, and fear of pirates—all are described in the stories of the Vietnamese. They repeatedly encountered indifference and rejection from ships on the ocean and countries where they landed.

In the refugee camps the Vietnamese again experienced hardship: shortage of food and water, sickness, boredom. In the interminable months in these camps they saw both the best and the worst behaviour of human beings. Eastern European refugees also lived for years in uncertainty as they waited for a country to accept them.

These young people have been strengthened by the hardships they survived during their escapes; these strengths have helped them survive the first difficult years in Canada. Their escape stories may help us to see immigrants with new eyes, understand and respect their experiences, and welcome their presence in Canada.

The Flag Sank

I boarded a small canoe with only my father, my older sister, two younger brothers, and a few other relatives. My mother, my older brother, and my youngest sister, who was five months old, were lost somewhere at a navy port in Saigon among the thousands of people who were trying to get aboard any kind of ship.

Two hours later, on board the big ship the captain announced that the ship no longer belonged to Vietnam, but to the United States and was subject to the orders of the American commander. Then everyone came out of their places, put on their best clothes, and stood there looking straight up at the South Vietnamese flag. There was a minute of silence to remember our native land. Some people cried; some tried to hide their sadness. I had come up to the bridge and stood there behind a number of civilians and sailors. After a minute of silence, we sang Vietnam's national anthem for the last time as the flag of Vietnam was pulled down slowly by two officers. The flag was folded neatly and was placed under the post. The American flag was pulled up, but there was neither singing nor music because nobody knew the American national anthem.

Then the captain came out to receive the Vietnamese flag with great care. He walked over to the side and, with no hesitation, he threw the flag into the sea. The flag floated for a few seconds and then sank down to the bottom of the deep sea. The captain stood there looking at the sea with great concentration. Nobody moved. Then he took off his captain's hat, his ranks, and his badges and he threw them down to the sea. All the sailors did the same thing. I felt like crying, but I didn't. This moment was one of the saddest that I had ever experienced, and I will remember it as long as I live.

Hung Nguyen
Vietnam

Stone of Fear

We left the place I had lived in for 14 years and headed towards the Hungarian border. I was extremely nervous because my father had told me that on the border we might be asked questions like this: "Are you going on vacation, or are you planning to leave the country?" I was afraid if they asked me I'd tell them the truth by accident. Fortunately, this did not happen, and a big stone fell down from my heart, the stone of fear that I might tell them our plan.

We had relatives in Vienna; so when we found them, they directed us to a hotel for the night. I was amazed how rich Vienna was compared to Hungary.

Joseph Csermak
Hungary

Question and Answer

As refugees, we were offered an opportunity to resettle in a third country. When we were interviewed by the Canadian delegation, I remember they were first surprised by the size of my family—my parents and eight children. They inquired about our ages, our professions in Vietnam, and our knowledge of English. These were the usual questions that every delegation asked. I had learned the possible questions and answers by heart. One of the Canadians asked me, "How are you?"

Quickly, I replied, "I am 16 years old."

He laughed. I was so embarrassed after I realized what he had asked.

My family was accepted for resettlement in Canada. We were so happy that we would finally become members of a country. Finally, we had a country that we could rely on and that could protect us. We were like orphans, grateful as we touched our foster parent.

Chau Lien
Vietnam

Too Late

The day before Saigon fell to the Communists there was great confusion. Many people ran or drove to the airport, even to the military airport, and to the harbour to flee. Thousands went to the American embassy because they knew that the American diplomatic corps would flee from there by helicopter. People were clinging to the helicopters and climbing on them.

All my family now wanted to leave the country because we thought when the Communists seized the city, they would get rid of all the wealthy people, the people who had relatives belonging to the former government, and the people who had left North Vietnam for the South in 1954. (People who had left the North in 1954 were considered to have betrayed their nation.) My family was wealthy. My brothers had been soldiers of the former army. Also, my father had come from North Vietnam to the South.

We asked our parents to leave Vietnam with us right away; we would not abandon them. Then we had an argument. My eldest brother asked my father, "Would you please make up your mind to leave now, Father? We don't have much time!"

Grievously, quietly, my father answered, "No. I was born in this country. I want to die here. How will I feel if I am in a foreign country? Of course, I will feel miserable. What about our properties? I had to spend almost all my life earning them. Shall I leave them now? I've already had to build up a life from nothing, and

so I know you will also have to work hard if you leave with empty hands. Also, what about the foreigners? What will they think of you? They will consider you beggars in their country. Don't think that all Americans are kind. You see, the American government only helped our country when they were still able to get profits, and they ignore us now. No, I'm not leaving."

One of my older brothers interrupted, "I think the first thing we should do is get some weapons so that we can protect ourselves. We left the army just to protect the family, and so why shouldn't we pick up weapons from the streets to protect ourselves? Then we can make plans to escape later."

Everybody agreed with his idea. We managed to pick up two machine guns, one revolver, a number of bullets, and several grenades. When we got home, my brother taught me how to hold the guns, how to load the bullets, how to aim and shoot, how to pull the bolt of a grenade and throw it; I had a chance to learn how to use these weapons when I was 15 years old.

After our self-protection was organized, we continued talking over our plan for escaping. My sister said first, "Father, Please go! We will have troubles if we stay here."

My father did not answer. Then, to my mother, she asked, "Why don't you persuade Father to go, Mother? I know if you leave, Father will leave."

"No," my mother said. "When your father leaves, I'll leave."

My sister was depressed. We, the younger children, did not take part in their conversation; we just put clothes into the suitcases so that we could escape the next day. My brothers wanted to intoxicate my father so that they could take him with them, but my mother would not allow them to do that. Then they went on disputing about their plan until midnight. Everybody was tired of quarrelling and fell into a half-sleep.

The morning of April 30th arrived. Still we had not been able to persuade our father to leave. In the afternoon of April 30, 1975, the president of the Vietnamese government declared that we had surrendered to the Communists and that we were now under the control of the Communists. Now it was too late to escape.

Van Tung Bui
Vietnam

Alone on the Ocean

My escape from Vietnam was the most dangerous and most difficult experience of my life.

At dawn on October 14, 1978, my mother, brother, cousin, and I left Vietnam, each of us carrying a small bag of clothes and another bag of dry food and water. We gathered together at the place where we had registered with the government and waited for the bus to the port. I was surprised by the number of people who were also waiting to leave.

The people were all excited when the buses came. We packed ourselves on the bus because we were afraid to be left behind. Our bus started to go, followed by my father, uncle, and cousin on motorcycles. Our hearts were all as heavy as the overloaded bus. When we arrived at an unknown port in a small village, we were met by some officers who called our names and studied our faces, matching them with the pictures on their lists before they allowed us on board.

That was the moment when I felt very concerned about leaving my father. I swallowed my tears and kept my eyes shut. My heart was crying bitterly inside as if hundreds of blades were cutting it.

Then my father said to me and my brother, "You have to listen to your mother and take care of each other. Do not complain about any hardships because the most bitter of the bitter you suffer will make you into the best people." I was as heavy as a stone when I heard these words.

Suddenly, I heard our names being called and we kissed each other good-bye. We dragged ourselves on the boat with heavy footsteps. We started our adventure on a small boat only 60 feet long; it carried 230 people. Our baggage and food were thrown into the cabin, and the women and children were forced to jump down into the cargo hold. It was all in darkness and we could just sit on the floor with bent knees. Soon the hold was filled with people packed in like sardines.

I fell asleep as the boat swayed. Soon everyone got seasick and babies began to cry. My throat was burning so much that I needed water. For two days I could not keep anything in my stomach. On the third day, I needed to go to the washroom, so

people on the deck pulled me out. I felt as if I were being freed from hell and that it had been years since I had had fresh air. Greedily, I inhaled the fresh sea breeze. I decided not to go back down into the hold anymore, and so I hid in a corner by the rail.

We were all alone on the Pacific Ocean. There was only an endless view of water and sky. I often saw some dolphins leaping around our boat, but to me they seemed evil rather than playful. In the night there was a storm with heavy rain pouring down and gusty wind blowing so sharply I was quivering and chattering all night long.

On the fourth day, we saw some large ships not far away. Eagerly we put up an SOS flag to ask for help, but they all steered away from us at full speed as if they had just seen a group of violent animals. I was so depressed by their indifference and selfishness. Perhaps they were afraid that they would have to share their food with us. With disappointments again and again and again, we went on and on and on slowly under the fiery sun.

Once we thought we were in luck because we saw a glistening boat which looked like an island. As we got closer, we found that it was a gigantic aircraft carrier. Even its life raft was bigger than our boat! We used all our strength to shout out to get the sailors' attention. When a few people came out, our captain spoke English to them to explain our situation and beg them to let us aboard because our boat had lost its direction, but they refused to accept us and pointed in the direction of Malaysia.

The next morning, we were happier because we saw some mountains and sea gulls, which suggested that there were people not far away. In a few hours, we saw two Malaysian fishing boats and the fishermen helped us land on an island. I had expected to be met with delicious food and drinks, but the Malaysians there did not welcome us and instead guarded us closely with rifles as if we were criminals. We had to continue our boat life even though we were on the land because we had to share the little food that was left over. That night, we slept on the sand facing the beach under the open sky. I felt sad because only beggars did that in my native country.

We were noticed by a patrolling boat the next morning. Some Malaysian officers landed with guns pointing at us and searched our baggage to see if we had any gun powder. They were very severe and ordered us to get back into our boat and leave that island, but fortunately our boat was damaged and could no longer move. Then they sent three motor boats to take us to a Vietnamese refugee camp which was far away from any town.

Bidong was an island with nothing but mountains and trees. By the time we got there, there were more than 10,000 Vietnamese occupying the place. The trees at the foot of the hills had been cut down for cooking, and spaces were built up for plastic tents. So we were assigned to go up and live on the mountain, where we cleared the land.

The Malaysian soldiers were corrupt. They changed our US dollars into Malaysian money and bought our jewellery for very low prices. Besides, they sold us necessary products such as food at very high prices. But we had no choice because we needed all these things to survive.

Life in the concentration camp was similar to Robinson Crusoe's. We had to build our tent with some long branches and sleep on the ground. We had to climb up over the hill to get a bath in a stream. We had to cut down trees to get wood for cooking and we had to get water from wells. If it was raining, we had to cook under the tent and stay outside in the rain. Life was so hard that we had nothing to worry about but the next meal.

The Canadian High Commission decided our fate. We had been waiting for two months to meet the Canadian delegation, but they visited the island just once a month and could only interview a few families. We were supposed to wait at least one year for an interview; however, we had brought proof of sponsorship of my aunt in Canada.

It was very hard to talk to the officials, because they did not meet anybody, except those whose names they called. One day my brother and I waited outside until one of them came out for some fresh air. Although we did not speak English that well at the moment, he understood us when he saw the sponsorship form. Immediately, he had an interview with my family and after asking some questions and filling in some forms, we were accepted! We were all so delighted that we could not sleep all night.

Our names were called to leave for Canada a few days after the interview. We could hardly believe it until our names were called again and again through the loudspeakers. We immediately packed up and left the evil island for a small town.

We were put in a big villa with about 200 people who were also accepted for Canada. We waited there for two months as they checked our health. The supplies there were sufficient, and we could buy some other things at the local stores. We enjoyed living there more than at Bidong, and so those two months passed very quickly. One day, our names were added to the list of those going to the capital for some documents and then for Canada.

The day I left Malaysia was the most meaningful day for me. When I stepped onto the plane I knew that all evil and hardship were left behind me forever and glorious days were waiting for me ahead.

I have been living now in Canada for two years and have grown to love this country, but I feel guilty about the material comforts and the freedom I enjoy here while my father is suffering in Vietnam. I will use whatever strength I have left to get my father out as soon as possible. I also pray that those still on the sea are secure. My escape from Vietnam by sea will haunt me until the day I die.

Donna Phung
Vietnam

Burning Desire, Secret Planning

My escape from Vietnam to Malaysia took us two years of effort and preparation. We had to risk our lives and leave our property to do it. I had to quit my school and live as a farmer in a small village. My second elder brother became a sailor on a fishing boat. Every member in my family had different functions, but we all aimed at the same goal—escape!

Two years after the Communists took over South Vietnam, our lives were completely changed. First, my father's business was closed, because now every business had to be nationalized, and if my father had risked running the business privately, he would have been arrested for being a capitalist. This was a common excuse that the Communists often used to arrest people who were against their policy. Second, after the war had broken out between Vietnam and Cambodia, the Communists wanted to recruit more troops. My two elder brothers were forced to join the army. That really upset my parents because they did not want their sons to be killed in a war, and they were also worried about the fate of the other five sons, who would be at the age to be drafted very soon. Under those circumstances they decided that we had to escape, no matter how hard or risky that would be. My father once said that he would rather die in the sea than live with the Communists.

To prepare for such a trip was a real challenge for us. We could not do it openly or else we could be arrested. We always had to be aware of our group leader, who was elected by the local government to keep an eye on several families. Whenever we wanted to go anywhere, we first had to ask him for his signature on the travel document, so that we could present the document to the local government for the final permission, and whenever we had guests staying at night we not only had to tell him about the guests, but also had to show him their travel documents. I remember he arrested our guest who had stayed only for one night after we had neglected to tell him about his staying. With such a dangerous, cunning, and sly person as our group leader, we were afraid that he would spot our plan and would smash it before we could make our dream come true.

The only way we could escape was by boat. My father first bought a piece of land which was located near the sea gate, so that we would have a chance to find a water route leading into the sea. I had to quit school to live as a farmer for nearly two years, and it was the toughest time of my life. I lived with my two older brothers. The three of us had never worked on a farm before. We not only had to learn how to farm, but also how to speak the local language because we did not want people to know that we were from Saigon. We had to plant vegetables, and fish for our daily food in the river which lay at the front of my cottage, because that was how the local people got their food, and we did not want to be different from them. Sometimes we had only one dish at a meal if we did not catch any fish that day.

The hardest thing we had to overcome on the farm was our loneliness. We had a burning desire to leave. Every morning when I put on my farm clothes and carried the plow on my shoulder to the farm, I felt as heavy as if I were pulling a wagon with my shoulders and I could hardly move my feet. I missed my parents, my school, and my friends very much. Besides working on the farm and planning an escape route, we also learned some English whenever we had time, because we hoped that we would need it someday. But we had to learn English secretly and hide our books under our pillows to avoid being seen by our neighbour on his unexpected visits. Our hope that someday we could leave this place had become an important support which helped us overcome our loneliness and hardship.

To escape, we needed a boat. My father conferred with his friend who owned a fishing boat. My second brother, who had no experience sailing, had to work as a sailor on the boat. He told me that he had vomited for three consecutive days on his first trip until he got used to the swaying of the boat. Even though he did not like sailing, he had to accept it because that was his job—to get used to the sea and get to know the officers who were in charge of organizing the schedule for fishing boats, so that we could easily get out to sea without arousing suspicion.

In Saigon, my young brothers still went to school as usual, and my parents lived with them. We did not move the whole family to the farm because we would need a place to stay if our plan failed. My father organized the people who wanted to go, most of whom were our relatives and some of my father's friends.

After two years' effort and much patience, we were ready to satisfy our burning desire to leave Vietnam. On October 16, 1978, we boarded several small boats on the river and sailed secretly out to sea where our fishing boat was waiting. We left behind some people who could not make it at the last moment. After two days' sailing, we reached Malaysia. We were accepted to resettle in Canada after living for six months in the refugee camp.

Chau Lien
Vietnam

Happy to Be Alive

I did not know exactly what I really felt inside me when I sneaked on the small boat which we hoped would take us to where free lands were, to where we would not be haunted by threatening thoughts of life under communist domination. My parents had planned our escape for nearly two years. After so many days of waiting and so many sleepless nights of worrying that the Communists might find out about the trip, my parents finally succeeded in getting us out of Vietnam.

We were on a small, wooden boat about 15 metres long and not more than 3 metres wide. I was afraid that it would not sail safely with so many people on it; however, I felt some relief because, at that time of the year, according to many experienced fishermen who were familiar with the ocean, the sea would be calm.

We set out in the middle of the night of October 16, 1978. There were about 80 people on the boat; some others had been unfortunate enough to have been caught by the Communists, who were patrolling the river banks. After waiting for a while, the people on the boat decided to leave without them.

I was on the deck of the boat while it sailed along a small river on its way to the sea. The boat was moving slowly and that made me feel rather worried that the Communists could easily come after us. After two hours of sailing, the land gradually disappeared. I saw ahead of me nothing but water and dark sky. I was extremely exhausted. I had had no sleep at all the day before because I had been busy preparing for the trip. I went down to the engine room and found a small space where I could sleep half-lying and half-sitting. Despite the noisy sounds of the engines and the uncomfortable smell of oil, I fell asleep shortly after that.

I was awakened some time the next day because of the uncomfortable position I was in. My back was sore and I could not fall asleep again, although I tried to. Besides, it was so hot in the room that my shirt was all soaked with sweat. So I left the engine room to go up to the deck to breathe some fresh air. It was early in the morning. I could see the sun emerge from the water some distance from the boat. It seemed to be a very good day for sailing. I had not had a chance to see the people on the boat because it had been very dark the previous night, but now I could see them. Some were sitting on the deck and others were down in the hold. They all looked exhausted and sad. I knew for sure that some of those people were leaving without their families. Some had left their parents, brothers, wives, or husbands behind to seek the freedom that they believed they would find somewhere outside their country.

We had prepared dry food, water, and oil for our trip in the boat. So the only problems we had to worry about were the ocean and pirates. We had heard many stories about the cruelty of the Thai pirates who were at large on the sea. We all prayed that they would not appear since we had nothing with which to protect ourselves. The sea was quite calm and the boat was sailing smoothly on the water.

After sailing for more than 24 hours nothing awful had happened to us. We were then in international waters, and so we were not afraid of being caught by the Vietnamese navy. The boat was heading towards Malaysia, where we had heard about refugee camps which would accept us.

When darkness came again the next day, I was frightened by the huge waves that kept slamming the sides of the boat. The sea was getting angry. Suddenly, a big wave lifted the boat up and then it went down again when a second big wave slammed right on the deck. Waves kept on crashing continuously against the sides as if they wanted to break the poor little boat into pieces. Everyone on the boat was frightened to death. Some were starting to vomit. Children were crying. The captain of the boat insisted that all people stay where they were to keep the boat in balance. In the meantime, he was trying to control the boat to avoid the waves that attacked relentlessly. The little boat looked the size of a grain of sand in the desert as it moved roughly and helplessly on the sea. Who knew what might happen to it when the sea was so powerful? I could not have visualized or imagined such a dangerous situation before the trip started, but I could see now that it was extremely risky and that we could drown at any minute if the boat sank.

The storm lasted until the sky above us became bright, showing that another day was beginning. The sea became calmer as the sun emerged. I almost believed that there must be some great power that had saved us from the storm that night. It had to be God who would have such power.

After another day of sailing, we could see in the distance some dark spots which we believed to be land. At dawn that day we reached the shore of one of the Malaysian islands. When our boat approached the shore, people on the land were shouting at us and some of them were throwing rocks at us. Suddenly, patrol boats of the local authority came out with three policemen, who asked us to leave immediately because we were not allowed to land there. They gave us some water and we departed again.

The joy of seeing land vanished as the boat moved slowly again towards the open sea. Again, all that I could see was water and sky. Everybody on the boat was disappointed. We felt like candles which had just started to burn and now were put out in a flash.

We saw land again after another day of sailing, but again we were asked to leave when we reached the shore. Since our engines had broken down and the rudder had been damaged, they allowed us to stop our boat and have the engines fixed.

We stopped there for another day. People on the boat were frightened because of what we had been through. They decided unanimously that we should not leave shore again since land was right in front of us. They did not dare to take any further risks, and besides, no one knew where else we could land. So at midnight, we rowed the boat to the shore and landed before the local authorities discovered it. We destroyed the boat so that we could not be pushed out to sea again.

The local police found out about us shortly after we landed. One of them was really angry. He slapped the captain of the boat when he tried to explain our situation. The Malaysian Red Cross arrived some time later and took us to one of the refugee camps.

It took us five days to reach land—five days of floating aimlessly on the ocean. We had risked our lives, hoping that we could find freedom and happiness. I thought of nothing in the future; I only felt happy that I was alive.

Thuan Lien
Vietnam

Life in the Refugee Camp

After we had landed in one of the large cities located in the south of Malaysia called Kuan-Tan, I realized that our hardships were not yet over. I had never expected that there would be other obstacles lying in our way to freedom. Life in the refugee camp was not easy. It was the first time in my life that I felt almost as if I did not exist in the world.

We were put in a camp located in the city. It had been a police station before the arrival of the "boat people." At the time we were sent to the camp, there were about 200 people crowded in this small, old building. People in the camp were isolated from the outside world, for nobody was allowed to go outside except in case of sickness. Local policemen guarded the gate every day and night. We received food and other life necessities daily from the world Red Cross. They also helped arrange for us to meet delegations of some countries willing to open their doors to us, who were without a country, without destination, and without benefactors.

I had thought that after we got out of Vietnam, we would be accepted to resettle in some countries ready to help us unfortunate people. But I soon found out how gullible I was to have thought this. I also found out that in order to resettle in another country, we had to have some qualifications: English or French fluency, a useful occupation, physical health, or a close relative who would sponsor you financially to come to his or her country.

Once every few weeks, representatives of some countries such as Australia, New Zealand, the United States, Canada, or Switzerland came to the camp to interview people anxious to immigrate to their countries; however, very few people were accepted. My family did not care much which country we went to. We only hoped to leave the camp to settle down in a free country as quickly as possible. Unfortunately, we were rejected by every country that interviewed us because of the large size of our family. Canadian representatives, however, said they would consider our application for immigration to Canada, but they told us to wait for their final reply.

Three months had passed since we had arrived in the camp. Life in the camp was quite good, except that we were locked inside. When the growing number of "boat people" made it too difficult, the Malaysian government removed all the refugees from the city to the seashore, where they could put all together the more than one thousand people.

Life was really rough in that camp. It was situated on a large expanse of sand surrounded by iron fences. There was absolutely nothing available for shelter. People had to set up tents and the materials provided by the Red Cross were insufficient. As a result, people lived crowded in little tents.

Obtaining water was another serious problem. Since the camp was a hundred miles away from the city, water was provided by trucks transporting it from the city. Obviously, there was never enough water for everyone. Every day, hundreds of people, with their containers for water, waited from early in the morning under the hot sun until darkness fell at night.

The shortage of food supplies also created another serious problem. People never had enough food; therefore, some were so desperate that they sneaked out of the camp to buy food, milk for the babies in the camp, and other necessities. Sometimes, they got caught by the soldiers who were in charge of keeping order in the camp. Anybody who got caught was brought back to the camp with wounds on the body. They were beaten up badly by those soldiers for leaving the camp without their permission.

Sickness was the worst problem of all. Because we were all living in a unhealthy environment and eating bad food, it was very easy to catch a fatal disease. Medical supplies were limited. I witnessed the deaths of one man and a child in the camp due to disease. I still remember the scenes that I saw. There were some famous doctors among the people in the camp. When they discovered what a serious disease the man had, they told the officer in charge that the man should be taken to the hospital immediately. The officer, who had always been hostile to people in the camp, said that there was no available vehicle to deliver the man to the hospital, despite the fact that there were some cars stopping outside the gate. Some people suggested that he call the hospital for an ambulance. The officer went back to his office for a while and then told us that he had called the hospital. The sick man waited painfully hour after hour and finally died without seeing any sign of an ambulance. I knew for sure that the officer had not called any hospital at all.

Difficult life always causes conflict. People living in unpleasant circumstances sometimes act disgracefully and easily lose their tempers. There were many squabbles and fights, very often over a minor matter such as distributing food or water. Besides, it was hard for people to control themselves when thousands of people were living together without laws or rules.

My family waited day after day for a reply from Canadian Immigration which would decide our future fate. Days passed. I sometimes wondered whether we had done the right thing in leaving Vietnam where, at least, life was not like the life I had now in this refugee camp. I even doubted whether it had been worth risking our lives for something that we were not sure existed. However, I did not want to complain or be sorry about anything because I knew about the situation in Vietnam. I did not think of grumbling about the hostility of and ill-treatment by those Malaysians and the negligence, the indifference of the world to us. We were, after all, people who had no country, who were unwanted, who deserved nothing. It was enough that we were alive. We easily might have died on the ocean or starved to death.

Despite everything, there were still people who cared. We finally were informed that Canadian Immigration had accepted us to go to Canada. After seven months of living in a refugee camp, I was anxious about going to another unknown place, but I was extremely eager to leave this miserable place. The sooner the better! The experience in the camp had disillusioned me so that I no longer expected to find perfection in people. No one is perfect. I also had learned how bitter it is to be a "refugee" with no country.

Thuan Lien
Vietnam

No One Cared

My father had talked about leaving Hungary many times. My mother did not agree with him. I did not understand anything. One day my father talked with me about it. He told me that life was much better in the West. The question of going was up to me. They said they would leave Hungary for me—for my future. I was very excited about what my father told me. I had never been abroad.

After a month we were on our way to Austria. We arrived at night on the train. I remember we just stood there with two suitcases and a bag. That was all we had with which to start a new life. We had not dared to bring more suitcases because that would have looked suspicious. We had the telephone number of a friend of my father who lived in Vienna, but we did not know how to use the telephone. We asked someone for help, but it was awkward because we did not speak German. We had the address of a Hungarian hotel and finally got there by taxi, but they did not have any room for us. It was night and we were tired because we had been walking on the streets of Vienna with the suitcases looking for a hotel.

Our plan was to stay in Austria, but we had no idea how we would do it. We met a lot of Hungarians in Vienna. We found out that there was only one way to have a chance to stay. We had to go to a refugee camp. In 1987 all the people from the Eastern block were refugees. Everyone warned us that the camp was a very danger-ous place. My parents were scared, but I was looking for adventure. We were separated from the outside world for a week because we were under examination about our destination. We lived in a big house where there were about 300 other people. Thirty people were put in each big room and we slept on iron beds. We talked and laughed. There was a girl in the same room with me and we played a lot. There were children running all around the room. Adults played cards and it was noisy all day. Everyone there was new and people were interested in one another.

After a week we were placed in another area for two days. We had to register to go either to America, Canada, or Australia. We chose Australia. Then we were placed in a boarding house in a village called Wallsee. The population was 2000 and there were 200 refugees. We got one room, which was pretty small. We lived there for two years. We were given food and a small amount of pocket money.

The first day I went to school, everyone stared at me and whispered about me. The teachers did not care about refugees and they looked down on us. During most periods I only sat and listened. Teachers did not give me books to study and did not seem to want to help me. I asked my English teacher to give me books because I wanted to study, but she did not give me any. I talked to the director and told him that I needed an education, but he was not interested in me. I tried to participate in class, but they did not let me. Sometimes the teachers made fun of us. Once my German teacher told the class: "I don't know why these refugees come to school." He said it in a humiliating way, and I never went to German class again. No one cared.

Almost every day I went home crying. At that time I felt my parents did not seem to understand me either. I really needed someone to talk to. I could not share my feelings with anyone. I changed a lot in Austria. I became shy and I lost my self-confidence. I had not known my parents in Hungary because I spent my time with my friends and my dog. I did not have much in common with my parents. In Austria, however, we were together in one room for a very long time. We got to know each other very well, but we did not understand one another. It was hard to live like that. My father always made me feel that I was the least important in the family and I could not say a word. He gave me orders that I could not stand, and he shouted at me. I had many friends with whom I played, but inside I was lonely and so were they.

Refugees were forbidden to work, but almost everyone did because they needed money and they could not stand sitting at home. Everyone worked "under the table." Sometimes my parents had a lot of work, but sometimes they didn't have any at all. They had to be thankful when farmers came and picked them up to work. They had to do the work that Austrians didn't do and they got low wages, but there was no other choice.

We waited for the mail every morning. After three months we received a letter from the Australian embassy telling us to get a sponsor. We wrote to a lot of places in Australia for help. Finally we got two sponsors. One was a Hungarian organization and the other was a man who owned a factory. For the following 13 months we lived in fear about our fate. At Christmas we got the letter saying that Australia had refused us. I died inside. I felt responsible for everything. My parents had left Hungary for me. For the first time in my life I saw my parents crushed.

Then we registered to go to Canada. I started to study English very hard on my own with the help of an Austrian woman. A church sponsored us in Canada. We had an interview in the embassy and a medical checkup. During the summer as we waited for our flight, I rode to the nearest camp two times a week to attend an English course taught by American students. When the list of flights to Canada was published, we weren't on the list. I felt desperate because I didn't want to miss the beginning of school in Canada. I worried about school very much.

Every single day spent in Austria is a bitter memory for me. However, perhaps the discrimination, the disappointments, the loneliness, and the problems I had to face have prepared me for life.

Krisztina Krisztics
Hungary

All Beginnings Are Hard

We waited seven years for permission to leave the Soviet Union. Then everything happened late on the night of November 7th. We were all sitting in the kitchen huddled in blankets, because the heat never seemed to reach the 14th floor of our building, waiting for my father to come home. We had already been waiting for over an hour when my mother suggested to my grandmother that we call the police.

"Mama, what if he's hurt? It's already 11 o'clock and he's never been this late before. Do you remember what happened to Alexander Vitzon last week? Let me call the police," repeated mother.

My mother was speaking of our neighbour, Vitzon, who had also asked permission to leave and who had been badly beaten by a Russian Patriotic gang on his way home from work. It was now dangerous even to walk in our streets. Manya, an elderly lady from our block, was hit over the head with a brick while going out to buy milk and remained in the hospital for two months. But my grandmother protested: "No, Lena, you mustn't call. Do you want to attract even more attention to yourselves? These policemen would rather destroy you than help you. Hasn't that gotten through to you yet?"

My mother just stood shaking and twisting her wedding ring. Her face suddenly looked old and haggard and her eyes seemed to be looking out into the unknown. My grandmother was trying to keep her composure, but she too was rubbing her hands nervously and muttering silently to herself. I buried my head in the pillow and sulked. Then, just as all hope was fading, I heard my father's metal-capped shoes tapping against the steps and at last arriving at our door. When my father walked in, my mother looked as if she had been renewed. My grandmother whispered to me: "God has answered my prayers."

My father, after removing his galoshes, turned on the tap in the kitchen, turned on the shower in the bathroom, closed the curtains, and walked over to us. He then sat down at the table and pulled out of his pocket an opened envelope.

"I had to go pick up the mail at Anatoli's house. Forgive me for coming late," he said touching my mother's hand. "Lena, we got it! Our visas have finally come! Seven years of waiting. It's all over. We will leave in a week. We will go to freedom and leave this wretched country once and for all." He then leaned over and kissed me.

The reason my father had to pick up our mail at Anatoli's was because we had had to trade apartments the previous year in order to be safer, so that no one would be sure where we lived. My father then motioned for me to go to sleep. The week ahead of us would not be an easy one. When my grandmother came to tuck me in, I asked her again if we were really leaving.

"Yes, God seems to have answered both of my prayers tonight."

Only six more nights in this bed, I thought. My room was very cold, but I didn't even notice it. My heart was thumping as I looked around my room carefully, selecting things that I would take with me on my journey to freedom. Suddenly my eyes fell upon my old address book, and it hit me that I would be leaving all my friends. No one other than my family, Anatoli, and my aunts could be told about our departure. It was planned that the night we left, my aunt and uncle-in-law would move in and pretend that nothing had happened and no one had left. Why couldn't my friends come with me though? Or why couldn't I have at least told them I'd be leaving? But my father's rules were not something I could disobey easily.

We spent most of the upcoming week packing. "Vera, you're going to have to leave all your crystal animals behind. There's no way they'll fit into our suitcases, dear," my mother told me.

"But mother...those are my very favourites."

"No 'buts,' Vera. We only have five suitcases. Be a good girl now."

I felt a sudden urge to kick my parents. Why couldn't I bring anything with me? Who cares if we only have five suitcases? Why can my mother bring all her belongings and I can't even bring my glass animals? I ran out of the apartment, slamming the door.

"She'll get over it. It's hard for a young girl," my grandmother said.

I wanted to scream. "No, I'll never get over it. It's the end of the world. Can't you see?"

I went for a long walk—past the Bolshoi Theatre, the circus, the children's theatre, the park, the store for children, and my school. Everywhere I went, I signed my initials: "V.R." and the date. Then I slowly walked home.

I went to school the next day and my friends greeted me: "Vera, where have you been? There's a new boy in our class. He's very cute. Come on, we'll show him to you. Hurry up."

My best friend invited me to a party she was going to give at her house. Nothing had changed. Except for me. My teacher even commented, "Vera, why are you so quiet? Is everything all right? I've never seen you sit in your seat all day without even passing a single note. Perhaps you're changing for the better."

I opened my mouth to tell her the truth, but quickly shut it. When the bell rang, I sprang up to give my teacher a gift. While she was opening it, I bit my lower lip not to cry. I gave her my crystal unicorn. She then hugged me and whispered something in my ear which sounded like "Good luck in the future, Vera, wherever you go." Perhaps I was just hallucinating.

My friend, Masha said: "Vera, I think your eyes are very watery. You're not crying, are you? Cheer up!" I wiped a tear off my face and kept walking with them.

When we got to my house, I gave them each a letter: "Promise you won't read it until midnight. It's very private." That way you could say I wasn't exactly disobeying my father. I was just bending the rules.

When I got home, I could tell that my mother had been crying. She must have walked around Moscow too. My grandmother was so busy preparing food that she almost ran out of the house in her bathrobe. The only thing that gave any of us hope was the look in my father's eyes. I had never seen them shine like that—like two diamonds. He had enough energy in him for the four of us. Finally it was time to leave.

I refused even to look where we were going and the last thing I saw of Moscow was the Leningrad railway station. I remember very little of our stay in Vienna, other than my father's constant speeches of freedom: "Finally, after 38 years of hell I am free. Do you realize what it means to be free, Vera? I can be whoever I want. We are *free*. No one here can punish you for being Jewish. Here you don't worry about going out at night and being attacked by Russian patriots. I feel reborn," he would often shout.

A week later we came to Canada. Two days after that I went to school. My parents took me to school. I didn't speak a word of English. "Don't worry, Vera," my parents kept telling me.

The minute I walked into the class, a middle-aged woman with a kind face came and took my hand. "Vera," she desperately tried to pronounce the Russian "R." "Come with me. This is our class and these are your new friends." I don't know for sure if that's what she said because I didn't understand, but that's what her eyes told me. That day I taught the whole class how to pronounce my name with a Russian "R," and we were all eager to learn from each other.

Everyone in this new country was so hospitable. I knew my father was right about Canada after all.

Julia Zarankin
Russia

Student Activities

Talking and Writing*

"The Flag Sank," "Stone of Fear," and "Question and Answer"

1. What incident does each of the students remember most vividly about his escape? In each case, explain why you think this incident is most important to him.

2. In your journal, list the incidents you remember most about leaving your native country. You may be able to develop some more fully in a chapter about your journey from your native country to Canada.

Talking and Writing**

"Too Late," "Alone on the Ocean," "Burning Desire, Secret Planning," "Happy to Be Alive," and "Life in the Refugee Camp"

What insights into the Vietnamese refugee experience are given by these stories? Consider the following aspects:

- making the decision to leave
- planning and preparing
- leaving behind friends and family
- struggling against storms, starvation, on the ocean
- surviving in the refugee camps
- working through the immigration process

"No One Cared"

1. Why does Krisztina consider her experience in the refugee camp a "bitter" one?

2. Why does she believe that her disappointments, loneliness, and experiences of discrimination prepare her for life? Do you agree with her? Give reasons to support your opinion.

"All Beginnings Are Hard"

1. How does the author communicate the sense of tension felt in the family before they leave Russia?

2. What do we learn of the reasons for the family's escape from Russia?

3. Why does Vera consider that leaving her home in Moscow is the "end of the world"? Compare your feelings about leaving to Vera's.

Writing Folder: Autobiography

1. In your autobiography describe your leaving from your native country. You might discuss

   - making the decision to leave
   - preparations
   - feelings about leaving
   - saying good-bye
   - journey to Canada

2. Before writing your first draft examine the structure and style of some of the stories in this section.

   - Narrating a single, important incident
        "The Flag Sank"
        "Stone of Fear"
        "Question and Answer"

   - Using dialogue
        "Too Late"
        "All Beginnings Are Hard"

   - Using descriptive details
        "Alone on the Ocean"
        "Happy to Be Alive"

   - Organizing the narrative
        "Burning Desire, Secret Planning"
        "Life in the Refugee Camp"
        "No One Cared"

3. After completing the first draft, ask your writing partner and teacher to suggest how you might improve it. Then edit your work. Choose an appropriate title for this chapter of your autobiography.

Continuing the Autobiography

1. Other chapters might focus on your experiences in Canada. Before writing, read and discuss stories on similar themes in the units "Adjusting to Canada" and "Family Roots." See student activities at the ends of individual sections for more specific ideas for discussing and writing.

   Possible topics:

   - First experiences
   - Learning English
   - Making friends
   - Adjusting to school
   - First jobs

- Living between two cultures
- Tradition vs. independence and freedom
- Pressures
- Achievements
- Who am I?
- Changes in me
- Challenges
- My double life
- Split personality
- Important events which influenced me
- My strengths and weaknesses
- My interests and hobbies
- Finding my roots

2. End your autobiography with a chapter on your future. For specific ideas see the student activities at the end of "Future Goals" in the unit "Becoming Canadian."

Publication of the Autobiography

1. After writing the first draft of each chapter and having your teacher and writing partner read it, use their corrections and suggestions in your rewriting.

2. Choose an interesting title for each chapter.

3. Include photographs or draw pictures to illustrate incidents in each chapter.

4. Include a table of contents at the beginning.

5. Design a cover page and a title for the autobiography.

BECOMING CANADIAN

Future Goals

New Canadian students think about the future very differently. Some are filled with fears—fears of failure, discrimination, alienation from children and grandchildren, and another world war. Others are optimistic as they consider the opportunities for higher education available to them, and their freedom to choose a career suited to their talents and interests. Some have a specific goal in mind, whereas others are still searching.

These young people imagine a future where they can contribute their skills to Canada through a rewarding career. Although some are fatalistic, the majority feel that their success in Canada depends on their talents and industriousness. Their goals are high, and they feel enormous pressure to succeed in Canada because of the expectations and sacrifices of parents. Sometimes they feel a conflict between choosing a career which will guarantee a secure future and following their interests.

In the process of becoming Canadian these young people become more intensely aware of their cultural roots. Already, they worry about their children growing up ignorant of their traditions and native language. But they recognize that Canada is their home and will be the home of their children. They rejoice in the freedom, independence, and peace that Canada offers.

Let God Decide

I never think of my future at all. I just want to get higher marks in examinations. In Hong Kong, my high school had a career association which helped the graduate students find jobs or told them what they could do after graduation. I didn't like this club because I didn't think it could help students much. At that time I didn't dream of my future. Maybe I am not mature yet. Perhaps there will be a World War III. Then we won't have to work any more. I don't dare to think of the future, for I am afraid that if I put my goals too high and fail to reach them, then I will feel angry and frustrated.

I live life by the proverb: "Let God decide it."

Amy Tam
Hong Kong

My Children

Although I may have a chance to go back to Hong Kong to live, I will never do so. I have decided to start my new life in this new country and have my children receive a Canadian education.

In the future, maybe five or ten years from now, I will get married and have children, who will become Chinese Canadians. Many older Chinese people do not like Chinese Canadians because their mother tongue is not Chinese, but English, and possibly some of them do not know Chinese at all. Our elders cannot tolerate this, nor can my parents. They do not want my children to be "dumb" Chinese. I would like my children to still remember their mother tongue, and I will teach them both languages: English and Chinese.

Cecelia So
Hong Kong

Now I Have a Country

Canada is full of freedom and happiness. It does not have the heavy pressure of political problems. In Hong Kong we do not really have a country. It does not yet belong to China, nor is it part of Britain. I am lucky for now I have a country. I am sure I will live here forever and let my children be good Canadians. I will teach them to have a strong sense of duty to their country, Canada. But I will not let them speak only English. I will teach them Chinese too, because, in fact, they are still Chinese. It is shameful if a person is Chinese but doesn't know Chinese.

Joey So
Hong Kong

I Have to Be Realistic

I do not have any future plans. In Korea I had one. I wanted to be a teacher, especially an English teacher, but because of immigrating to Canada this dream has gone. I think I have to be realistic; therefore, I will have small goals, but I will never be a failure in life.

Mi Suk Pong
Korea

A Strong Passion

The future is a great challenge which I take seriously. I have chosen to go into medicine because I want to be a doctor. The medical field is considered to be one of the most respected and important professions. It has dignity and security too. Above all, it is my parents' wish that I be a doctor. My father, who is dead, wanted me to be a doctor. His last wish remains in my heart with a strong passion. I am a hard-working person, so that I believe I can have this dream. In Canada, there are many opportunities for me and I don't wish to lose them.

Mohammed Khan
Pakistan

It is Up to Me

My future seems so far ahead that I will never reach it. I have been avoiding thinking about my future because I am afraid that I will not be successful. I feel that I have done nothing, and it is too early to think about the future. Despite this, I have been deeply concerned about my future. There are a number of concerns I have which include health, career, education, language, and family.

The idea of "success" is difficult to pin down because it is differs from one person to the other. Each individual has a unique point of view about success. To me, it is whether my goal is fulfilled as a result of my effort.

I strongly believe that if I am to have a happy, meaningful life, I have to be healthy and fit. Sickness adds misery to life and restricts activities. I think of myself as being healthy at the present time and I wish to keep my health or even better it in the future. I am concerned with the food I eat and the hours of sleep I get. I do not think I will become a smoker.

As far as education is concerned, I expect to finish university. I want to get as much education as possible. In the past, I was not sure what career I was going to have. Up to this point, I am still undecided. The answer is not at all easy to find and it may be too early for me to decide. My ideas change from time to time. But I think it is better to find out as soon as possible what my career will be so that there is a goal towards which I can work. I have wanted to be a scientist, or have a related career in the field of science. Actually this goal may be an illusion because I doubt my ability to become a scientist, and I realize more and more how difficult it is to reach this goal; however, I still keep this wish. I do not want to tell others about my dream because I am afraid of being laughed at for being unrealistic and too ambitious.

There are many reasons for my wanting to be a scientist. I have always been interested in the nature of things: how machines work and why. I am curious about nature and I have an eagerness to learn. I respect and envy scientists because they try to solve some of the problems facing the world. Also, mathematics and science are my favourite and best subjects at school now.

One thing which is increasingly alarming to me is the language problem. I emigrated from a Chinese-speaking country to an English-speaking country. As a result, I have to learn a brand new language. I realize the position I am in is very dangerous because I feel trapped in the middle between Chinese and English. Over the past years I have only learned a fraction of the English language. I believe that language is needed in order to enjoy life and get the most out of it. Communication is vital for human beings. In my case, I must be fluent in English so that I can compete with Canadians and participate in Canadian society. At the same time, I want to preserve my native language.

As far as family is concerned, I will choose my wife on the basis of her character and education. Appearance is also a factor to consider, but it is not the most important one. My children are going to have two languages—English and Chinese. At home, they will speak only Chinese as much as possible.

I am lucky and grateful to experience two countries with different societies, cultures, and customs, and to be able to speak two languages. I think it is wonderful because it helps me understand human relationships. I have learned something which I could never have learned in any other way. I enjoy life better because there is more colour in my life. I have two countries at the same time—Canada and China. Canada is a great nation because it is peaceful. Although I am living in Canada, I will never forget my native country, and I will always feel great love for China.

My future is vague because it is so distant, but I hope my life unfolds as I expect. I am aware that it is all up to me to make my dreams come true.

Gary Oue
China

Dreaming

I don't care whether or not my goal will be reached, but I always dream that some day I may become a doctor or an engineer. Whenever my mother, father, or sister get sick, I think if I were a doctor, they would not suffer so much pain. I'm very interested in math and science. I'm going to go to university after graduating from high school and learn more about what I don't know now. It is clear that going to university will not be easy for me, especially in medicine or engineering because I have a language problem. But I have made up my mind—I'm going to try.

Going to university means I face more hard work, but I'm willing to do it. No matter how long it takes, if I have opportunities to learn, I will continue to study even after I graduate from university, because no one can create a better life for me except myself. I'm not religious, so I don't think praying to God can help me in any case. I believe that my future depends on my efforts

I was surprised when one of my teachers asked me whether I was going to have a Canadian boyfriend. Maybe that was because I never thought about it. I think it isn't time for me to think of a boyfriend and I should concentrate on study while I am at school. Nevertheless, I see that many girls who have a Canadian boyfriend speak English very fluently. Perhaps having a boyfriend isn't such a bad idea! I may have a boyfriend who can teach me English. All I hope is to learn English faster.

I have no idea whom I will marry. My family never talks about this kind of thing at home. I don't like to talk in public either. But for sure, I won't get married too early because my career may be more important than marriage. I think if you are uneducated, you will not find a good husband and you won't have a happy family. On the other hand, the longer I live in Canada and the more I see, the more I feel that being a single person means more freedom. You can travel anywhere and have lots of fun. You have nothing to worry about but to take care of yourself. It is ten times better than being tied to a small family. In the Chinese tradition, parents choose husbands for their daughters. I hate this idea; I would like to make my own choice. If my parents allow me, I'll find one I love.

Unlike most Chinese families, I don't plan to have too many children: two is enough, maybe one. They will learn English at school and I will be a good home teacher of Chinese because I don't want to be a translator for my children when we go back to visit China.

I will live in Canada permanently because the society, the life-style, and the education system are much better than where I came from. I love Canada and I love my motherland, too. I will go to visit my country, but not before I finish university. My old teachers and friends are hoping I will bring them information on modern science.

My friends, there are too many thoughts in my mind and too much I would like to tell you. I can't express myself on this small sheet of paper. I'm putting my pen down now, and I'm not going to write any more about dreams. Stay with me, friends, to see my real future.

Binhua Wang
China

I Want to Be Independent

Every individual has at least one dream which makes her feel great. It does not matter whether the dreams come true in real life or not; they always give hope and consolation in times of depression. Sometimes, I dream that I am the cleverest student in school, the cleverest pilot, or a well-known vocalist. Besides these dreams, also I have another dream which I must try to achieve.

Unlike most young people in Burma, who dream of being doctors, I do not want to be a doctor, since I am scared to touch anything live from a cockroach to a crocodile. In Burma, my sister had to take intravenous glucose frequently since she was weak, and whenever the doctor was about to insert the big long needle into my sister's vein, I quickly hid my face or turned away. With this attitude, how could I be a doctor?

What I most want to be is an independent person. That is one of the reasons I came to Canada. If I lived in Burma, inevitably I would have to marry someone to support me, since I could not live with my parents forever, and it is impossible for a woman to be in business or get a job from the Burmese Government, even though she is highly educated. Even if she had a job, she would not earn adequate money for herself. If I had to depend on my husband, I would have to listen to him, my parents-in-law, and even to my sister-in-law. I would have no voice. I could not do anything for my own parents, or if I wanted to go out, I would have to ask their permission. If I could earn sufficient money for the family, I could positively have some voice or even some control in the family since money decides most things, but unfortunately, I cannot earn money in Burma.

I used to see my female cousins and my own sister asking permission from their husbands to go out or to buy clothes. However, I have never seen men ask such permission from their wives. The hypocritical answer of men is that since they earn the money for the families, they have power to do anything they want and the women who cannot earn have to listen to them; therefore, since I was young, I vowed to myself that I was going to lead an independent life in order to be different from those women.

When I was in Burma, I fought frequently with my fourth brother about his admiration for his friend, who had trained his wife to take his shoes off every time he came home, to serve him a soft drink and to fan him when he felt hot. He never took his wife out when he went to a movie nor let his wife go to a movie. I had never met him, but I loathed him because he gave this lesson to my brother. Well, I also taught my brother a lesson.

In 1978, I decided to come to Canada where I could find a job to earn money in order to be independent. I dream that I can earn a great deal of money, live in my own house, and even have my own car. Maybe I will get married, maybe not. Even if I get married, I will not always listen to my husband and to others. I will do what I want to do and only when I want to do it. I do not mean that I will not respect to them. I will, but my respect will be limited.

To be able to do what I want, I need a decent job for which education is essential. That is why I am trying to be educated no matter how hard it is. I am going to fight against the macho attitude of these ridiculous men from Burma, and one day my particular dream will come true.

Jodie Chen
Burma

Uncertain

My future seems very uncertain. It might be gloomy, bright, or ordinary. In my dreams it includes a healthy life, a happy family, and a satisfactory job. I do not know whether I can make this dream come true or not. I do not know what my future will be.

There have been different periods in which I have had different dreams for my future. In Vietnam, I never thought of my future until one day my father said to me, "Pei Yuen, you are in high school now. Later, you will graduate. What are you planning to do after your high school education? I hope you can do what your sixth uncle did. You should go abroad to study." I started to dream of university and the black gowns that the students wore triumphantly at the graduation ceremony.

Once a friend of mine said, "You possess a teacher's solemnity; you look like our geography teacher." I then began to wish to be a teacher who was respected and adored by the students.

After I arrived in Canada, I realized that that dream of mine would never, never come true. First, I felt I had only such superficial knowledge. Second, English was a great obstacle, and I felt I could never overcome my problems in English. I felt really depressed and disappointed.

However, I still have other dreams. I dream of being a nurse sometime because I like the nurse's white dress and the name that people usually call a nurse—"White Angel" and the nurse's respectable job. I remember when I stayed in the hospital looking after my aunt, I always looked at the nurses with admiration. I like to deal with people, though I am not very expert at this, but, on the other hand, I do not like the sight of blood. Also my friends always say that I get nervous so easily, and I cannot deny this fact. These problems make me so confused that I cannot make up my mind about what I am going to do in the future.

I am not doing too badly in school now. The fact is that I have not failed any subject yet, but those marks on my report cards are obtained by hard work only. The knowledge that I force myself to absorb is only temporary. It will not stay in my brain permanently so that I am afraid I am not smart enough to go to college where I have determined to go.

"No matter what is important to you," my father always says, "remember the first thing you must think of is your health; otherwise, you will never succeed completely in doing anything. Health is the greatest necessity." I had not appreciated his advice until I really got sick with mononucleosis. Ever since, I have been afraid of being tortured by sickness. If I neglect my health again, it could prevent me from receiving an education and getting my job in the future.

Now, I have my family, with my parents and my brothers and sisters. Then, in the future, I will have another family. It does not mean that I will forget my present family. I will never forget my parents and will still support them. In the Canadian society, the old, Chinese feudal concept, which forbids a woman to support her family after she puts her feet into her husband's house, can never exist. My children will receive both Chinese and Canadian education. They will go to a Canadian school because I do not want them to be disdained by the others, and it is also necessary for their future life. Also, I will send my children to Chinese school because their roots will always be Chinese. They cannot forget their ancestors.

The future is so far away. Now, I am a student. But what will I be in a few years? All I can do is struggle to achieve what I dream of and do everything I can to provide for my future.

Diana Tang
Vietnam

Searching

For a long time I have wondered what I will do in the future. At the moment, I want to be a scholar, specializing in culture and philosophy. My first choice would be to become a musician, or any kind of artist, but I know I do not have the talent to do this professionally. Music will always be a hobby for me.

At my school in Japan there were two kinds of students. One group did not have their own thoughts. They were interested in nothing and studied because their parents wanted them to do so. They were the ones who would be the elite in the future and gain as much money as possible, without thinking much about what they were doing. The other group did not have dreams either. But at least they were trying to find joy and think for themselves. I felt comfortable with this group. I really thought they were my friends. But in each other we were just looking for comfort. In the meantime, I was playing music in a band, which was the only thing I was seriously interested in.

With neither dream nor ambition, but enormous expectations, I came to Canada. I was expecting to have a different kind of life in Canada, although I had no idea what I would do or what would happen to me. Since coming to Canada, I have learned much and become interested in many things I knew nothing of when I was in Japan. And I am interested in almost everything that I learn now. But particularly, I am obsessed by arts, politics, philosophy, and culture. They are connected in my mind. And I want to combine them all in my profession.

These days I often find beauty in my life. When I am talking or walking, no matter what I am doing, I suddenly feel as if I am out of this world and watching the world from somewhere different. At this time the world seems wonderful. And I often just keep looking at something beautiful, hoping time will never move. The is the joy of art, I believe. And music is just as wonderful to me.

This is what makes me think that science is not important. Happiness can be attained without technology. But happiness cannot be attained without art. Real comfort does not come from convenience, in my opinion. People can be happy in poverty or under political repression, if they can discover or create beauty in their lives. This is the wonder of art.

Also, to me philosophy is a kind of art. I love to examine how people think about life. But actually these studies are for those who cannot be artists, including myself. Knowing that I cannot be an artist, all I can do in my life is study about the arts. I am still not quite sure what I will major in. But whatever I do, I want to feel, and let others feel beauty as much as possible in life.

Yuichi Kawomoto
Japan

Entrepreneur

Living in a society without making any decision for the future is like sailing in a big ocean without knowing the direction. Whenever I try to think of my future, I always feel troubled. Honestly, I have no idea whether I should continue my education in university or not. In fact, I do not enjoy studying at all.

When I was a little boy, I never thought of being a doctor, a teacher, or an engineer. What I really hoped was to be an entrepreneur who goes out with his own driver, talking about money. Also, I dreamed of being a powerful man who lives in a high-class society. When I was an eight-year-old boy, I loved stories about the great business leaders in the world, and what really impressed and surprised me was that most of those rich men had not graduated from high school, but were nevertheless successful. From then on, I began to believe that education was not very important for me. For this reason, I became lazy and never paid attention to the teachers and always skipped classes.

But when I came to Canada, everything changed in my life. I felt that I would not achieve anything in this society if I did not go to school. In addition, I knew that no one would accept me if I had neither experience nor education. More importantly, I felt some responsibility to my family, especially my parents. They always ask me to finish my education in university.

So finally, I have decided to continue my education in university. But still I dislike school as much as I used to. Since I have to go to university, I know it is very important to analyze carefully the courses I am going to take. First of all, I have considered engineering because I do well with subjects which deal with numbers and calculations. Also I am particularly interested in mathematics, physics, and chemistry; however, I believe I will go into business. I want to take business because I intend to open my own business later and travel all over the world. Instead of working for other people, I want to work independently. I intend to work as hard as I can to reach my goal.

Cam Hung Vuong
Vietnam

Canada—The Home I Have Found at Last

Canada has so many opportunities. In front of me stands a possible future world of happiness and success. There are, however, too many choices, and the world of the future is too complicated. There is such a great diversity of jobs that I can hardly choose which is better for me. Sometimes I want to be a doctor, but maybe I lack the ability to achieve this. To be a teacher? It is not of interest to me. To be an engineer? I am not sure that I will be able to succeed in it. To be a pharmacist? Maybe this is my choice for the future.

It all depends on me whether my dream becomes real or not. I believe that confidence and patience will always win at last. Therefore, I will seize my goal and try to sweep out of my way all the obstacles.

What will I do after I have realized my dream? When I arrived in Canada the first day, I decided to stay here permanently. You may ask me why I never wanted to return to my country. No, it is not my country. I never had a country. When I was a child, I knew only war which lasted so many years. Nowhere in my country can I live in peace. Peace has been the only thing I have searched for in a long time. Peace has been my passion since war revealed to me its horror. I have lived through this horror and now, I just hope to live in a country where it is peaceful. Canada is the home I have found at last.

Thuy Van Luong
Vietnam

Proud to Be Canadian

When my mother recalled my third birthday, she said she had been so happy to see me pick up a pen among various articles. Traditionally, older people believed that if a child chose the pen rather than other objects, this prophesied his future as a scholar. She was proud when people around cheered for me as I chose the ideal profession. It was totally luck; however, I put my faith in this story and dreamed of myself being a knowledgeable scholar.

Once my father sighed, "When I was young, I dreamed of many things and my dreams never came true, partly because my family was poor and my dreams were too impractical." Therefore, he was greatly concerned with my future and carefully selected a good school and then encouraged me to study in the medical field in the future, as he had dreamed that he would be a doctor. I was inquisitive about the noble life of a doctor. I admired the doctor's knowledge. During my years in middle high school, I was always proud to say that I would be a doctor when I grew up. I tried to develop my interest by reading books which related to the human body or by reading my father's books about health.

A few years later, my ambition to be a doctor seemed to be forgotten when I started to learn writing. It attracted my interest when one of my efforts appeared in a Vietnamese newspaper after about ten of my "masterpieces" were rejected and thrown into the wastebasket. I was fascinated with writing and decided to write more. Looking at my grandfather's poetry, I imitated his style. Sometimes my obsession took time from schoolwork. When I told my mother that I hoped to learn to write very well and later become a famous writer, my mother was pleased by my strong ambition.

When I was in Grade 9, my new Vietnamese teacher, who was chosen for his correct political ideas, taught lessons that I did not enjoy. From that time on, I felt that I was involved in a school that saw me as an outsider. School was now for the proletarian classes and for the original Vietnamese, and I felt every political lesson was directed against myself and my family. I found I was their opponent and thus I felt like an alien in school. My essays never got good marks and gradually I lost my interest in writing.

I was saved from the loneliness of my youth by coming to Canada. I grew up to be mature with the scars of life in a refugee camp and started my life in this new country. Now I have my life to begin again and I have more ambitions than ever. Canada, the country that I will live in for the rest of my life, holds many opportunities. Instead of being a doctor or a writer, I hope I can successfully study computer science so that after I graduate from university, I will work as a computer specialist, preferably overseas in developing countries. Perhaps, one day when Canada and my country agree to take further steps toward the normalization of their relations, I may have a chance to work in my country where I will be proud to be a Canadian.

I am optimistic and believe in a bright future as I can see a wonderful life in my dreams.

Dan So Giang
Vietnam

Student Activities

Writing Folder

Autobiography

1. In the final chapter of your autobiography, write about how you see yourself in the future. When you read the stories in this section, you will see how other students have developed the following themes and you will become familiar with the vocabulary and structures you need to talk about yourself.

Themes:

- Dreams and goals
- How personality, interests, values, and parents' expectations influence your choice of career
- Marriage and family
- Raising children
- What success means to you
- What you value most

2. After writing the first draft, get suggestions from your teacher and writing partner on how you might improve your writing.

Future Goals and Present Decisions (a project for senior students)

In an essay discuss your future career goals and your reasons for choosing particular colleges/universities. Analyze your personality, interests, values, and feelings in the process of weighing the merits of alternative careers and the decisions you must make now concerning college/university applications.

In your research you might

- interview a high school graduate who is at university or college
- talk with a guidance counsellor and find out answers to your questions
- read university/college booklets in the guidance office

You need to find out detailed information about

- educational background needed for careers you are considering
- entrance requirements
- cut-off average (*It is important that you analyze whether your goal is realistic given your academic performance to date.*)
- English requirements
- job opportunities (*The Guidance Department has statistics about the number of graduates who have obtained jobs related to their speciality.*)

You may have made already decided on a career. If so, give the reasons for your choice. Even if you have made a choice, it is important to have a backup plan should you are not be able to attain your first choice.

In your essay you do not need to come to firm conclusions if you are still undecided about your future. What *is* important in this essay is to weigh the arguments for and against different plans.

The essay will be evaluated for content and style. You should hand in an *essay plan* and *first draft* with the final essay in your writing folder.

Voices of Graduates

The adults who speak here range from those who have recently graduated from secondary school and are still at university to those who graduated some time ago, completed college or university, and are launched in careers, marriages, and raising children.

They have helpful advice to students still in high school. Khuong Doan counsels students to take advantage of their school years and not to be lured away by the desire to have fun and make money. Hwan Lee, in a valedictory address, worries that students who speak English as a second language ignore the humanities because of their lack of confidence in English. He advises students to study a wide variety of subjects in the humanities, as well as in the sciences and mathematics.

The process of "becoming Canadian" is long and complicated. Even when problems of communication no longer remain, there are still barriers created by cultural differences. For example, Richard Yu continues to feel "out of tune" with Canadian society and explains how differences in values have caused problems in his medical studies. His culture emphasizes respect and deference to the elderly, but he must learn now to interrupt his older patients during clinical interviews, if necessary, in the interests of time. On the other hand, Tze Kan Yeo believes that he has integrated successfully into Canadian society. Canadian families have welcomed him into their homes, and he has developed close friendships with Canadians at university. However, balancing between two cultures continues to create tensions. Although he feels accepted as Canadian by others, at home his mother still sees him as Chinese. "Now if only my mother would accept me as Canadian," he comments.

These young adults recognize that their children will feel more Canadian than they do. As they contemplate raising their children, they worry about their growing up in a society where there is so much freedom. Binhua Wang states: "I grew up in a society with strong moral values and strong family ties. These I believe are very important to keep in my family in Canada." They hope that their coming to Canada assures a more hopeful future for their children.

In the process of becoming Canadian, these immigrants seem to discover their roots and become more intensely aware of their cultural heritage. They wish to share their traditions, especially with their children and with others. They recognize that an intimate knowledge of two cultures and two languages is a great advantage. They reflect on the changes they see in themselves since coming to Canada. Michael Morad, an immigrant from Lebanon, realizes that he feels much more in control of his destiny since coming to Canada.

Do these young adults feel Canadian after spending their adolescence and early twenties here? Jason Lien, who came to Canada at the age of 14, leaving his family behind in Vietnam, found that his sense of belonging to Canada became stronger when he returned to Vietnam for a visit: "I had been away ten years and had spent my adolescence in Canada. I felt like a Canadian." When Winston Loui, a native of Trinidad, first arrived in Canada, he felt a need to behave as Canadians did, but was uncomfortable doing so. Now, while he recognizes that he will always be different because of his skin colour and his accented English, he also sees that Canada is a blend of the cultures and the traditions of different people. He concludes, "To be Canadian, I simply have to be myself."

Valedictory Address

A friend of mine came to Canada from Korea a few years ago. He excelled in mathematics and sciences, for he studied only those subjects. Many people around him thought that he was going to be an engineer or a scientist because...well, what else could a bright Asian immigrant be?

One day, just by accident, he picked up Dostoevsky's *Crime and Punishment*. After reading some of it, he was amazed by a world of thought he had never encountered before. He was overwhelmed by the endless questions the book inspired: Should society treat the capable and incapable equally? If there were a war, should we send a potential Nobel Laureate, who could contribute so much, to the war field just as any other civilians? Do we deserve to judge the good and the evil and to act according to our judgement? And on what standard do we judge these things?

Not getting many definite answers, he decided to study nineteenth century Russian literature. He began to isolate himself in the library. Turgenev's ideas of nihilism and Dostoevsky's profound thoughts on the extent of free will struck him, while Tolstoy's religious work made him ponder the existence of God. The more he read, the more questions he had. And the more questions he had, the more he read.

At the end of the term, he failed all his school subjects since there wasn't any course entitled "Nineteenth Century Russian Literature." He had to repeat the school year before he could go to college.

Many people say that he was unfortunate to become suddenly "crazy" about such a subject. I say he was extremely fortunate. Throughout the year, he learned that not every good book in the world is about calculus, not every great intellectual is like Newton, and not everything can be expressed by numbers. He explored a whole new dimension of knowledge that he might have just passed by.

Unfortunately, the first priority in our society, it seems to me, is speed. Life is like the hundred-meter dash. Whoever reaches the finish line first—this is all that matters. Who goes to medical school first. Who goes to law school first. Who hits Wall Street first. Who makes the first million.

This emphasis on vertical growth and relative de-emphasis on horizontal growth can be especially troublesome to immigrant students who speak English as a second language. Since they have to move quickly to take the prerequisite courses, they first eliminate all humanities from their course selection lists. They feel that unless they go into the sciences, they will be hungry in the future with their limited English knowledge in this speed-oriented society. They never experience the beauty of humanities. They become afraid of the humanities.

No wonder there is such a rift between students of science and humanities. Students of humanities think that their world is so beautiful compared to "boring" sciences. Is this true? In my biology course, I once saw the structure of a fly through a scanning electron microscope. When magnified, the small fly was a tiny universe in itself. I realized that when I kill a fly, I'm not just killing an insignificant insect, but I'm actually destroying a small world that has an endless array of cells that house much smaller organelles that are composed of atoms that have myriads of electrons revolving around the nucleus. And it may go further; we just haven't found out yet. There might be another such sophisticated world in one tiny electron. To me, the structure of a small fly is just as beautiful and amazing as that of a poem. Science is beautiful.

Many science majors, on the other hand, tend to believe that the humanities are unnecessary. Are the humanities really a luxury? Let me answer this by an example. Many people believe that the airplane was invented by imitating the bird. I disagree. The motion of the bird might have been the inspiration for the invention of the airplane. But by imitating the bird, we could only think of moving the wings; we could not think of fixing the wings and moving a propeller—a brand new concept. I don't think this revolutionary idea came from calculus or Newton's laws. I believe it was the result of the endless imagination nurtured by education in the humanities. Long before the airplane was invented, such imaginative forms of the airplane had already existed in the mind of poets who always "dream things that never were and ask,'Why not?'" Even at the heart of science we can see the trace of the humanities.

Science without the humanities is incomplete. So are the humanities without science. We may not have to be experts in both fields, but at least, we need to be explorers of both. Some thirty years ago, in an attempt to narrow the gap between intellectuals and politicians in our society, John F. Kennedy quoted a mother who had said, "Don't teach my boy poetry. He is going to run for congress." In response, he commented, "If more politicians knew poems, and more poets knew politics, the world would be a little better place in which to live."

If more physicists knew philosophy, and more philosophers knew physics, the world would be a little better place in which to live.

Hwan Lee
Korea

Too Much Freedom?

I like the political freedom in Canadian society. Anyone can openly discuss international or domestic politics and politicians. This was not the case in my motherland, China. I also enjoy personal privacy in this society with regard to life-style and personal belongings such as bank accounts.

However, I feel that in some respects Canadians get carried away with freedom of expression. For instance, we, especially the younger generation, are exposed to excessive violence, obscene language, drugs, sex, and infidelity in movies, television programs, magazines, radio, and books. As a result, we may question our family values and weaken in our sense of responsibility towards others and towards society as a whole.

I cannot help but remember my golden years as a teenager in China. Unlike many teens in Canada who are in too much of a hurry to be like adults without fully realizing the implications, I loved my childhood. In those green years I learned many new ideas and enjoyed invaluable experiences in a safe and innocent environment where drugs and sex were never heard of. I grew up in a society with strong moral values and strong family ties. These I believe are very important to keep in my family in Canada.

Belinda Binhua Wang
China

Part of the Cultural Mosaic

I feel more Canadian today than I did a decade ago. When I arrived in Canada in 1979, my new homeland was completely strange to me. Language obstacles, harsh February snow storms, and other social and cultural differences made me aware that it would be a long journey to becoming Canadian and feeling Canadian.

The first immediate challenge I faced was the English language. I could not imagine what life would be like in a place where I was unfamiliar with the language. I knew it would cause all sorts of hardships and inconveniences in my daily life. I remember well what happened to me on the first day I arrived in Toronto. I went into a fast-food restaurant only to find out that I had to use gestures to order my lunch because I could not read the menu. A man talked to me while I was walking on Yonge Street. I responded by shaking my head since I did not understand what he was talking about. The subway was like betting on heads or tails. I sometimes ended up travelling in the direction opposite to the one that I wanted. Experiences like these made me realize that studying English ought to be my first priority.

Being Canadian gives me a sense that I belong to a great land of opportunities, that I am one of the many ethnic minorities who make up the cultural mosaic which is the fundamental character of this country. Most importantly, I feel that I am part of the Canadian family.

I am proud to be a Canadian and I feel fortunate to live in one of the greatest countries in the world. Being a New Canadian does give me all the privileges a native-born Canadian enjoys. But there are also responsibilities which I must assume. Although I am still learning the English language, and still do not feel 100% Canadian, I know for certain that my children will definitely feel more Canadian than I do.

Chauncee Tang
Cambodia

Canada is My Home

After I finished my final exams at college, I decided to go back to Vietnam and visit my family. I had not seen them for ten years. I made the decision on Sunday, purchased the ticket the next day, and departed the following Wednesday. I had to cash in my savings bond and take out my entire savings to finance the trip.

As the airplane prepared to land in Vietnam, my heart began to beat faster and faster. I was saying to myself, "What should I say? How will I react to the whole situation?" After some thought, I decided to be tough, strong, and not to cry. After a long inspection by the Vietnamese customs and immigration, I proceeded to the exit gate.

There stood my mother. Her face showed years of separation, years of longing for her son. My tough, strong stand was no more, I looked into her face and I cried.

For the entire trip home, my mother did not take her eyes off me. She clasped my hand firmly as if to hold me beside her forever. As the car pulled up to the door of my house, I saw my father waiting. I lunged out of the car and grabbed hold of him. Emotion choked back our words. Onlookers offered congratulations. My sister and brothers emerged from the small crowd that had gathered at the front door. We greeted each other like strangers. Everyone said that I looked different and didn't even sound the same. It was true. I had been away ten years and had spent my adolescence in Canada. I felt like a Canadian.

Everywhere I went, kids followed me and people looked at me with curiosity. They laughed at the way I dressed and commented on my light complexion. They treated me like a total foreigner. Little did they realize that I had been born in Vietnam and had spent half my life there.

After three weeks in Vietnam, it was time to go home. My sister said, "Where are you going? Your home is here!"

I told her, "My home is in Toronto and it will be yours too in the near future."

During my short stay in Vietnam I never felt at home simply because I was treated like a foreigner. My sense of belonging to Canada became stronger. Canada had been my home for ten years and it will be my home always.

Jason Lien
Vietnam

Where Are You From?

Discrimination isolates and differentiates the individual from the rest of society.

I have encountered some discrimination in Canada from both children and adults. However, at least Canadians are conscious of discrimination, since Canada is officially a multicultural society. (This is in contrast to a more traditional society where xenophobia may perhaps be born of an instinct for cultural survival). Generally, Canadians are a very generous and open-minded people, but there are always those who hate or fear others simply because they are different. Yet, there is nothing simple about discrimination, for as I have learned in my first decade in Canada, intolerance comes in all shapes and sizes.

I initially experienced prejudice during my first year in Canada. I remember that as I was walking home from school one afternoon, I happened to pass by a boy playing in the street. Suddenly, without warning and for no good reason, this boy of no more than seven or eight began taunting me. This little Canadian boy, a complete stranger to me, stood there across the street chanting in a sing-song imitation of a foreign language which neither of us had ever heard before. At the time, I thought to myself: "What did I ever do to you? I don't even know you, much less you, me!" My English was poor, but the insult was unmistakable. Of course, his blind stereotyping of me grew out of the assumption of my ignorance. Those who knew me, such as my Grade 6 classmates, hopefully understood my deficiency in English did not make me as a nitwit. I was quite startled that a little boy would go out of his way to mock me, and it must have hurt, because I remember the incident still. Was it for this that my family and I had jumped into a leaky boat, got shot at, abandoned our home, and fled our country?

Another common reaction I get from Canadians is the inevitable question: "Where are you from?" When I first came to Canada, the query was naturally expected. As a newcomer, I was happy and even flattered to answer such a kind questions. However, after a while, I have found the question mark on my person more and more offensive, rather like a racial putdown. Having spent more than half my life in Canada, I consider myself a Canadian, and find the question altogether tiresome.

Discrimination in Canada comes about as a result of a disagreement over what makes one a "Canadian." We cannot all be the same. We cannot all share the same values and beliefs. We do not even expect it of our own family. Why then do people not show more tolerance toward others less fortunate than themselves?

Nevertheless, there is common ground that all Canadians can stand on. We all believe in the fundamental human values of life, liberty, and equality, if not fraternity itself. This common tie should bind us together, despite any physical differences. There is a need for open communication among all Canadians, regardless of ethnic origins, if we are to stamp out discrimination in Canada, and make our multicultural society work.

Ang Meng
Laos

How Will My Children Turn Out?

Do I ever regret coming to Canada? My relatives and my best friend used to ask me if I ever thought of moving south. They offered to help me with all the bureaucratic red tape if I immigrated to the United States. It didn't take me long to answer them. I let them know that I was willing to visit, but not to live there.

When I was in the refugee camp, the Canadian visa officer asked me why I chose Canada. I answered, "Canada is a big land, a young land near the North Pole. Best of all, in Canada there is no war. All through our lives we have experienced war, and so now we wish to immigrate to a peaceful land." That was all I knew about Canada. He smiled and approved our application to Canada.

My future and the future of my children was determined by that decision. All Chinese hope their children will be "dragons," or famous people. Now, day after day, as I look at my two sons growing up, I am happy and proud although they are just little children. But I worry about them too. It is the fate of parents to always worry about their children. A Vietnamese folk song says: "The mother soothes her child and sheds tears; the older a child becomes, the more the mother worries." In Canada, I worry about the abuses that have invaded the souls of many teenagers. How will my children turn out?

I love Canada. In Canada I hope that my children will have a beautiful future.

Ba Hong Lam
Vietnam

Out of Tune

In my first year of university study, I gained a new perspective on Canadian culture. Perhaps immersing myself in an absolutely Canadian environment by living in residence during the first year was the biggest challenge of my life. I experienced intimidating noise and loud party music in the residence. Making friends was particularly difficult at first. Coming from a quiet family and perhaps a submissive culture, I found myself totally out of tune with residence life. I was not sure if I was being shy or antisocial.

I knew I had to do well in the first years at university in order to get into medicine. I had a duty to myself and my family to study hard and to achieve my goal. With this in mind, I kept contact with the students in the residence and the university community to a minimum . I felt neither isolated from Canadian students nor close to them. I did make one good Canadian friend in the residence, and, in later years, in university two or three others who came close to being my good friends, but I am still doubtful about using the word "friend." Perhaps, they were just acquaintances after all.

My definition of being a Canadian is to be friendly and respectful to people from other cultures. In that sense, I believe I may be qualified to be called a Canadian. I believe it is important to keep what one believes is right and not to change one's personality and traditions as a result of outside forces or influences. I have learned respect for the elderly and have been taught not to interrupt their speech and not to talk loudly in front of them. However, the elderly patients I see often like to chat and talk excessively, and since there is a time limit in clinical interviews, I must learn to interrupt and stop the patients. This is not a pleasant task for me.

Personally, I have not encountered discrimination in Canadian society. However, I have heard stories of such discrimination from friends. One incident was in a hospital where a middle-aged man with a heart attack refused to be attended by a Chinese intern.

Going back to Hong Kong after five years in Canada was wonderful. I felt a sense of belonging there that I can never experience here in Canada. There, the language, buildings, people, culture, and friends are all part of me.

Richard Yu
Hong Kong

Lucky to Live in Canada

I had been looking forward to going back to China ever since my arrival in Canada more than ten years before. The trip from Hong Kong took little more than an hour. When the train finally glided slowly to a halt, I could hardly believe that I was back in my homeland again. I was excited and curious to see how China had changed.

I was caught by surprise when I saw a large number of high-rise buildings standing alongside more traditional architecture. Together they formed a surprisingly unique picture. I thought to myself, China has really accomplished quite a lot in a short period of time.

The hotel I checked into was, no doubt, world class. Everything from decoration to service was superb to the last detail. If not for the people around me, I could imagine that I was still in a western country. I was more than impressed. One night I decided to go down to the disco in the hotel. When I lined up to get in, a number of Westerners and Hong Kong tourists were allowed in with welcoming smiles, but when it came to the couple in front of me, the situation reversed. The two young people were noticeably residents of China. They had more than enough yen, but no foreign currency. Thus, they were refused admittance. It did not matter how rich they were or how well they behaved. The door guard simply told them to leave and threatened to call the security if they kept on arguing. I was shocked and embarrassed. How could Chinese treat their own "comrades" like nobody and foreigners like "Gods"?

It was then that I realized, that in China, there was still so much inequality despite economic reform. Although China had improved economically, in the process it had lost its spiritual goodness.

As a child, I was told that when the British were in China, they posted signs outside parks such as "No dogs and Chinese allowed." I was so angered every time that story was told. I told myself that I have to do well to show the world that I am proud to be Chinese and forever erase this shame. Now, the same scene was happening right in front of my eyes, yet startlingly different in principle. I had heard that the people in China were materialistic, but I never expected they would reach the point of discriminating against their own people.

I turned away from the disco, leaving behind the arguments and the disappointed couple. At that moment, I felt very lucky to be a Canadian.

The rest of my stay in my motherland was pleasant. When I think about it now, it is the politics and policy-makers in China that I find unbearable. An ancient Chinese proverb states: "A son never dislikes his mother's looks." While I am happy to be Canadian, a part of me will always miss my innocent childhood and the many beautiful memories back in my motherland.

Chris Tai
China

Advice to High School Students

Why did we leave Vietnam? It was because there we had no future. We came to Canada, a country where we are free to be whatever we want. If we want to be a doctor, or a mechanic, we can. By staying in school, by investing time and energy now, we can have security in the future.

I know it is not easy to do. It is hard trying to study when your friends are out there having a lot of fun. They go to movies every day and they have a lot of money. When they are in school, they don't bring a little brown lunch bag. But because you spend your time studying, you have no money.

At times I wanted to quit school so that I could work, make money to buy fancy clothes, have an attractive girlfriend, and never have to use my head too much. But I decided to stay in school. There were several reasons. Knowledge is a never-ending river, and I wanted to expand my knowledge. I also wanted to help my native country in the future.

You are the key to help Vietnam if it ever wants to catch up with the world outside, and if we are ever welcomed back. I believe that it is important to do your best at school and never turn your back on people who want to support you. A curious mind, a willingness to accept a new life-style, and respect for your parents—these are the attitudes which will make you happy and will help you make a worthwhile contribution to Canada.

Khuong An Doan
Vietnam

Language and Culture

As I went out the classroom door, I called to my first English teacher, "Have a good weekend."

"I sure will!" said Mrs. McIntyre.

"I sure will" kept echoing in my mind all weekend long. In fact it bothered me. I could not understand at the time how anyone could be so *sure* that they would have a "good" minute or even a "good" second, let alone a whole weekend. But then again I had only been in Canada for four months and indeed had only spoken English for four months.

I do not intend to comment on the language here. Language was not the issue. Culture was.

In Lebanon, where I was born and raised, if you wished someone a good weekend or a good anything for that matter, the common answer was, "I hope so."

This is indeed a doubtful statement suggesting a passivity, an inability to shape the future. One may wonder why a Lebanese would not say, "I certainly will," when being bid a good weekend. After all, surely it must lie within the individual's power to determine the future. The Lebanese do not lack a strong will—indeed far from it. The fact is that for a Lebanese, subconsciously perhaps, fate seems to be an essential element in any plans for the future and arrogant is the person whose certitude allows him or her to actually be "sure" about any moment of the future.

At the time I did indeed feel that Mrs. McIntyre was being arrogant when she said that she would have a good weekend. But now, about one hundred moons later, I have grown to perceive the expression of "will" differently. In fact, I actually say, "I sure will" whenever I am wished a "good time." I now feel that it is fine to "will" and not just to "hope" although I know that the outcome in either case is bound to be the same!

Michael Morad
Lebanon

Educational Opportunities

It is surprising to me when I start to count the years and realize that I have been living in Canada for six years now. To live and function in a new and unfamiliar environment is never easy. When I came to Canada I was sixteen, and I had no ideas of the difficulties that lay ahead of me or the variety of possibilities open to me.

As I look back, what I am most thankful for are the educational opportunities that have been available to me in Canada. Had I not come to Canada, I might be working aimlessly somewhere now after high school graduation instead of taking my Master's degree. Every night on the way home after studying five or six hours in the library, I say to myself that I am tired of studying. But I know that hard work does pay off eventually. It is a matter of recognizing that the reward is "eventually," not "now."

What is also beneficial to the younger generation in Canada is the tremendous encouragement and help one can get from the government. Loans and grants are always available to the needy, so that a good education is not restricted to the privileged or to geniuses. The only problem a student has in pursuing further studies is the overwhelming number of choices.

In my case, I guess luck was on my side, too. I was accepted into a very good high school, where I gained a great deal of self-confidence. In the multicultural environment of the high school, I learned that it is all right not to be part of the majority culture and not to understand everything around me. Different cultures and languages made our school interesting. I realized that what is important is to ask questions, for you learn while you are asking. My confidence came from the realization that I didn't have to leave my identity behind in order to succeed or to be accepted.

In fact, now I find that being an immigrant is an added advantage, because I know at least two cultures and two languages. This means that I have more choices in daily entertainment and job opportunities than do native-born Canadians.

Although I have been in Toronto for six years now, I still miss my native country occasionally, but I know I would also miss Canada tremendously if I went back. Slowly I have built around me a world which is a part of me and of which I am a part. I consider myself very lucky and blessed that my parents brought me with to Canada six years ago.

Ephrem Shui
Hong Kong

A Multicultural Nation

What does it mean to be a Canadian? Does an official document make one "Canadian"? I have often wondered why people question their own identity and why I need to question my own.

Fifteen years ago, I arrived in Toronto with my family. It was a cool summer evening. I felt a chilling freshness in the air; it was different from the warmth of my tropical island home town in Trinidad. In the days that followed, I busily observed the wonders of the big city. But, everywhere I went, eyes stared at me, or so it seemed. Was it the colour of my skin or was it my accented English? I was intimidated by these thoughts. I did not want to brave the new any more. For some time, I only wanted to stand quietly and observe. Fortunately, I began to discover people's friendly natures. They showed interest in my background. They even offered their friendship.

In the meantime, I still had doubts about fitting into Canadian society. But I was determined to establish myself (prove my existence) in some way. I felt impelled to follow what "Canadians" did. Yet somehow, I was not comfortable doing that. It was then that I realized that the Canadian culture is a blend of the cultures and the traditions of the different people living in Canada.

To be Canadian, I simply have to be myself. If I cannot accept myself or appreciate others, how can I expect to live in this multicultural nation? To make my life in Canada worthwhile, I must share my unique heritage.

Today I do not question myself. Canada is my home. And, certainly, I do not have to label myself with a sign that says, "I am Canadian." Why should I? After all, I am one of those different people living in Canada—a Canadian.

Winston Loui
Trinidad

Accepted as a Canadian

It was late November. As the Air France jumbo jet approached Dorval Airport for a landing, I looked out of the window. There was a blanket of white snow on the ground. It looked beautiful, and I knew I would like my new home, this vast country called Canada. White snow was my first impression of Canada and that is probably why I love white snow. I was full of hopes, dreams, and expectations, and yet I felt uncertain at the same time. I began to wonder how I would master the English language, how I would make new friends, how I would adapt to and integrate into the new culture, and whether I would be accepted as a true Canadian.

For the first two and a half years in Canada, which I spent finishing secondary school, I made new friends mostly with new immigrants and refugees. I did not have Canadian-born friends because I was afraid of making a fool of myself with my limited English. I could not understand them fully when they started speaking in slang and using idioms. I could not laugh with them because I could not understand the jokes and interpret the sarcasm. I felt out of place among them. The fact that I did not really have close friends did not matter to me at first. I was busy with a part-time job, and besides, there was always television. My social life revolved around my parents and my sister's family.

As time went on, I began to realize that Canada was still a foreign country to me because I had failed to integrate into the mainstream of Canadian society. Part of the problem was that my parents were worried that I would be come too "Canadian-ized," and I would not do anything that would upset them. After all, I was indebted to them for the sacrifices they had made for my future by immigrating to Canada. I decided to attend a university out of town away from home because it would give me a chance to learn "the Canadian way of life" without upsetting my parents.

I went to Queen's University in Kingston. It was a dramatic change in my life-style, living away from home for the first time, free from the control of my parents. I had no choice but to speak English all the time and to learn quickly the customs and norms of Canadian society in order to fit in with other students who came from all regions of Canada. The infamous orientation rituals of the Engineering Society at Queen's provided a good environment for establishing close friendships with other first-year students. I made friends with students, most of whom came from small towns I had not even heard of. They were very understanding of my limited Canadian cultural background and explained to me anything I did not understand. They would in turn ask me questions about my native country—the seasons, the food, the customs, and the politics.

The engineering department I enrolled in traditionally had been closely knit, and I was the only Chinese there. I participated in departmental and student activities as much as I could. I gained invaluable cultural experiences socializing with my friends. In time, it became natural and effortless for me to speak English without hesitation and for me to express myself clearly. I began to pick up connotations and subtle differences in the use of words. I learned social etiquette, informally. I felt that I had integrated into Canadian society.

My experience at Queen's University was certainly memorable and worthwhile. I had two close friends who came from northern Ontario, and I visited them in Chelmsford and Sudbury. Their families made me feel at home. When they got married, I was honoured to be invited to each of their weddings to share in their joy. All in all, I can truly say that they have made me feel accepted as a Canadian.

P.S. Now if only my mother would accept me as a Canadian...

That's another story!

Tze Kan Yeo
Burma